Words of Praise for *Elza's Quest*

"Faith meets persecution head on in this dramatic account. Kay Kuzma transports us to one of the darkest times in history to show us how faith in Christ carried one family through. The story is written with such vivid detail that I felt I was right there with the Kuzmas. As you read, you'll examine your own walk with God and answer his call to commitment."

~ **Jon Fugler,** *Chief Content Officer for Trans World Radio, and Christian Author*

"*Elza's Quest* is a powerful true story of a devoted young couple, successful in literature ministry in Poland before World War II, who found themselves caught up in the murder and mayhem of the Nazi occupation and then the Soviet onslaught. This compelling book provides a window into the horrendous decisions that faced regular people caught between competing totalitarian powers. Harassed by Nazi soldiers and the Gestapo, and then by rogue Soviet soldiers and the KGB, the family navigated unspeakable violence and hatred, enduring labor camps, hunger marches, and hostility from all sides because of their stand for Bible truth.

"Follow their incredible journey as the father escapes the tyranny of a Nazi forced labor camp, and the mother chooses family unity, attempting an impossible escape with four children across the closed communist border to rejoin her husband—only to face the challenges of living in German displaced person's camps for years. God watched over this family, miraculously preserving their lives and bringing them to America where He wrote their next chapter. Be inspired as you see how God protects His children, and how good ultimately triumphs over evil."

~ **Conrad Vine,** *DMin, President at Adventist Frontier Missions, and YouTube Personality*

"The true stories written in this inspiring book by Kay Kuzma, one of America's greatest Christian authors, unveil a thrilling odyssey of the unwavering faith of a remarkable woman, the relentless vision of a father's dream, and the power of God's amazing miracles. The experiences lived and revealed here in exquisite detail not only show that when you trust in God the impossible becomes possible, but assure you will discover the peace that passes all understanding. Read; be blessed and inspired!"

~ **Carlos Pardeiro,** *President/CEO & Founder of SAFE TV®*

"Reading Kay's book, I feel blessed all over again—for I was there with the Kuzma family in the Wentorf Camp for Displaced Persons. (In the "chapel picture" I'm the only boy in the second row of children.) Our families went through similar disappointments. But here in America all of us Hintz children, Hannah, George, and I, were given good Christian educational opportunities, the freedom of worship, and so, so much more. God has truly blessed us. What a fantastic job of reporting, researching, and writing Kay did. Her book brings back so many memories."

~ **Roman Hintz** *(Romek Hinc in Polish), World War II Survivor, Retired Math & Science Teacher, Video Producer*

"An inspiring, thrilling story of what happened when Elza and her family, in the midst of war, terror, and persecution, put ultimate dependence on their loving heavenly Father. Reading Kay's narrative will capture your attention and you'll never be the same."

~ **Dan Matthews,** *TV Producer, and Speaker Emeritus of Faith for Today/ Lifestyle Magazine*

"Being Polish, knowing the Kuzma family, and being involved in a book publishing ministry makes this whole story very special to me. What an amazing journey! It will leave you inspired and in awe of God's incredible leadership through the complex realities of life during and after the war. This family story is a tribute to God's leading and the human spirit's ability to endure and triumph over adversity. It's a story of hope, resilience, and the unyielding effort to find freedom and a better future."

~ **Robert Kuczek,** *President of Springs of Life Foundation, Poland*

"Reading this book is like sitting at the kitchen table and listening to Kay share captivating stories of family, love, deception, religious persecution, escape, unquenchable faith, and even more love! Call the kids—especially your teens. They'll want to hear every word. Never again will the Second World War be just history!"

~ **Dick Duerksen,** *Busily Retired Pastor, Storyteller Extraordinaire, Writer, Photographer, and Friend*

"Very inspiring and challenging!"

~ **Douglas Na'a,** *Director of SALT (Soul-winning and Leadership Training) at It is Written School of Evangelism*

"Like Bible characters of old, the protagonists in *Elza's Quest* are passionate, raw, and at times morally chaotic. Yet their story is an inspirational testament of faith, determination, and God's ability to use humans to dramatically fulfill His will."

~ **Shane Anderson,** *Lead Pastor of Pioneer Memorial Church at Andrews University, PM Church.TV*

"This historical account of a family's journey from war and religious prejudice to freedom is inspiring and gripping. The story of Elza and her family reminds us that the assurance of salvation found in Jesus, and the blessed hope of His soon return, offer critically needed encouragement and guidance through the darkest times of relational struggles, religious persecution, and political upheaval."

~ **Elizabeth Viera Talbot,** *PhD, Speaker/Director for Jesus101.tv*

"This book—engagingly written, as you'd expect from Kay—is a potent reminder of the power of the message of scripture, as well as the sacrifices on which this movement has been built. You'll find portions of it will be reminiscent of your walk, while others will provide you with new ground you've not walked before; it will help you see how God works tirelessly in the background of your service."

~ **Shawn Boonstra,** *Director/Speaker for The Voice of Prophecy*

"A dramatic story of longing, heartache, persecution, human suffering, and the miracles that allow love, faith, and freedom to triumph. Walk with Elza through the pages of her quest and be inspired."

~ **Brenda Walsh,** *Director of Brenda Walsh Ministries, Dynamic Speaker, Author, and TV Producer*

"I loved reading *Elza's Quest*. It's just a great story. It's about real people, but reads like a page-turning novel, especially as it got deeper into her life during the war. Would they ever get married? Would they survive the war? Would they find each other after the war? Elza becomes a great model of resilience, using her deep faith to find a way to cope with whatever hit her family. A great, inspiring book by a wonderful writer!"

~ **Dan Smith,** *International Evangelist, Co-Founder of Grace FORCE Ministry*

"Kay Kuzma has captured the essence and resilience of the human spirit with an authentic journey of life, love, and loss. *Elza's Quest* is a compelling narrative of the Kuzma family's commitment to family and faith, and it serves as a powerful reminder of God's faithfulness amid pain and even persecution."

~ **Jill Morikone,** *Vice President of Three Angels Broadcasting Network (3ABN), Author, and Speaker*

"This is not just a great human interest story, but a well-told true narrative that will make you appreciate the blessings we have in our lands of freedom. It's a story that will give you a practical look into the reality of God's protection and care when you choose Him to lead you through all of life's hard issues."

~ **Monte Church,** *Speaker for Native Life TV Series*

ELZA'S QUEST

The true story of a courageous woman
(and her family) living by faith, longing for love,
and risking everything for freedom.

Kay Kuzma

World rights reserved. This book or any portion thereof may not be copied or reproduced in any form or manner whatever, except as provided by law, without the written permission of the publisher, except by a reviewer who may quote brief passages in a review.

The author assumes full responsibility for the accuracy of all facts and quotations as cited in this book. The opinions expressed in this book are the author's personal views and interpretations, and do not necessarily reflect those of the publisher.

This book is provided with the understanding that the publisher is not engaged in giving spiritual, legal, medical, or other professional advice. If authoritative advice is needed, the reader should seek the counsel of a competent professional.

Copyright © 2024 Kay Kuzma
Copyright © 2024 TEACH Services, Inc.
ISBN-13: 978-1-4796-1796-8 (Paperback)
ISBN-13: 978-1-4796-1797-5 (ePub)
Library of Congress Control Number: 2024939328

Scripture quotations are taken from the New King James Version ®. Copyright © 1982 by Thomas Nelson. Used by permission. All rights reserved.

Published by:

www.TEACHServices.com • (800) 367-1844

Dedication to Jan W. Kuzma

I dedicate this book to a most amazing man, Jan W. Kuzma, who loved me. And he loved Poland, even though it was in Poland where his family suffered overwhelming persecution and experienced the terror of war. This book is his family's story—and the fulfillment of my promise to him when we first met in 1961.

Kay and Jan Kuzma, 1963.

Contents

Dedication 7
Acknowledgments 11
Introduction 13
Chapter 1 : Dreams, Doubt, and Disappointment 15
Chapter 2 : Elza Meets Her Match 22
Chapter 3 : The Storm of Opposition 30
Chapter 4 : Wladek's Search for Truth 37
Chapter 5 : The Lie That Sealed the Deal 45
Chapter 6 : Sold for Chickens 52
Chapter 7 : Together—at Last! 62
Chapter 8 : Brodnica: Working Together in Ministry 66
Chapter 9 : Leszno: Love and Soul Success 71
Chapter 10 : Warsaw: Golden Apple of Opportunity 82
Chapter 11 : Sierpc: Living in the Fire of Persecution 88
Chapter 12 : Plock: Trapped in the War Zone 101
Chapter 13 : Plock: Surviving Nazi Occupation 109
Chapter 14 : Plock: Living next to the Nazis 121
Chapter 15 : Plock: In Sickness and in Health 132
Chapter 16 : Plock: Family, Challenges, and Celebrations ... 140
Chapter 17 : Escape from Nazi Forced Labor (Wladek's Story) ... 148
Chapter 18 : Trying to Outrun the Russian Front (Elza's Story) ... 159
Chapter 19 : Belgard: Caught by the Communists 172
Chapter 20 : Belgard: Post-War Survival 181

Chapter 21 : Slawno: The House with the Red Gate 194
Chapter 22 : The News That Changed Everything 203
Chapter 23 : Szczecin: Escape from Poland 214
Chapter 24 : Germany: Existing as Displaced Persons 224
Chapter 25 : America: The Land of the Free 243
Epilogue 260

Acknowledgments

This book started with a promise: Jan Kuzma and I were dating, and after hearing him tell his family's story of surviving the Nazi invasion of Poland and then escaping from communist Poland, I said with a twinkle in my eye, "If you marry me, I'll write your story!" Over sixty years ago (in 1963) he married me, not because of my proposal but because we had fallen in love! And now it's my turn! This is the book I promised him.

Between 1972 and 1974, Jan realized his parents were getting older. To capture their story, he sat down with "Oma" and "Opa" in our living room in Redlands, California, turned on a small cassette tape recorder, and began asking questions. They answered in Polish and German, and Jan translated it into English while I typed as fast as possible! Then, before I forgot what all the abbreviated words and partial sentences meant, I typed my notes into my very first computer! (Those were the old days before "talk to text" or digital language translation!) At about the same time, Jan asked his siblings (Donna, Christine, and George) to record their memories. To continue our search for facts, we made numerous trips to Poland to visit each place the family lived and speak with family members and friends. In addition, Nina Kuzma Sapiejewska (my husband's cousin) gave me interesting details about my father-in-law's family background. This truly has been a family project—and I want to thank everyone for sharing and allowing me to write their story.

Two friends of the Kuzma family have been most helpful: Lydia Klutz Boyanic and Roman Hintz[1]. Their families knew the Kuzmas in Warsaw, then were together in the Wentorf Displaced Person's Camp near Hamburg, and finally, all three families immigrated to the USA.

And to my Polish friend, Robert Kuczek, who through his ministry in Poland (Springs of Life Foundation), has translated into Polish and published many of my books, I want to give a special thanks for his encouragement and offering the help of his colleague, Katarzyma Krok,

---
[1] known by Hinc (instead of Hintz) before emigration

who contacted Peter Cieslar, whose father, Paul, lived in Poland at the time this story happened and knew many of the people mentioned. His confirmation of facts and names was most valuable.

At the end of my writing journey, I needed new eyes to read the manuscript, to correct errors, and to make sure the text was clear. A special thanks to my cousin, Noelene Patterson, and friend, Judy Gargulio, for volunteering and sharing valuable insights.

What an honor it has been to work with the talented staff at TEACH Services. First, Timothy Hullquist, my friend from Loma Linda days, said yes to my manuscript, then his team of talented professionals shaped my words into the book you're now reading. I have worked with many publishers, but this has been my dream team. They deserve the highest respect and praise.

And finally, God has been good to me. I praise Him for allowing me to meet Elza's son, Jan, on a blind date just because his sister thought I looked like his "old" girlfriend. Jan always saw potential and possibilities in me and was, as the old saying goes, "the wind beneath my wings" through a lifetime of ministry. This is my gift to Jan's memory and to the growing Kuzma clan, and is my loving testimony to the goodness of God.

Introduction

I'm not Polish, but few things have touched my soul as much as this story of a struggling Polish family whose greatest desire was to pursue Bible truth and embrace their faith regardless of what others thought or did to them. I especially identified with the wife and mother—Elzbieta, or Elza, as her family and friends called her. As she got older and was surrounded by her grandchildren, we called her Oma.

Since I grew up in America with its amazing freedom and countless privileges, it was difficult for me to imagine the horrors of living in Poland before, during, and after the Second World War: the threats, the abuse, the bombs, the killing of innocent people and the loss of everything they owned—not once, or twice—but three times! *However, there were also miracles.*

I hope this book about a mother's faith, a father's dream, and God's amazing miracles will encourage you to stand for truth and freedom for all, regardless of circumstances. When you believe God is in control and that with Him, anything is possible, as it says in Mark 10:27, you have no need to fear.

For most, Poland is just a country in the middle of Europe whose boundaries and very existence came and went depending upon the outcome of war after war after war. Facts, however, don't feed your soul or cause you to cry out against lies, injustice, and cruelty. *But this story will.*

Chapter 1

Dreams, Doubt, and Disappointment

(Christmas, 1928: Ostrowo[2], Poland)

Elza, meaning "God is my joy," was born in Lotz, Poland, on February 1, 1903, to Pauline Gebeorin Mai and Emil Gartz. How prophetic her name would turn out to be! Discovering God's love, knowing more about Him, and following His will, was her heart's desire—and her greatest joy. Here is Elza's story.

Elza stood alone, looking out the window of her family's farmhouse. *Nothing!* In the distance, the cathedral's steeple bells were faintly ringing over the crystalized snow covered hills of rural Ostrowo, Poland.

"He would be here soon. Surely he would come." But over the years, love had a way of flirting and fleeing from Elza.

It was Christmas day, and she was alone. Well, almost alone.

Elza could hear her mother in the kitchen, clinking cups and saucers in the suds-filled sink—cups that just a few hours ago held sweet, creamy coffee and saucers that cradled delicious thick slices of monkuken, that yummy poppyseed strudel that made their family's traditional Christmas brunch such a delight.

Guilt swept over Elza as she once again glanced out the window. She probably should be helping her mother—but the last thing she wanted was to be alone in the kitchen with Pauline. She feared her mother was once again preparing her "old maid" lecture which she delivered to her eldest daughter far too often. Plus, Elza was in her yellow silk dress waiting for a

---

[2] Ostrowo (pronounced "oh-stroh-voh") was the German name for what is now the Polish town of Ostrow Wielkopolski. It is in west-central Poland, about 25 km southwest of Kalisz and 144 km west of Lodz.

guest! Christmas was for merriment, celebration, music, and stimulating conversation, not lectures and housework!

Elza sighed as she tried to process why, with her mother and father and seven siblings, she felt so lonely. "You'd think," she fretted, "my brothers and sisters who no longer live on the farm would at least drop in for a visit on Christmas! And why wasn't her father home?" He was probably at some tavern—celebrating with his drinking buddies.

Elza wondered, *"Was it an economic necessity that her father spent so much time away from home or an acceptable excuse for his lengthy absences?"* Marriage was so complicated! She sighed, "It probably wasn't Tata's[3] idea in 1906 to move from the bustling textile capital of Lotz to this tiny farm just because Ostrowo's economy was healthy and the town was expanding and becoming a vital railway hub. Pauline was the one who wanted a cow, chickens, and a garden to feed the family. Emil was a fun loving city boy and a traveling textile salesman—but he wasn't always a good provider! Plus, Mama's sharp tongue could make life difficult, so it was no surprise that he simply disappeared for long periods of time.

Elza remembered their first few years in Ostrowo when she and her two oldest brothers had to scrounge for food in the garbage in order to survive! That was before the farm started producing, and Pauline began her "black market business," selling Polish products to the Germans and importing foreign goods for the Poles. She was good at it—a born wheeler-dealer. No one would ever suspect her of dabbling in illegal activities.

Tata? It wasn't as if he didn't love his family, for he had a habit of appearing at the most surprising times, bringing his wife a simple bouquet or some sweets and gushing with regret that he had been away so long. "Yes," Elza mused, "he had come often enough to keep his wife either pregnant or nursing babies for most of Elza's growing years.

"And he wasn't always an absent father." Her earliest memory of her tata was snuggling up on his lap in the rocking chair with him telling her his favorite story about when she was little. He and Mama managed a gaststube in Lodz, which was an inn with a restaurant, tavern, billiards, and a large room that could be rented out for weddings and other special occasions.

His story went like this: "When you were a tiny girl, I would lift you into the air, kissing your nose and saying, 'Come, my little Elza; come and help Tata at the tavern. Mama must feed baby Emilek, so you shall be my

---

[3] Tata is Polish for Daddy.

helper.' And how Mama would object, "No, Emil, she is too young. The tavern is no place for a child!"

Elza laughed, remembering him saying, "So I just took Mama in my arms and smothered her with kisses, and then I'd whisk you away to 'happy hour' and lift you up on the tavern's bar, and your little feet would go tapping to the lively beat of the accordion player's polka with the crowd clapping and your tata urging you on, saying 'Dance my little princess, dance.'"

What a precious memory. Unfortunately, this carefree lifestyle would not last long.

What Pauline and Emil didn't know when they started their gaststube in 1901 was that Lodz was about to experience a major recession. Trying to run a successful business was a challenge in the early twentieth century in a town that was experiencing an economic collapse, worker's strikes, and Russian/Tartar control. They managed for five years but eventually lost the inn in 1906 to the Russians, and that's when the family moved to the farm in Ostrowo.

Elza was now twenty-six and no longer a dancing princess! Instead, she felt more like an aging spinster!! Elza hated it when her mom reminded her, "I married at twenty-one, and by the time I was your age, I had two children. If you wait much longer to marry, nobody will want you, and you'll end up an old maid!"

> *If you wait much longer to marry, nobody will want you, and you'll end up an old maid!*

Elza glanced over her shoulder at the cuckoo clock. She sighed. "It's getting late."

And then, just as Elza was about to give up, telling herself that once again she had been stood up or forgotten, she heard a gentle tapping on the door.

Instantly, she flashed a smile. Her eyes sparkled. Now, that was more like the compelling, vivacious Elza—sunshine, butterflies, and daisies even in the midst of winter! Her charming personality was irresistible. She smoothed her auburn hair and adjusted the long braids that encircled her head as she rushed to open the door.

"Paul, you came!" she exclaimed. "I'm so glad! I was so afraid your parents would object to you leaving them alone on Christmas."

"Of course, I came. After all, I promised your mama I would play some German carols for her. I know how much it means to her. And Christmas only comes once a year. It's such a shame to see your pretty little organ being neglected day after day with no one playing beautiful music on her keys.

If only my parents could afford such a luxury! Having to trudge over to the Evangelical Church[4] every day to practice is a terrible inconvenience."

Elza laughed, "Paul Kolata! You poor, poor boy!" she teased as she hung his coat and hat on the rack by the door. "Now I know why my mother and I are so fortunate on this Christmas day that you have come to fill our house with music: *You love our organ!*"

Paul hung his head, but all he could think of to rebut her jest was, "Well-l-l-l, I guess I do!" making Elza laugh.

"Mama," Elza called as she opened the organ cover and gestured for her guest to sit. "Paul's here to play for you."

Paul gave the organ stool a whirl and pushed it back a bit to accommodate his long legs. Then he placed his feet on the pedals and began pumping while he pulled out his favorite stops. Soon, the old familiar strains of "Silent Night" rang through the house.

Leaving her kitchen duties, Pauline found her way to the rocking chair and sat down with a sigh of pleasure. She, like her oldest daughter, loved music. "Ah, yes," she addressed Paul, "Now it's truly Christmas!" And together they began to sing: *"Stille Nacht, heilige nacht, Alles schläft; einsam wacht...."*

Elza's thoughts whirled around her head as she hummed an unfamiliar verse that Paul and Mama were singing. She loved hearing Paul play. Her face flushed as she remembered how he had hinted about marriage the last time they were together. *Was he the one?*

"Silent Night" blended into "O Tatumbaun." Elza was intrigued when Paul, after years of knowing him at church, finally mentioned marriage. But love? She wasn't sure. Everyone said he was perfect for her. They were alike in so many ways: He went to church every Sunday, was obviously talented, and was kind and polite to her—as well as to her mother. Why, then, was she so reluctant to just let go and fall in love like so many of her friends had? Confused, she began to second guess whether she was actually more in love with Paul's music than she was with him. She really, really needed to talk with him. They had been friends for so long! What was holding her back from falling in love? And why didn't Paul give her the attention she craved? Why was he so reluctant to commit?

Hearing a little ruckus in the back bedroom, Pauline sighed, stopped rocking, and got up to check on her two youngest children.

---

[4] In Poland (and throughout Europe), the Lutheran Church is known as the Evangelical Church or the Evangelical Lutheran Church. The vast majority of Polish citizens, however, are Catholic. Because Pauline had a German heritage, she and her children attended the local Evangelical Church.

Almost immediately, Paul stopped pumping—and the air whished out of the treasured instrument as the melody of *"Three Ships Come Sailing In..."* vanished, like the wind to the sails, into the silence left behind with Pauline's departure.

"I must talk to you," Paul looked earnestly at Elza, "about getting married."

"What? About marriage?" (*Was this the romantic proposal she had been yearning for since she was a teenager?*)

"Yes, about marriage," Paul almost whispered (just in case Pauline could hear them). "I've been thinking that we have known each other for years. We both attend the Evangelical Church. We both love music—and you sing so beautifully. And we both grew up on farms, but I-I-I," he hesitated and began again. "You see, I have a feeling my parents may not approve!"

"What do you mean?" Paul's sudden declaration had startled her. "I know you said they had hoped you'd marry someone from a well-to-do family, but we have so much in common—and I do have a good paying job at Tschapka's Konditorei[5] in town!"

"Well," he declared with an air of alarming authority, "we certainly wouldn't want to marry if one of our parents objected, would we?"

The shock of hearing these words turned Elza's world upside down. "But I thought since we had known each other so long..." her voice trailed off into a whisper as she rose from her chair and began to pace around the room. Then silence. She wanted a declaration of love—and instead, she was thrown a bucket of ice water! *What kind of a proposal was this?*

Paul twirled around on the organ stool and tried to repair the breech. "Elza, I really like you. Let's not talk about it right now. After all, it's Christmas. I'll go home and see if I can get my parent's approval to marry you." He hesitated then and added, "Please come and sing with me," and he began to play the old German carol, *Lo, How a Rose E'er Blooming* (Es ist ein Ros' Entsprungen).

But Elza was not into "blooming roses." She finally swallowed hard and willed herself to weakly respond with a sigh, "I agree, Paul. We shouldn't marry if your parents disapprove!"

After solving the ruckus in the back bedroom, Pauline reentered the parlor and again took her place in the rocking chair.

And then it happened.

There was another knock on the door, but this time it seemed urgent. Elza, needing an excuse to retreat from the intensely awkward situation, quickly got up and opened the door.

---

[5] A konditorei is a confectionary or pastry shop and sometimes serves as a café.

At the door stood Ania, one of Elza's Sunday school students, all bundled up and breathing hard as if she had been running. "Elza, Elza, I'm so glad you're here!"

"Come in, come in! But what are you doing here? And why are you in such a hurry?" gasped Elza.

Ania stomped the snow from her boots, entered, and quickly shut the door behind her to keep out the cold.

"Are you OK?" Elza inquired with a worried look. "It's Christmas! You should be home with your family!"

"Yes, I know, but wait till you hear..." Ania nearly exploded with excitement and made no move to take off her coat. "Elza, there's something strange going on at my house. *You need to come right away!* My dad figured you'd be at the farm since it's Christmas, so he sent me to get you, and he won't take no for an answer. We've got this book salesman who came to celebrate Christmas with our family and friends (*even though he wasn't invited*). After dinner, he started talking about things in the Bible we'd never heard of before, a-a-about Daniel and some big image with a head of gold...and about Babylon. So my dad challenged him, 'I don't know if what you're telling us is true. But I know a Sunday school teacher—she's the teacher of my two girls at the Evangelical Church—and she's pretty smart when it comes to the Bible. If you can convince her that you're right, then I'll let you continue telling us about the Bible. But if she says you're wrong...then you'll need to leave!"

Ania took a deep breath, "So Elza, you've got to come. It's very, very important. I can't go home without you!"

Elza knew her Bible—that was true. If anyone could set someone straight about what was in it, she could. *What should she do?* She looked confused and turned to Paul, who by this time had stopped playing the organ in order to hear what was happening at the front door. He sensed Elza's struggle—for he also knew how much the Bible meant to her.

"I don't know what to do." Elza shrugged her shoulders and glanced at Paul for an answer. An internal struggle was raging. She was almost in tears. Could she possibly turn away from someone begging her to study her favorite book? Yet, it was rude to leave Paul when he had come so far to see her, and they so desperately needed to talk.

"Go!" Paul said, knowing his home was several kilometers away. "It took me forever to get here on my bike because of the icy roads, so I'll just play a few more carols for your mother and then start home so I can make it before dark. Plus, I need to talk to my parents about... (He cleared his throat)…you know what! As soon as we have discussed our situation, I'll come back and tell you their decision. Go. You need to go!"

Elza grabbed her well-worn Bible—the one she and her brother Emil Jr. had read from cover to cover as they spent lonely hours watching their grandparents' goats graze on the hillside pasture when, in the 1920s, the Bolshevik-Russian Army invaded Poland and threatened the Ostrowo area with violence. Fearing for their teenage children's safety, Emil and Pauline sent their two oldest, Elza and Emil Jr., about 200 kilometers to the north to stay with Pauline's parents, Oma and Opa Mai, on their 200-hectare[6] farm in Poland's remote countryside, where they not only had goats but grew grain and had a mill. Days turned into months and months into almost two years before it was finally safe for the teens to return home. By then, both Elza and Emil had become knowledgeable Bible scholars.

After returning home, Elza continued learning new Bible facts as she taught her Sunday school class weekly. Now, after years of study, she felt confident in her knowledge of the Bible—and perhaps—a little arrogant. She knew she could prove Bible truth to this person who was upsetting people with strange teachings. Silently, she prayed, *"God, what should I do?"*

Finally, feeling called to a sacred mission, she thanked Paul for coming and pulled on her boots. "Please wish your parents a merry Christmas," she waved as she grabbed her coat and muff and shut the door against the cold wind that had begun to blow.

Then, holding tight to Ania's hand, the two girls slipped through the icy snow to…what? New adventures? New friends? New Bible insights to challenge Elza's quest for truth? Her destiny? Elza glowed with excitement thinking about the encounter she was about to experience…and thoughts of love, music, Paul, and rejection vanished.

---

[6] about 500 acres

Chapter 2

Elza Meets Her Match

(Christmas 1928: Ostrowo, Poland)

In the late 1920s and '30s, Wladyslaw Stefan Kuzma (known to most as Wladek[7]) was a dedicated Christian bookseller, going door to door spreading what he called "happiness for families!" At that time, few people in Poland had Bibles, so in addition to healthy lifestyle magazines, he sold Bibles and books filled with Bible truths such as salvation by faith, the literal second coming of Jesus Christ, Bible prophecy, and the importance of the Bible's fourth commandment to keep the seventh-day, Saturday, holy. He also offered free Bible studies. They called him a literature evangelist. He loved his work—and was good at it! This is how he became part of Elza's story.

For the last month, Wladek had been knocking on doors from early morning until after dark, selling Bibles and life-changing literature that he knew would make excellent Christmas gifts.

God had blessed! This definitely was his calling! In fact, he remembered the very moment it happened. He had just been baptized by immersion in 1923—and had prayed, "OK, God, what do You want me to do now?" He was sure that his mission wasn't to make shoes, even though he came from a long line of cobblers (his grandfather, uncles, father, and two older brothers) and was about to finish a three-year cobbler apprenticeship.

Then one night, he had a "life-changing" dream. He saw Jesus handing him a basket filled with pieces of bread, saying, "Feed my sheep!" *That's all it took!* Instantly, he knew God was calling him to share the gospel by selling Bibles and Christian books, giving Bible studies, and starting churches, just like the literature evangelist who had sold him his first Bible! *He was to feed people who were hungry for Bible truth.*

---

[7] pronounced "VAH-dek"

"What a week!" exclaimed Wladek now. "So many people were interested in studying the Bible!" His adrenalin was flowing! He bent lower on his bike, pushing hard against the steepness of the hill and the chill of blowing snow. "Lord," he prayed, "may my testimony and the books I've sold make a difference in people's lives!"

Snow was falling again. The icy wind was blowing giant flakes into Wladek's face, making his dark lashes and bushy mustache frosty as he pushed the pedals harder and breathed a little faster as he anticipated snuggling under the feather-filled comforter in his room at The Lutheran House. "Brrrr," he shivered. "Thankfully, tomorrow is Christmas."

He rounded a corner and recognized his neighborhood. The street was quiet—except for the chimes from the distant steeple reminding parishioners to attend midnight Mass. Even carolers had gone home to their families. He imagined the smell of homemade pastry and the sight of neatly wrapped presents under decorated trees—but he had no family nearby—no pastry and no tree!

Wladyslaw Stefan Kuzma was alone. There would be no one looking out a frost-covered window anticipating his arrival. As his boarding house came into view, he thought, *Maybe my New Year's resolution for 1929 should be to find a wife!* He smiled, *"My mother would probably like that!"*

As Wladek parked his bike and grabbed his almost empty leather satchel, he exclaimed, "I wonder what the New Year will bring? How many people will I be able to reach with the good news that Jesus is coming again? How many souls will be saved with the Bible truths held in the books I sell?"

Christmas morning, Wladek awoke with the sun shining through the frosty windowpanes and the aroma of freshly baked bread wafting from the kitchen. Most of the residents were already eating. He dressed quickly and headed to the dining room where Mrs. Anderson, the matron, had thick slices of fresh bread and marmalade and a huge skillet with scrambled eggs seasoned with Polish sausage for the residents …and a special dish of eggs with no sausage marked "Kuzma." His buddies thought he was crazy to pass up the "good stuff" just because it was on God's Leviticus 11 list of "unclean meat." Even his brothers and sister back home teased him about his strange eating habits. They couldn't understand how not eating "unclean" meat, like pork, had anything to do with being a Christian. Just a few years ago, he would have thought the same thing. But once he read 1 Corinthians 6:19–20 about your body being the temple of God, it was a no-brainer. If God said, "Don't eat it," he didn't!

With his tummy full, Wladek needed to decide where to spend the day. He would have loved to see his family again but the tiny village of Tuszewo near Grudziadz on the Vistula River in northern Poland was a day's train ride away! Besides, ever since he had started studying the Bible with the Seventh-day Adventist bookseller, his devout Roman Catholic parents, especially his mother, had gone ballistic! In fact, she was so upset when Wladek announced he was joining a church that worshipped on Saturday (the "Jewish" Sabbath) and believed Jesus was coming soon, she had gone to the priest asking, "What shall I do?" Wladek still remembered the shock he had felt when he learned what had happened next.

The priest had replied, "Well, if your son dies before he becomes a Seventh-day Adventist, he will be saved." That comment planted an insane thought in this devoted mother's mind: she had brought Wladek into the world and was responsible for his salvation. *To save her son, would she have to kill him?* Finally, one afternoon, when he was napping in his downstairs bedroom, she took a butcher knife and started down the stairs. Thankfully, at that very same moment, her sister, Julia, came through the backdoor, saw Anna with the knife, and stopped her!

As strange as it seemed, Wladek understood his mother's odd behavior. He thought back to his childhood when he and his mom were both devout Catholics in Andrychow[8]. They faithfully attended Mass at the beautiful Rzymskokatolicki Church, built in the ninth century. In fact, he had been an altar boy for two years, assisting the priest during Mass. He eagerly professed his love and service to God. He enjoyed the reverent atmosphere of the church with its beautiful stained glass windows, the religious frescos, and the statuary of saints and expressed an interest in entering the priesthood. But in all that time, Wladek had never seen a Bible. He had asked the priests, but they always said the Scriptures were given by God to the priests to interpret—not to people who didn't understand. Instead of accepting that excuse, it ignited Wladek's curiosity—until finding a Bible became his passion.

> *That comment planted an insane thought. To save her son, would she have to kill him?*

Wladek seldom took the time to reflect on his early life, but this was Christmas morning and he had the time. He smiled as he thought back to how God led him to discover Bible truth. "All I want to do is follow what

---

[8] Andrychow is a small town in southern Poland. Until 1918 it was located in the Austrian province of Galicia, so the Kuzma family spoke German as well as Polish. Kuzma is an eastern European/Slavic name that probably originated from Russia or Ukraine.

the Bible says, yet I'm so frustrated because I don't know anyone with a Bible," he had confided in a friend who was an ex-priest.

"Well," said his friend—pausing as he considered how to respond—"what you need to do is find a Seventh-day Adventist, because all their beliefs come directly from the Bible."

Wladek now smiled to himself as he thought back on his passionate search for truth. Even as a teenager, he had known that if he ever met a Seventh-day Adventist and became one, he would be ostracized from his family. However, he never forgot what the ex-priest had told him about these Bible-keeping Christians.

Then, because of economic necessity, Wladek's family had moved from Androchow to the Grudziadz[9] area of Poland, where his father and older brothers were cobblers. Everyone had expected Wladek to follow in their footsteps. But Wladek felt abused and rejected in his home, so when he was fourteen, he had moved out. He was smart, loved to read, and was a quick learner, but because of the chaos of World War I, he had only attended four years of formal schooling.

Wladek never had much in common with his brothers, who enjoyed drinking, gambling, and partying as teenagers. He was more serious, loved God and music (he played the mandolin, violin, and harmonica), and enjoyed reading books about history, art, and poetry. He was short, wiry, and determined, yet kind and sensitive with a spiritually inquisitive nature—so, unfortunately, he grew up lonely and misunderstood.

When Wladek left home, the railroad looked exciting and was fast becoming the number one industry in the Grudziadz area. His first job was stoking fires to fuel the train's steam engines. It was hard work and not at all fulfilling. After a year or so, Wladek quit that job and joined the army. But that was even worse—and lasted only the required year. At last, Wladek succumbed to his family's urging and went back to his old hometown of Andrychow, where his father had arranged an apprenticeship for him with a well-known cobbler.

Wladek became an excellent cobbler, but his passion for finding a Bible far exceeded his interest in shoes. What made the three-year apprenticeship bearable, however, was his mentor's library. Searching the shelves one day, Wladek found a book with an intriguing title, *The Great Controversy between Christ and Satan*, by Ellen G. White. The owner, although he had never read the book, gladly lent it to Wladek, who devoured it. But because it quoted so many Bible texts, it only increased his desire to find a Bible of his own.

---

[9] Grudziadz is a city in northern Poland on the Vistula River.

Then, one night, Wladek had a dream about a man knocking on his door with a briefcase full of Bibles. Immediately, he knew this wasn't an ordinary dream. A few weeks later, a traveling bookseller knocked on the door of the house where Wladek was staying. The owner sent the bookseller away. Wladek, however, recognized the man as the same one he had seen in his dream, and he ran down the road after him. When he caught up, Wladek breathlessly asked, "Do you have a Bible in your briefcase?"

"Why, yes! I have a number of Bibles and some other books that help explain the Bible." He showed Wladek a copy of the *The Great Controversy*, the book he had just read.

That sealed the deal. Wladek bought the man's entire inventory, which led to Bible studies and the conviction that, at last, he had found Bible truth. Wladek had then asked to be baptized the Biblical way—by immersion.

Enough reminiscing, he thought to himself. *Now I've got to figure out how to get invited to someone's house for Christmas!* He then remembered the railroad executive in Ostrowo who had recently purchased a book from him for 34 zlotys. It was the most expensive book Wladek sold! The man's wife had been so kind! *Why not visit the Streibels? Surely, they wouldn't turn me away on Christmas—and they might purchase more books! Yes,* he decided, *that's where I'll go!*

Around noon, Wladek arrived at the Streibel's house, which was full of guests. But thankfully, Mrs. Streibel invited the lonely bachelor to stay for dinner. After dessert, not wanting to waste an opportunity, Wladek began to talk to the guests about the book of Daniel and the prophecy of the image in Daniel 2. Everyone listened politely. But as soon as Wladek started sharing the dream's interpretation, the railroad official got nervous.

"Ahem," he said as he cleared his throat. "I'm not a Bible student, so I can't really judge if what you're saying is true, but I know who can. There's a young woman whose family lives down the road. Elza is an excellent Bible student. In fact, she's the Evangelical Church's Sunday school teacher for my daughters. And Ania, my oldest, is her friend."

"Mr. Kuzma," he turned and addressed Wladek, "since it's Christmas, she's probably with her family right now. What if I send Ania to ask her to come over to hear what you have to say?"

Mr. Streibel continued, "If you can convince Elza Gartz that what you are telling us is true, then we'll be more interested in listening. Otherwise, I think we should change the subject—and you should probably leave."

Wladek agreed, "Good idea. I think she will enjoy my presentation."

So Ania put on her heavy coat and boots and immediately left for the Gartz farm. About an hour later, Ania returned with what seemed to Wladek, the most beautiful girl in the world. When Elza removed her coat, and he caught sight of her in her beautiful yellow silk dress, her stylish gold rimmed glasses, and her beautifully braided hair, his heart leaped.

Immediately, Wladek announced to the guests, "I have so much material to cover that I will share the first part now and the second part on Thursday night, which is two days away."

Ah-ha! Wladek thought, *Now I will have an opportunity of seeing Elza two nights this week, instead of just one!*

Elza, on the other hand, was so absorbed in the Bible story about the image with the different body parts representing different world kingdoms that she hadn't paid much attention to the speaker other than thinking, *The man is rather short—and definitely not my type—with his faddish Kaiser mustache and his well-worn suit.*

But he did seem familiar to her. *Where have I seen him before?*

Instead of the man, however, she was fascinated with the message from the second chapter of Daniel: The gold head of the image representing Babylon; the silver shoulders and arms were Medo-Persia; then the bronze belly and thighs, Greece; the legs of iron, Rome; and the ten toes of iron and clay, the divided nations of Europe. She turned to every text Wladek mentioned and read it from her own Bible.

As Wladek ended the lecture and began shaking hands, he was unaware that Mr. Streibel had turned to Elza and asked, "Well, what do you think?"

"It sounds very interesting," she said. "In fact, I was impressed!" She paused and added, "Of course, I'll have to refresh my knowledge about the progression of major world empires in history. But as far as I can tell, he seems to be onto something and has made a meaningless prophecy very enlightening."

"I felt the same way," Mrs. Streibel joined the conversation. "Yes, it was very interesting. I just wonder why I've never heard of the prophecy before."

"Well," smiled Elza, "I guess we'll just have to come back and hear part two. I've got to get back to my mother's place now, reflect on what I've heard, and look up each text I wrote down!"

Just then, Wladek approached Elza as she was about to leave and politely inquired, "Miss Gartz, I was wondering if you would like me to walk you home? It's on my way to The Lutheran House where I live, and it will soon be dark."

"How kind of you," Mr. Streibel replied, so Elza could hardly decline. As they prepared to leave, Elza turned to the Streibels, "Thank you for the invitation and tell Ania goodbye. I'll see you again Thursday night."

As Elza and Wladek turned to walk toward the Gartz farm, Elza commented, "Now that I realize the prophetic significance of Nebuchadnezzar's dream, I'm curious about how many other Bible prophecies I have missed in my Bible study."

Elza was impressed with Wladek's broad knowledge—and he was excited to hear of her interest in the Bible. But it was not until he saw the Gartz farmhouse that he realized why Elza looked so familiar.

"I've been here before," he exclaimed, "with my friend, Pastor Kosmowski! I think it was about a year ago when I first came to town. The lady of the house had invited my coworker and his American friend to lunch, and at the last minute, the friend had another appointment, so Pastor Kosmowski invited me to join him. I remember the lady was a terrific cook—and we had an interesting Bible study together."

Suddenly, Elza remembered. "Yes!" she exclaimed. "That was my mother, Pauline. I actually recall that day. I live in Tschapka's boarding house next door to the Tschapka Konditorei[10] where I work, but that day, because it was Sunday, I was visiting my mother. You came just as I was leaving, so I didn't pay much attention to my mother's guests. But I do know she was highly interested in the Bible studies the pastor had with her. What a fascinating coincidence!"

At the door, Wladek politely said, "Elza, thank you so much for coming to the Streibel's house today. I'm looking forward to seeing you again on Thursday night." Then, because a cold wind was blowing, he got on his bicycle and rode away as she turned and entered the warm, cozy farmhouse.

Wladek was impressed by Elza's beauty, but when he realized that she was far more interested in his message than she was with the messenger, his main focus turned to sharing Bible truth with her! In fact, courting didn't even enter his mind, but this was soon to change.

---

[10] Tschapka's Konditorei was well-known in Poland and Germany and was the official bakery for Kaiser Wilhelm (German Emporer and Prussian King from 1888 to 1918). When Elza met Wladek, she had been working at Tschapka's Konditorei for more than six years and rented a room in Tschapka's boarding house next to his konditorei. Because it was close to her family's farm, she often spent vacation days and weekends at the farm.

The next weekend, Elza's friend Paul visited the Gartz farm as promised. He only stayed a few minutes.

His message? "Elza, I'm so sorry, but my parents do not approve of us getting married. I know this decision is not what you wanted to hear. But they feel I should marry someone younger to help me take care of our 200 hectare[11] family farm."

No, this was not what Elza wanted to hear. But she had no choice in the matter. With a heavy heart, she responded, "I had a feeling it wasn't going to work out. Thanks for coming all this way to tell me. God knows what's best. I've appreciated your friendship over the years—and your music."

"Thanks for understanding," Paul replied as he turned to go.

"Happy New Year," Elza called. "I'll see you at church!"

Then Paul, nodding his head with a final glance toward Elza, got on his bicycle and rode away as she closed the door on that chapter of her life. Except for a few fleeting glances across the crowded Evangelical Church, Elza never saw Paul again.

---

[11] about 500 acres

Chapter 3

The Storm of Opposition

(1928–1929: Ostrowo, Poland)

What neither Wladek nor Elza knew as they walked toward the Gartz farm that Christmas night was that, by morning, a major storm of religious opposition would be brewing in Ostrowo that would deeply affect them both. Here's what happened:

The day after Christmas, Mrs. Streibel called Pastor Ruiz of the Evangelical Church and told him about the Seventh-day Adventist man who had given them a Bible study on the image of Daniel 2. She then mentioned that their Sunday school teacher, Elza Gartz, appeared very interested. "Should we be worried?" she asked.

"Yes!" Pastor Ruiz replied. "All heresy must be stopped!" He took a deep breath. "Who is this man, anyway? Obviously, he's a heretic sent from the devil to confuse our good church members. We must do everything possible to get rid of him."

"Well," continued Mrs. Streibel, "I think he's staying at The Lutheran House!"

"What?" the pastor yelled. "He can't be! He's a wolf in sheep's clothing! We must evict him at once!"

Pastor Ruiz then called Mrs. Anderson, the manager of The Lutheran House, and threatened her, "Mrs. Anderson, you're going to lose your job if you don't force Mr. Kuzma to leave our boarding house immediately. We are providing this facility to help Lutherans and Mr. Kuzma is NOT a Lutheran. In fact, he is teaching Adventist doctrine like keeping holy the Jewish Sabbath instead of the Lord's Day, which conflicts with what the Evangelical Church teaches."

"But," replied Mrs. Anderson, "Mr. Kuzma is a kind man and never complains; I like him. He's been here almost a year, and I've never heard him trying to confuse the other boarders. He loves the Bible and has an amazing understanding of Scripture. He doesn't argue or speak against our church. He just quotes Scripture. *Why are you doing this?"* Mrs. Anderson questioned. "I don't think kicking him out is very Christian!"

Mrs. Anderson tried her best to reason with her pastor, but Pastor Ruiz's decision was final. "Mr. Kuzma must leave immediately. In fact, I want him out of there tomorrow!" the pastor shouted.

Wladek, after hearing about the conflict he had created, packed his belongings and left. He found a room in a boarding house owned by a kind Polish lady who was very accepting when he explained, "I don't eat pig meat, so please don't cook with bacon." The accommodations, however, weren't nearly as nice as the room he had enjoyed at The Lutheran House.

But even worse than losing his lodging, as word spread that the Adventist man was trying to "steal sheep" from the Evangelical Church, the Streibels canceled the Thursday night Bible study.

Wladek was disappointed, but not wanting to add fuel to the fire of controversy, he decided to concentrate on selling health magazines and Bibles in Ostrowo rather than doctrinal books. *However,* thought Wladek, *I don't want to cancel the meetings. So many people are interested in hearing more Bible facts.* He decided to go to Tschapka's Konditorei to consult with Elza.

Elza was shocked to see him. "I'm busy right now," she said, "so I can't talk."

"No problem," he answered, "I'll wait since I have nothing else to do."

After she finished with some customers, she came over to Wladek. "What a surprise! Is something wrong?"

He then told her about Mrs. Streibel calling Pastor Ruiz and about the pastor kicking him out of The Lutheran House and the Streibels canceling the Thursday night Bible study. He ended with, "I know you're interested in studying the Bible. What do you think we should do?"

"Well," Elza took a deep breath, "I told my mother about what you said about Daniel's image, and she was interested in learning more, so why don't we join the Bible study group Pastor Kosmowski has every Sunday at my mother's house?"

After some discussion, Wladek agreed. "This, indeed, might be the answer," he said. "After all, the pastor is such a popular speaker the meetings might even be more interesting if the two of us combine our efforts."

For the next six weeks Elza never missed a meeting. Before each session, Wladek would go into the woods and kneel. "Lord, I need wisdom and Your blessing. I pray for souls for Your kingdom. Help me to know what to say so the people with whom we are studying will want to return. Amen."

God answered Wladek's prayer by inspiring him to end each study with a question that was to be answered at the next meeting. Elza's curiosity was sparked—and the others who were attending kept coming back week after week.

Elza recognized Wladek's teaching skills and expressed her admiration to her mother, "Wladek is gifted in the way he answers questions so no one is offended. I don't know how he does it. I wish I could do the same." She thought for a moment and then added, "He's an amazing Bible teacher. His love for God seems to make it easy for him to have a conversation with others and answer questions in a way that really meets their needs. He can talk to anyone and steer them to God's Word."

While the meetings were going on, Pastor Ruiz never contacted Elza or her mother about his concerns. He did, however, complain to Elza's boss, Tschapka, who was not only a church member but also an elder of the Evangelical Church. "Be careful, Tschapka," he warned. "This man is dangerous and will make you pay him tithe." (This, of course, wasn't true!)

Tschapka then pleaded with Elza to give up this religious foolishness so things could return to normal. But nothing he could say would change her mind about the Bible studies. The truth was the truth. If God said it, she believed it, regardless of what others thought. She felt trapped in the middle. If only her pastor would study these issues for himself instead of spreading lies about people just because they believed differently!

> *I don't care if what they say is true or not. I just want them gone!*

As time went on and the meetings continued, Pastor Ruiz began bribing his parishioners by promising them money if they could drive Mr. Kuzma and Pastor Kosmowski out of town. "I want to make it clear," he announced, "I don't care if what they say is true or not. I just want them gone!"

When Wladek heard about the pastor's irrational declaration, he was sad. Religious persecution had been going on for centuries. He remembered reading about the crusades in the Middle Ages, where the papacy tried to take the Holy Lands from Muslim control and all the people they killed in the process. The "church" even persecuted people like Martin Luther, who dared to believe differently. Now he was finding that the Protestant Evangelical "Lutheran" Churches in Poland were also prejudiced and he was in the middle of what appeared to be a spiritual battle between Bible truth and the doctrines of established denominations.

Elza responded by studying her Bible more earnestly to make sure what she was learning was Biblically correct. She was shocked to learn that the day of worship had been changed from Saturday to Sunday by the Roman Emperor Constantine and the Catholic Church in the fourth century. "No way," she exclaimed. "That can't be true!" Elza was determined to find a Bible text to prove Wladek didn't know what he was talking about. But her study just made her more convinced that Saturday (the seventh day of the week) was the day on which God commanded His people to worship. The Bible in Genesis 2:3 says that after the six days of creation, "Then God blessed the *seventh* day and sanctified it, because in it He rested from all His work which God had created." The fourth commandment in the Protestant Bible says in Exodus 20:8–10, "Remember the Sabbath day, to keep it holy. Six days you shall labor and do all your work, but the *seventh* day is the Sabbath of the Lord your God...." When she read Luke 4:16, it was clear that Jesus' custom was to go to the synagogue each Sabbath to worship. Even though Elza searched, she couldn't find where Jesus changed that custom after His resurrection. Instead, she learned this change came directly from the Catholic Catechism, which claimed that although God's day of worship was Saturday, the Catholic leaders had the power to change the day of worship to Sunday to honor the Lord's resurrection.

When Elza realized that men—not God—changed God's day of worship, she once again was convinced that what Wladek was teaching was correct. Others began to believe, too. Soon, the attendance at the studies grew to about fifty people.

> *Elza was devastated when she realized that after all the years of serving her church as a much loved Sunday school teacher, the leaders accused her of believing Adventist "lies."*

As the weeks went by, many of the members of the Evangelical Church noticed that Elza did not attend their church as faithfully as she had before the meetings, and they began to ask questions. This prompted the general superintendent of the Sunday school to write Elza a letter saying: "We cannot understand why the Adventists are taking away one of our best Sunday school teachers. The Adventist people don't know what they're talking about. They're not educated. They're negative people. And they're poor. Since you have been our Sunday school teacher for so many years, we don't want these people to confuse your mind. For your salvation, please stop attending the Adventist meetings. Our children need you."

Elza was devastated when she realized that after all the years of serving her church as a much loved Sunday school teacher, the leaders accused her of believing Adventist "lies." How could she make them understand that everything she was learning was in the Bible? She appealed to Pastor Kosmowski, "Please help me use Bible proof texts in my answer."

Her letter, however, made no difference to the Evangelical leadership. Instead, they sent two more letters with more accusations, which she again answered using Scripture to defend her position.

The Evangelical leadership never acknowledged her thoughtful Bible-based answers. Instead, after three letters, they gave up trying to convince her of her error and notified her that she could no longer teach in their Sunday school.

Elza could not believe her friends from church were punishing her for believing the Bible! She loved teaching the children. She wept when she realized she was being shunned by people whom she had known and worshipped with since she was a teenager.

The Evangelicals, however, were not the only ones who didn't like what was happening in Ostrowo. When the Catholic leaders heard that Wladek and Pastor Kosmowski were teaching Bible facts to a large gathering at Pauline Gartz's house, they were incensed, called them "Red Devils," and warned people not to attend. The announcement, however, only stirred up people's interest, and instead of stopping the meetings, attendance grew.

Word about the religious controversy in Ostrowo soon reached the Seventh-day Adventist Polish Union leaders in Bydgoszcz (where their office was located in 1929), and they sent Georg Czembor and two other conference officials to try and pacify the opposition. But as soon as they left town, the conflict intensified between the established churches and the meetings. Elza felt as if she were caught in the middle.

During the weeks that the Bible studies were being held, Wladek and Pastor Kosmowski visited Elza at Tschapka's Konditorei a number of times. They loved Tschapka's famous buns, which were only five groszy, which meant they could get twenty for one zloty! However, the real reason the men went to Tschapka's shop was that they felt it was important to make as many contacts as possible with their Bible students.

The visits to her workplace didn't go over well. First, Elza wondered if they were spying on her, and second, the visits incensed her boss and ended up causing tension between them. Elza felt ostracized from her church but also persecuted at work.

She did, however, notice that her personal intensive Bible study was causing her to fall more deeply in love with Jesus. How amazing; at the same time, she felt the increase of criticism and rejection of her friends, she also sensed a closer relationship with God. She desperately wanted to share what she was learning with her family and friends, but the devil was doing everything possible to prevent this from happening.

Soon Elza became convinced that the Seventh-day Adventist Church taught God's true message because everything could be defended text by text from the Bible, and she made her conviction known at one of the meetings. Because there were others who felt the same way, Georg Czembor, an administrator from the Polish Union, came again. This time he held a special meeting to help establish a Seventh-day Adventist Church in Ostrowo. Elza, along with a few others, decided to do what the Bible said and be baptized by immersion. They wanted to become Seventh-day Adventists and charter members of the Ostrowo congregation.

The Fateful Decision

Elza was the first person from Ostrowo to become a baptized member of the newly organized church. She was baptized in June 1929 by R. J. Cunitz, the President of the Silesia-Galicia Conference[12] in a public swimming pool at the conclusion of a Seventh-day Adventist young people's conference in Bydgoszcz, a beautiful town on the Vistula and Brda Rivers—and a popular location for professional meetings and church assemblies.

Elza was excited about her new faith, but her happiness was clouded by the rejection of her family. She hadn't told any of her siblings about being baptized because she knew they would try to talk her out of it. Her brother Emil, who was her most influential sibling, had moved to Rybnik where he had started what was to become the family business, Firma Delicja[13]. Before he moved, he knew about the Bible studies at his mother's home, but being a leader in Pastor Ruiz's Evangelical Church, he chose not to attend. Her brother Alfred, who was seven years younger, attended many of the studies and knew the most about the Adventist message, but he wasn't interested in being baptized. When Selma, who was eleven years younger than Elza, heard her sister was joining the church, she told Elza, "It would have been

---

[12] The Adventist Polish Mission Conference was made up of three smaller conferences, one of which was The Silesia-Galicia Conference which included the town of Ostrowo. In 1930 the Adventist work was reorganized and the administrative office was moved to Warsaw and eventually became known as the Polish Union Conference.

[13] This successful business produced caramel candy and a sweet powdered fizzy drink (something like bubbly Kool-Aid). The factory flourished until the World War II's Nazi occupation took over the factory and forced it to close. All the Gartz family, except Elza and her father, had at times worked at the factory to help make it successful.

better if you would have gotten pregnant and brought home an illegitimate baby than for you to become an Adventist." Her comment deeply hurt Elza.

Elza's mother, Pauline, knew about her daughter's baptism but wasn't able to attend.[14]

Even though Elza's family missed what Elza felt was the most important day of her life, the friends who had followed her spiritual journey were there: Wladek and Pastor Fabian Kosmowski and those from the Bible study group who had also chosen to be baptized. Together, they would form Ostrowo's new Adventist Church. Plus, Georg Chambor, the distinguished administrator of the Polish Union, was there! Despite her family's rejection, it was a memorable day.

---

[14] Pauline was convinced that what she was learning in her Bible studies was true, but being an Adventist meant a major lifestyle change, and she wasn't ready to make that decision. Eight years later, Pauline was baptized, but by then, she was helping to run the family business in Rybnik, and even though she believed Bible truth, she found that not doing any work on the Sabbath was difficult. She was never a strong member of the Adventist community.

Chapter 4

Wladek's Search for Truth

(1895-1929)

"Tell me about your family," Elza asked Wladek one Sunday night while walking home after the Bible study at the Gartz farmhouse. These walks had become a meaningful routine, giving Elza uninterrupted times to probe her friend's mind about the new Bible facts she was learning.

When Wladek didn't answer her question about his family, Elza prodded. "You know everything about me. You've met most of my family, and you've been an incredible Bible teacher. But you never talk about yourself. I know very little about you or your family. That's not fair!"

"Well," Wladek hedged, "There's not much to tell."

"What do you mean?" Elza playfully teased. "Everyone has a story—start with your childhood! What was it like?"

Wladek hesitated, "Well, mine wasn't exactly a happy one. In fact, I was so miserable I left home when I was 14."

"Really?" Elza was surprised. "That's so sad. Tell me more."

Wladek sighed and rolled his eyes, "I don't really know where to start."

"At the beginning," she said. "Tell me about your parents and your siblings."

"You can't possibly be interested in all that?"

"Yes, yes," Elza urged. "After all, it was you who brought me to a new understanding of the Bible and a new relationship with Christ. I will always be grateful. Why wouldn't I be interested in the circumstances in your life that made you willing to go through this crazy persecution by other Christians just to share Bible truth with people like me?"

"Well, I guess my story is an example of what God can do when you give your life to Him because I came from a very poor, hardworking, dysfunctional family of cobblers who had a strong Catholic heritage."

"OK, tell me more. Where were you born…and when?"

"I was born in Androhov, Poland, in 1895—the last of eight kids," Wladek began hesitantly—"but only four survived. Two died at birth, and another died so young none of us kids remember her. And I never knew my oldest brother, Jan Stefan, because when he was six years old, he fell off a teeter-totter and died six days later from a brain injury. My dad was never the same after that. His grief was so severe that he ended up neglecting the rest of us."

"I'm sorry," Elza lamented. Then, trying to lighten the mood, she said, "My dad delighted in telling me family stories. Did yours?"

"The only story I remember my dad telling happened when he was a teenager selling the shoes his family made. He would take a wagon full and sell them in various villages. One day, as he was going through a dense forest, he was attacked by gypsies. They stole every shoe he had. Well, that's it! Not much of a family heritage!"

"There must be more…" Elza interjected.

Hesitantly, Wladek continued, "As a kid, I lived with a lot of emotional pain, so I don't remember much. I do know my parents didn't give me much attention. In fact, no one, except maybe my sister, Angelica, understood me, so I spent a lot of time alone. My mother was especially stern and ridiculed me as a method of control. I felt I could never do anything right. I wasn't like my brothers. I was more serious and spiritually sensitive and internalized all the bad stuff instead of acting out. I loved books, poetry, music, and nature. They were more of the rough and tumble, loud, and demanding type—and ended up drinking, gambling, and partying as teens while I was timid and obediently went to mass every week with my mother, and she was proud when I became an altar boy. Actually, when I was a teenager, I even considered becoming a priest! I only went to formal school for four years. During the Great War[15], life was chaotic, and getting an education wasn't a priority."

"Wow," Elza exclaimed. "I would have never guessed you went through all that as a child. You're so knowledgeable—and such a great teacher. I would have thought you had gone to the best schools in the country!"

Wladek laughed. "Well, I always loved learning, so I read a lot, and I admired educated people, but my quest in life was to find out more about God. That's why my passion became finding a Bible so I could read God's Word for myself. My real education started when I read the book,

---

[15] now known as World War I

'*The Great Controversy between Christ and Satan*. It's a big book—over 400 pages! And it's filled with fascinating stories of martyrs—stories that you don't find in regular history books. And the more I read, the more I began to see God in a whole new light. I was amazed to discover He was a loving God. Plus, the book is filled with hundreds of Bible texts—which fueled my passion to find a Bible and read God's Word for myself. Well, that book opened up my mind, and suddenly, making shoes—which I was learning to do at the time—was the last thing I wanted to do.

"I guess living with conflict all my life, and hating it, made me sensitive to all those who had been persecuted because of their belief in God. The stories touched something in my soul, and I began to pray more earnestly for a Bible since it had become clear to me that, in each case, the person was martyred because of his or her belief in the Bible. There was just something within me that made me yearn for God to speak to me personally like He did with Moses in the burning bush—which, by the way, is one of my favorite Bible stories."

"All this when you were just a kid," Elza reflected.

"Well, I was in my twenties, so I thought I was grown up!" laughed Wladek. "I told you how I had been praying for a Bible. Well, that was my first burning bush experience."

"What do you mean?" Elza asked with a somewhat surprised look on her face.

"That's when God spoke to me for the first time in a dream. I had been reading about Daniel having dreams from God...and Joseph—and I wanted one, too. Only my prayer was to find a Bible so I could connect with God's awesome power. Maybe then, I wouldn't feel so inferior and could actually make a difference in this world.

"And that's when I had the dream about the literature evangelist knocking on the door and having a Bible in his briefcase. That dream was a life-changer! If God was that personal that He would hear my prayer and give me an answer in a dream—or a new insight that I had never considered before—I wanted more of that kind of power. I guess my feelings of inferiority as a child suddenly paled with the realization

> *That dream was a life-changer! My feelings of inferiority suddenly paled; I could make a difference in this world.*

that with God, I could make a difference in this world, even though I'm short and rather timid. Certainly not a courageous warrior like David!"

"Wow! What a great testimony! I guess I really want that power, too," reflected Elza. "And the second time God spoke to you in a dream was when you were uncertain about what God wanted you to do as a lifework, right?"

"Yes, that's when I had the dream about Jesus giving me a basket filled with pieces of bread and saying, 'Feed my sheep.' I suddenly was no longer in doubt as to what I should do. God was calling me to be a literature evangelist and share the gospel by selling Bibles and religious books, giving Bible studies, and starting Bible-believing churches, just like the literature evangelist was doing!"

"How awesome that you can live so close to God that He actually influences you or tells you what to do. I want that, too!" Elza admitted. "Oh, one more thing! How did you get started selling books? Did you have to go to school?"

"No! I just started…as they say, 'cold turkey!' (in Polish: *bez przygotowania*!) It's actually quite a fascinating story. Are you sure you have time for it?"

"Yes, yes! Don't keep me in suspense."

Wladek took a deep breath. "Well…I contacted Brother Bigalke, who at the time was the Publishing Secretary of the Adventist Polish Union, the Seventh-day Adventist Church branch that hires and supervises literature evangelists. I had an interview and started my career on Monday afternoon, three weeks before Christmas in 1923. My two mentors, the publishing secretary and another literature evangelist, took me by train to the little village of Tuchola (population 3000) in northern Poland. It was about 50 kilometers north of Bydgoszcz and 70 kilometers west of Grudziadz, where my family was living.

"When we arrived, Brother Bigalke explained to me, 'We will go down the road to the left, and you can go to the right. We will meet again at the train station in four days.' Other than the books and a receipt pad, all I had with me was my overcoat and hat—and my faith in God. It was freezing cold, and I started off in the direction I was told to go. To keep as warm as possible, I pulled my hat down as far as I could until it almost covered my eyes.

"And as I was walking along the road, I stumbled into a hole and struggled to climb out with my heavy case of books. It was a tough way to begin a new career. It was as if the devil was doing everything possible to discourage me. But I felt a calling from God and kept walking toward the village. When I got to the first house, I knocked on the door, and the person who answered asked, 'Are you selling something?'

"'Yes,' I answered enthusiastically, 'I have a good plan for you for Christmas to learn more about Christ our Savior.' I then gave my canvass and sold a book for 4.50 zlotys. Then the man asked, 'Do you have a Bible?'

"'Oh, yes! The Bible is a wonderful book,' I said. 'It has sixty-six books in one book for only three zlotys.' I then sold the man a Bible.

"At almost every house in the village, the people asked me for a Bible. I couldn't understand why. Later, I learned that someone had come to their village and told them that the Bible was the book that directs people to heaven. That's why everyone was so eager to have a Bible. I wondered if that 'someone' might have been an angel preparing the villagers to accept the books I was selling.

"It was about 9:00 that night when I went to the last house of the day. The moon was out and shown on the snow covered ground and trees. It was a beautiful, clear, freezing cold night. After the man of the house ordered some Bibles, he asked, 'Do you have a place to sleep tonight?'

"No," I replied.

"Then you can stay in our house," the man offered.

"That night, I talked to the man until quite late. I even had an opportunity to share with him the Bible message that Jesus was soon coming again to this world, this time to take us to heaven.

"As I went to the different homes, the Lord gave me the words to say. God gifted me with an understanding of how to interest people in the books I was selling. I'll admit, I was so eloquent at times I surprised myself! I got to the point quickly and in such a way that the people didn't want to let me go until they had purchased a book." Wladek laughed. "God made sure I was incredibly successful. In fact, I was so good I knew it wasn't me. It was obviously the Holy Spirit impressing me with just the right words. It made me realize what God can do in a person's life. As a kid, I would have never thought I could be a salesman. I was shy and certainly not assertive enough to talk to strangers and try to sell them books, as I'm doing now."

"So, what did your mentors think of your success selling books?" Elza asked.

Wladek laughed at the memory, "They were shocked! After four days, when I met up with them at the train station, they asked where my books were. I reported that I had sold over 1,000 zlotys worth of books. That was more than both the publishing secretary and his partner sold altogether. The men were quite impressed!

"But what was even more surprising was my mother's reaction. When I got back to my parent's home in Grudziadz, my mother, who had never complimented me on anything, asked, 'What did you do with all of your books?'

"'I sold them,' I announced.

"'What?' she exclaimed. 'You apprenticed as a shoemaker, and that's the trade I thought you'd follow—like your father and his father.' Then I showed her the money I had made. As she counted the zlotys, she began to shake her head in disbelief and commented, 'I can see now that the Lord has called you to this work, and He has blessed you.' I think that was the first compliment my mother ever gave me!

"So, on that positive note, I felt it was time to permanently move out of my parent's home and find a place of my own where I wouldn't be harassed and teased. I shared with my family what I had learned about the Bible, but they weren't interested. They were obviously impressed with the money I was able to make, but not with Bible truth. My presence and the lifestyle I was now living only made my fragile relationship with my family more delicate. So, now I am here in Ostrowo, where God has blessed us with a new Bible-believing congregation."

It was getting late. They were now standing by the front door of Elza's house, and Wladek was preparing to leave.

"Wait a minute," Elza called, "You can't leave until you tell me where you learned to give such insightful Bible studies."

"Oh," said Wladek, taking a few steps back to the door. "I'll try to make it short. My training began right after the dream about the literature evangelist with the briefcase full of books. The man asked me if I was interested in Bible studies. He was my model. That's when I learned that the doctrines of the Seventh-day Adventist Church came directly from the Bible. I also learned that this Adventist movement is a growing one. In fact, it's so new that it wasn't until about thirty years ago that the Polish people first heard this message, and an Adventist Church was started in Poland. After that, I absorbed the teachings of the Bible like a sponge and realized that what the Bible said was different from the teachings of many established churches. I was so excited about my discovery that as soon as my cobbler apprenticeship was over, I returned to Grudziadz to share my findings with my family. But, as you know, I was ridiculed for my strange beliefs and my new lifestyle. That's when my mother, based on something the priest had said, thought it was her responsibility, in order to save my soul, to kill me before I actually became an Adventist. Praise the Lord that my Aunt Julia talked some sense into her and my life was saved.

"In spite of my family's negative reaction to my new lifestyle and religious views, I remained convinced that the Seventh-day Adventist message was true because every belief could be found in the Bible. So I finally renounced my Catholic heritage, was baptized by immersion—like the Bible says—and joined the Seventh-day Adventist Church.

"And that's when I had the dream of the basket of bread and Jesus telling me to 'Feed my sheep.' So, I became a literature evangelist and have had many miraculous experiences. But after four years, I decided that I needed more training. My only knowledge of the Bible had come from my own study. Now, I longed to obtain the theological training necessary to become a Bible worker so I could be more effective in leading people to Christ and organizing churches.

"I talked to the Publishing Director and received permission to attend Mission Seminary Friedensau, located in Mockern, Germany, about two and a half hours by train from Berlin. At the time, it was the only Seventh-day Adventist Seminary in Central Europe. Friedensau was a life-changing experience for me. I loved the intellectual stimulation. I was like a starving man who couldn't get enough to eat when it came to the truths in the Bible. I studied late into the night so I could understand how the different texts fit together so I could give more meaningful Bible studies. I questioned my professors and felt an amazing sense of fulfillment in knowing how to prepare others for the soon return of Jesus. Actually, when I went to Friedensau, it was as if someone took a file and polished me so I could more effectively work with the public in presenting Bible truth."

"Wow, so Friedensau really made a difference in your ability to share the gospel?"

"Yes, a huge difference. While I was there, I made some meaningful contacts. For example, I became friends with another Polish student, Jan Martin Waspawny, who was studying to become a pastor. Jan told me about his cousin Francziszek Lyko, who lived in Zakopane, Poland's popular southern vacation destination at the foot of the Tatra Mountains near the border of Czechoslovakia. Both cousins had been in the Polish army during the Great War, but in two different locations.

"Jan was captured during the war and was a POW in Russia, where he learned about the Seventh-day Adventist message and joined the church. After his release in 1917, he went to Zakopane to share what he had learned about the Bible with his cousin, Francziszek, who was very interested, but Jan could only stay a few days. Ten years later, we were talking about Francziszek when Jan suddenly looked at me and said, 'What he needs now is someone who can provide him with religious literature and Bible studies. After you graduate, since there isn't an Adventist Church in Zakopane, why don't you go there and get one started? I'd go, but I'm already committed to another church district.

"I accepted the challenge, and as soon as I got my diploma, I headed to Zakopane, where I looked up Francziszek Lyko, sold him some books, and started Bible studies. Soon, a small group of people began to meet regularly to study the Bible together, and in 1927 we were able to start a small church.

"I was then asked to make my headquarters in Poznan, but it turned out to be a very difficult territory with strong religious opposition, which, I guess, was good training for what we have encountered here in Ostrowo."

"So after Poznan, they sent you here?" Elza inquired.

"Well..." Wladek started to laugh. "Actually, the director wanted to send me to Bydgoszcz, where his unmarried sister was living. (I think he was considering doing a little matchmaking on the side.) But instead, he suddenly said, 'No, I'm impressed you should go to Ostrowo. It's a nice town of 35,000, and there are no Adventist members in the region. It would be a perfect place for a literature evangelist.' And so I came here and have been sharing Bible truth as I knock on doors, sell life-saving books, and share my faith! And now, that's the end of my story!"

With that, Elza and Wladek decided it was time to get some sleep. Elza said goodnight as she turned to open her door and Wladek waved and headed down the street to the room he was renting.

It had been a life-changing night for Elza, learning how powerful God had been in directing Wladek's life. She went to bed determined to live so close to her Savior that she, too, could enjoy the same relationship with God that Wladek had experienced.

Chapter 5

The Lie That Sealed the Deal

(1930–1931)

Elza

There was something intriguing about Georg Chambor, one of the top administrators of the Adventist Polish Union. Elza had seen him when he came to Ostrowo to calm the storm of conflict caused by the meetings Wladek and Pastor Kosmoski were holding at Pauline's house. Then, he showed up again to establish the Ostrowo Adventist Church. The third time she saw him was at her baptism.

Who was this man? Elza wasn't blind! He was tall and good looking with wavy dark hair, and she could tell by his accent (as well as his name) that his heritage was German.

He seemed well suited to his job. He listened to people and made good decisions but was diplomatic. Her only reaction was that he seemed rather young to hold such a high church position. But she didn't think to ask anyone whether or not he was married.

Since Georg had shown Elza no special attention the times she had seen him, she just considered that it was his job to be there on those special occasions.

Now back in Ostrowo, with the Sabbath morning church services starting and the Bible study meetings continuing at Pauline's house, Georg Chambor's name would sometimes be mentioned in conversations about church business.

Because the administrative offices of the Polish Union had moved from Bydgoszcz to Warsaw in 1930, the church employees, like Wladek, now traveled to Warsaw if they needed to consult with their superiors or if they needed to attend special meetings.

Wladek

A few months later, R. J. Cunitz, the President of the Silesia-Galicia Conference[16] and the pastor who baptized Elza, was in Warsaw while Wladek was there for special meetings. Pastor Cunitz sent word to Wladek that he was anxious to meet with him and arranged an early morning appointment.

Six a.m.? questioned Wladek. *What on earth does he want to see me about that is so important that it's scheduled at 6 a.m.?* The message merely said, "I need to talk to you about a very important matter."

Wladek's curiosity was peeked. "It must be extremely urgent!" He began to worry. "What possibly does Brother Cunitz want to discuss with me?" Wladek could hardly sleep that night thinking about the early morning meeting. When the alarm rang, he got up quickly, dressed, and arrived at Cunitz's office five minutes early.

What a shock when Brother Cunitz began the meeting by asking, "Wladek, how much longer are you going to be a bachelor?"

Wladek nearly choked! "Well, sir. I really don't know! I don't even have a girlfriend."

"Why wouldn't Miss Gartz be a good wife for you? She speaks Polish and German, and she's a business lady, too. I want you to think about this. Go see her for more than just Bible studies."

Obviously, President Cunitz felt that if Wladek was ever going to get married, he needed an official push!

Suddenly, others seemed to be on his case. Even his friend, Pastor Luedtke, and a number of other coworkers were asking, "When are you going to get married and settle down? You better ask Elza before someone else comes along and steals her away from you!"

Wladek's head and heart were telling him it was time to start thinking about marriage—*and now his colleagues were pushing him!* The problem was Elza. Although she was a good friend and an interesting communicator, she had shown NO interest in a more serious relationship.

Elza

At the time that Wladek was being "pushed" into the idea of marriage, Elza was being pressured by her family—especially her mother—that if she wasn't careful, she would be an old maid. And the older Elza got—the more Pauline pushed! She was always saying, "Haven't you found someone yet?"

---

[16] At the time the Silesia-Galicia Conference was one of three conference offices under the Adventist Polish Union.

Recently, she even reminded Elza of the old platitude, "A single girl over twenty-one is like a wagon full of cow dung!"

"Mama!" Elza retorted in frustration. "I can't believe you'd say that! I've had suitors. It's just that the right man hasn't come along. For example, there was Paul Koleta—but if I'd married him after his parents disapproved, my life would have been miserable. Plus, even though I admired his music, I never really loved him!"

"And then there's Tschapka! For months, he's been pressuring me to marry him! I'm actually getting tired of avoiding his proposals!"

"Well, OK, so you've had a couple of suiters, but Tschapka is old enough to be your father. That would never work!"

"Not only that," Elza replied, "His family is high upper class. He knows people who know the Kaiser's family! I'd never fit in. Plus, his sister is constantly complaining about my lack of proper etiquette. She actually wants to send me away to charm school. I'd be absolutely miserable trying to please that family!"

"But Elza, you're not getting any younger!"

"Well, it's not as if I'm not dating. Remember how Emil tried to set me up with his border-control friend?"

"Yes, he wrote such beautiful poetry to you. And eight different times, he traveled a very long distance to visit you here at my house!" Pauline replied. "I liked him!"

"And I thought I would never get rid of him!" Elza sighed. "Thank goodness, Emil found someone else for the poet…and he's now happily married. He definitely wasn't my type!"

Elza took a deep breath and gave her mother a hug. "Don't worry, Mama, I will find someone at the right time. Besides, I'm a different person now than I was last year. I have different beliefs. And I'm meeting new people and making new friends. I'm happy with the way things are. Plus, we must never forget that our God is a God of miracles!"

Wladek

It wasn't long before Wladek was surprised to find that he was thinking more about Elza. Was he beginning to have feelings for her? He obviously liked her but he had no experience with falling in love. He was unsure of himself. This was unfamiliar territory, so he just harbored the warm feelings in his heart.

Their friendship was growing…perhaps it would just take more time. They did enjoy talking together, especially about the Bible. When she pushed him to tell her about his conversion, that was about as personal as their discussions ever got—and that was all about him. He realized he really didn't know much about Elza's likes and dislikes, let alone her hopes and desires.

Was he falling in love? He never declared his love for her. He never said he couldn't live without her. He didn't even say he was attracted to her. In fact, when he finally mentioned marriage (which was months later), it was more like a contract than a love relationship. He was far more practical than romantic. All he knew was that they were good together. Their friendship was growing, but it was a complimentary relationship—not an emotionally expressive one. And it was certainly not the magical romantic relationship that girls, including Elza, fanaticized would happen to them when they fell madly in love!

Wladek simply knew that Elza was the kind of woman who would support the work God had called him to do—and in his mind that was reason enough for marriage.

Practicality was vitally important to Wladek because he not only felt called by God, but he also loved selling religious books and giving Bible studies, and not every wife would be content to have her husband gone weeks at a time. In addition, Elza would be an asset to him in his ministry. She sang beautifully—in fact, they had even enjoyed singing together for various meetings. Plus, she was an excellent translator for him when he was lecturing to a group of both Polish and German-speaking people. It was easier for him if he could just speak in Polish and she could translate what he said into German, then for him to speak both languages. She had an engaging presence when she was up front, but even in a crowd, her smiles lit up the room. The kind way she treated people was amazing. Everyone was drawn to her. And obviously, he was too! But Elza was longing for a romantic love relationship—and it just wasn't there.

It wasn't long, however, before Wladek convinced himself that Elza would indeed be a good wife. There was only one problem; he had to convince Elza that she should marry him and he had no idea how to transition from a friend to a suitor. Instead, he "dug" himself into a deep, deep hole. *He told a lie that would haunt him for the rest of his life!*

It happened a few months after Elza was baptized. With the church headquarters now in Warsaw, the church administrators had organized a conference-wide Polish camp meeting to be held there. Everyone was excited. It was to be a week of good preaching, revival meetings, classes about evangelism and Bible prophecy, and the renewing of old acquaintances and the making of new ones.

So, Wladek asked Elza if she would like to go. "I would like to introduce you to some of my coworkers, and I know you will enjoy the meetings."

She happily accepted his invitation and was eager to make new friends. What Wladek wasn't expecting was that taking her to camp meeting would expose a beautiful, talented, newly baptized Adventist girl to a population of bachelors who were far more experienced and open in expressing their feelings than he was.

Elza looked amazing when she made her entrance to the first meeting. "Who is that?" Elza heard the whispering.

"Oh, that's Elza Gartz. She's a new convert. Someone said she was from Ostrowo and is quite the Bible student."

"I don't know about that—but she is very attractive. I don't think she'll be single for long!"

It was true! Elza, in her stunning blue dress and confident presence, was not only very attractive but also friendly and talented, which was noticeable when she sang a solo for one of the meetings. Georg Czembor, an administrator in the Polish Union (who just happened to be a very handsome and charming man), had met her three times before. Still, since Brother Czembor had been on official business, it was just a casual acquaintance. In fact, Elza had no idea he was single until Georg met her at camp meeting. Suddenly, they both experienced an immediate attraction to each other. He went out of his way to speak to Elza and give her special attention. She enjoyed this attention immensely and looked forward to the next time she would meet him on the camp meeting grounds. She couldn't believe this gorgeous man who was a leader of the Polish Adventist Church was single!

Elza never considered the train ride to camp meeting with Wladek as a date. Wladek was her friend and her spiritual mentor—nothing more. He was merely her escort to the event, and once she got there, she felt free to get acquainted with others rather than hang on to him. She was having a wonderful time meeting people, sharing her story, and making new friends—including the friendship of top administrative church leaders like Georg.

Wladek immediately noticed what was happening between Elza and Georg. He saw the "spark," but he didn't really know what to do about it. A couple of days later, however, when Georg and Elza's friendship seemed to be escalating, it really began to bother him. Having someone else pay obvious attention to the woman he had brought to the meetings as a friend made him realize just how much he really did care for Elza—especially when that someone was Georg Czembor, who was good looking, had a charming, charismatic personality and also held a prestigious position in the church!

Wladek was jealous! In fact, he was so jealous that he decided he had to say something. When he had the opportunity to speak to Brother Czembor in private, he blurted, "I don't think it is appropriate for you to pay so much attention to Elza!"

"Why not?" Brother Czembor asked. "If she is free, then there should be no problem!"

Now Wladek was trapped. He really had no right to tell his rival, "Hands off! I'm interested in her." So, without realizing the lifelong ramifications of his answer, he replied, "Elza is not available…because she's mine."

"What do you mean she's yours? Just because you gave her Bible studies and introduced her to the Seventh-day Adventist Church, it doesn't make her your property."

Wladek should have admitted at that moment that he had no hold on Elza. He should have merely said that he was falling in love with her and was planning to ask her to marry him. That would have been the truth.

But Wladek wasn't blind. He could see that there was definitely an attraction between Elza and Georg that was much more than his friendship with Elza. Suddenly, it dawned on him that because of his hesitation to declare his interest in Elza, it was very likely that he could lose her to a more aggressive man. He couldn't take the chance, so he blurted out the lie that would haunt his and Elza's relationship for a lifetime, "We're engaged!"

> **Wladek was so jealous that he decided he had to say something.**

"What?" Georg exclaimed. "I had no idea! You should have told me before. Elza is a very talented and beautiful woman. She will make a wonderful wife."

Brother Czembor immediately apologized to Wladek and backed off. "If I would have known, I would not have tried to pursue a friendship with her."

The problem was that Elza really liked Georg and was eager for a friendship. He was the first man she was truly attracted to and she was enjoying his attention. Even though Wladek had invited her to the camp meeting and she had come with him, he had never said anything about dating—let alone marriage, so she felt no obligation to him other than as a friend. She had enjoyed getting to know other men and even flirted a little. Now, she was puzzled. *Why had Georg stopped paying attention to her?*

Georg Czembor wasn't the only man attracted to Elza at the camp meeting. One of Wladek's friends, Brother Klutz, who was pastoring in the town of Kalisz just a few kilometers away from Ostrowo, was very impressed with Elza and wanted to get better acquainted. His wife had died, and Elza reminded him of her. After the camp meeting was over, he even made a special trip to Ostrowo to see Elza. But she kindly let him know that she wasn't interested. Wladek was thankful for that, but he never admitted this fact to Elza.

What Elza really wanted in a marriage partner was to fall head-over-heels in love with the man of her dreams. She wanted to be swept off her feet in a fairytale romance and courted by someone who made her feel like she was the center of his universe. And it wouldn't hurt if the man just happened to have a distinguishing presence with his dark, wavy hair! Wladek was short with straight brown hair. He was nice looking, but his appearance couldn't be described as dashingly handsome.

Here is the question: *Will Elza find the love she's looking for? Will Wladek become the man of her dreams? Or will her love for God, her age, and the pressure she was getting from her family cause her to give up her romantic fantasy? Will God give her the desires of her heart as He promised in Psalms 37:4, or will He impress her to yield her will to Him because He knows the end from the beginning and has a better plan for her life?*

Chapter 6

Sold for Chickens

(1930–1931)

The news about Elza getting baptized and joining the Seventh-day Adventist Church spread quickly through the town. No one but Elza and Wladek seemed to be happy about her decision. People all over Ostrowo were gossiping about the Adventist Bible worker who had stolen the Evangelical Sunday school teacher.

The opposition may have caused some to give up their faith, but not Elza. Nor did it cause Elza to change her mind about Bible truth or give up her friendship with Wladek. Instead, it drew them closer together. Elza felt so rejected by her former friends and coworkers that she once tearfully confided to him, "It is so hard for me; everybody is against me!"

By this time, Wladek really cared for Elza, and it broke his heart to see the rejection she was experiencing. He wanted to protect her and take her away from the conflict, so he began to bring up the subject of marriage. "Marry me," he urged. "We have the same religious beliefs and so much in common. We are a good ministry team. I can speak and you can translate for me. And we even sing together! There is no reason we shouldn't get married. I'm falling in love with you—and in time, you can learn to love me."

Elza respected Wladek for the strength of his convictions. She didn't want to hurt him because she owed him her newfound joy in the Lord. After all, if it hadn't been for his knowledge of the Bible and his willingness to take the time he did to share this Bible information with her, she would have never fallen overwhelmingly in love with Jesus, her Savior. Wladek had shown her a God of love who accepted her unconditionally—and she felt free and energized and truly happy in God's love. She would always be indebted to Wladek for that. But when it came to marriage, she had in her mind a romantic ideal—and her friend and mentor didn't measure up to who she had visualized as a life partner. So whenever he brought up the subject of marriage, she kindly responded, "I'm sorry, Wladek. You are a good friend—and I highly respect you. But I'm not ready to marry you."

Wladek, however, wouldn't take no for an answer. He had told Georg Chambor a lie that he felt he was obliged to rectify. He had said he and Elza were engaged. Now, he felt pressured to make it come true. And as he prayed, in spite of his lie, he felt more and more convinced that Elza was the girl God had chosen for his wife. So again and again, he broached the subject. And again and again, Elza turned him down.

At the same time, the hostility of the members of the Evangelical Church and the Catholic Church toward what Wladek had done in "stealing" Elza from the Evangelical congregation was so strong that Brother Cunitz, who was president of the Adventist Silesia-Galicia Conference—and was the pastor who had baptized Elza and urged Wladek to court her, thought it would be best for the survival of the small Adventist Church in Ostrowo, for Wladek to back off and let the conflict caused by the town's people settle down.

"No, that won't work!" the stubborn administrator retorted. "I'm moving you to Dzialdowo, NOW!"

To make sure Wladek would "back off," Brother Cunitz traveled to Ostrowo with a shocking message for him.

"Wladek, I have no choice," he began, "there is so much conflict in this town that I fear we are in danger of losing the new church plant. The only answer is to move you to another distract immediately and allow this theological crisis to pass."

"W'w'what?" Wladek stammered. "Why are you doing this? Pastor Kosmoski and I have worked hard to start this new church, which still needs leadership. And besides, just a few weeks ago, you called a very important 6 a.m. meeting with me because you wanted me to court Elza. How do you expect me to do that from a distance?"

Brother Cunitz only commented, "Moving you should stop the conflict!"

"You can't mean it! I've been successful here, and I'm doing exactly as you asked me to do. I'm *courting Elza*. You can't move me now. Please give us time to cement our relationship, and then we can move together."

"No, that won't work!" the stubborn administrator retorted. "I'm moving you to Dzialdowo, NOW!"

"Dzialdowo! NO!" Wladek exclaimed. "That's 300 kilometers away! This is no way to treat your star literature evangelist! And you can't possibly expect a man to court a woman from halfway across the country!"

But no matter how much Wladek pleaded, President Cunitz held his ground. If Wladek wanted to be a literature evangelist, he could not stay in Ostrowo. Period!

Wladek was devastated. Elza was also devastated when he broke the news to her about Brother Cunitz moving him 300 kilometers away.

"What?" she exclaimed, "That's not fair!"

Elza even complained to her mother. "Just because he's the president of this conference, how can he do this to Wladek, the only person who really understands me? How can he do this to me?" Elza was growing in her feelings for Wladek and saw the injustice of this act. This administrator was basically punishing Wladek for being successful! In addition, she felt that she, a new convert, was being betrayed. He was taking away her mentor, the person who brought her Bible truth and was now her major supporter and source of encouragement. So many of Elza's family and friends had turned against her, even her boss! It didn't seem fair that her friend and mentor was being sent so far away! Elza deeply resented this decision, especially since Wladek had just begun seriously courting her.

How could she be courted properly when he was 300 kilometers away? Elza may have been a new church member, but that did not stop her from voicing her strong opinion, "If Brother Cunitz had wanted to move Wladek, he could have chosen an acceptable town near Ostrowo where Wladek could be a Bible worker and literature evangelist and our friendship could continue to grow. Instead, this insensitive man is sending him to a place so far away that it makes it almost impossible for Wladek to continue building a relationship with me." She deeply resented the loss. And she blamed the president of the local conference for manipulating their lives. If he really wanted them to marry, he would have never sent Wladek so far away!

But Brother Cunitz wouldn't listen. His mind was made up. And the countdown to Wladek's departure day began. Wladek was desperate to salvage the relationship with Elza, which was just beginning. *What should he do?*

The first thing Wladek did to win Elza's heart backfired! He had gone to Tschapka, Elza's boss, and confided, "I've been transferred to Dzialdowo, 300 kilometers away. I am alone and lonely, and I am interested in marrying Elza. I hope you will understand and not interfere with our growing relationship." Wladek's intention was to "in a subtle way" let Tschapka know that he wanted to marry Elza and that Tschapka should be a gentleman and "back off." But it had the opposite effect, and Tschapka began to put more pressure on Elza to marry him instead of Wladek.

Chickens for Pauline

Since Wladek's first plan didn't work the way he intended, Wladek next decided to work through Elza's mother. If he could win over Pauline Gartz, he might have a chance with Elza. Even though Pauline had taken Bible studies and believed many of the things that Elza now believed, he knew that she had been against Elza becoming an Adventist and was certain to oppose her daughter marrying an Adventist. So Wladek started "courting" Pauline. Whenever he was in town he would pay special attention to her and help her with her chores.

Elza had confided in Wladek that her mother had for years been pushing her to get married. Since Elza was getting older and there were no new suitors, he figured that Pauline must be even more concerned now than when Elza had just turned twenty, and had begun her campaign to get her daughter married.

Wladek reasoned, *If I can just convince Pauline that I can provide a good living for her daughter—and even have enough money to help her family—then maybe she would decide I wouldn't be such a bad son-in-law after all.* And that's when he came up with the idea of the chickens.

He knew Pauline raised chickens, probably for the black market, and the more she had—the more money she would make by selling eggs—or by selling the chickens for meat. So before approaching Pauline with his request to marry her daughter, he bought Pauline two live chickens as a gift.

Most men would have brought candy or flowers, but Wladek knew Pauline would be more impressed with a practical gift. Candy doesn't last long, and flowers wilt, but chickens could go on producing eggs for years—and eggs meant more chickens—and more chickens meant more money.

It was a shrewd move on Wladek's part—and it had the exact effect on Pauline that he hoped it would. She was so impressed with this unusual gift that she told Elza, "No other men who have come and courted any of my daughters have brought me food for the family. He will make a good husband. He can take care of you and knows how to treat a girl's mama with the respect she deserves!" And then Pauline once more reminded her daughter that if she wasn't careful, she would be an old maid. "At least Wladek could make a good living and support you—which is a lot more than your tata has done for me. And look at how hard my life has been! Is this what you want? Give up your silly ideas of finding love and marry for security. He's a good man!" In a way, Pauline was saying, "A bird in the hand is worth two in the bush." Or, in this case, "Two chickens now are much better than hoping for something better and ending up empty handed!"

The next time Wladek proposed, Elza thought of her mother's words, and it was as if all her resistance had been beaten down to nothing. It was one thing saying no to Wladek but another saying no to Pauline. She felt betrayed. Years later, when she at times got angry with her husband, she was known to exclaim, "I can't believe my mother sold me into marriage for two chickens!"

One reason Elza refused Wladek's previous proposals was that she secretly hoped that Georg Czembor would pursue her when she returned home from the camp meeting. But after a couple of months, when she didn't hear from him, she gave up hope.

Intellectually, she knew that Wladek would love, respect, and support her. Was she foolish to give this up for her dream of romance? Maybe it was time she got married? After all, she reasoned that she was 27 years old and had already been rejected by Paul's parents because they thought she was too old for their son. So, after a deep sigh of regret for all that would never be, she accepted Wladek's proposal.

Wladek was ecstatic. He had successfully won the approval of an amazing woman. And it was just in time because it was only a few days before he had to move to Dzialdowo to begin his work there as a Bible worker and literature evangelist. Their courtship would have to be a long distance one. So for the next two years, although they wrote regularly, they only saw each other a few times.

Sometimes, however, the hand can write what the tongue cannot say—and in each letter, they learned more about the person they were about to marry. Their friendship blossomed, and they fell into a gentle, accepting agape-type love. Sometimes, distance has a way of accomplishing what proximity cannot.

But this is getting ahead of the story!

Tschapka

When Tschapka learned that Elza was planning on marrying Wladek, he exploded! "What? Why are you marrying a sleazy salesman who doesn't know anyone important? I'm well known, and I have a home. I can take care of you. I can't believe you are marrying this guy just because of religion! Have you lost your mind? You don't have to go through with this. Marry me. I know people in high places. With me, you'll be rich and famous. Don't throw your life away on a nobody!"

Tschapka now became a man with a mission. He wanted to stop Elza from marrying Wladek. So after he cooled down, he proposed again, this time with great passion. He not only wanted Elza to be his wife, but he wanted to rescue her out of the hands of this Adventist bookseller who had stolen her from him and what he considered the "true" church. He wanted to bring her back to the Evangelical Church where he was an elder and felt she belonged.

Elza replied to Tschapka, "You have been good to me these eight years I've worked for you. You have helped my brothers and sisters. And I appreciate everything you taught me, but you come from a well-to-do family. They are friends with important people I don't know. I have nothing in common with these people. Plus, you have money and prestige. I wouldn't fit in, so it wouldn't be good for either of us. And you, I hate to admit, are as old as my father. Likely, after a few years, you'll die, and I'd be a young widow! I'm sorry, Tschapka, but there is nothing you can do to make me change my mind and marry you."

Tschapka wouldn't take no for an answer and continued to pressure her. Finally, Elza decided, after eight years of employment, to quit her job at Tschapka's Konditorei.

"I'm sorry," she told her boss. "I will not marry you. And I'm tired of you not understanding the reason I'm declining your marriage proposals. Therefore, I have decided that it would be better to be unemployed and move back into my mother's house than to be subjected to this continual pressure for me to do something I don't believe is God's will for my life. I'm thankful for all you have done for me and my family in the past, but I think it is best that I move on."

"You're not going to quit on me!" Tschapka exclaimed.

"Yes, Tschapka, I'm quitting!"

Elza Becomes a Literature Evangelist

Three hundred kilometers away, Wladek received the news that Elza had quit her job with great joy. He felt sorry for her because her job had provided a stable income. Still, for weeks now he had entertained the crazy idea that Elza would make an amazing literature evangelist, but he didn't want to say anything that would persuade her to do something she didn't feel was God's calling.

Now, with Elza unemployed, he immediately contacted Brother Felte, who was the Director of the Home Missionary Department and was responsible for training new literature evangelists and provided a glowing report of Elza's virtues. "She's a hard worker and has great people skills. I think she might even be able to outsell me!" he joked. "Please contact her and give her a chance. I'm quite sure she won't disappoint you."

A few weeks later, that's exactly what Brother Felte did. He visited Elza on a Sunday morning at her mother's home in Ostrowo with one objective in mind: He wanted to prove to Elza that she was the right type of person to sell religious books door-to-door, as the star literature evangelist, Wladeslaw Kuzma, had boasted.

When Brother Felte took Elza out on a trial basis, she proved to be amazingly successful. At a Polish factory, the workers even gave her five zlotys in addition to the money for the books she sold because they enjoyed her presentation so much. After that experience, she was encouraged to continue this work. People were generally good to her and appreciated what she was doing. Sometimes, when she had to ride long distances on her bicycle, people would give her apples or some other fruit for the journey. In the two years she worked selling books, she was very successful. In fact, in the Adventist Polish Union periodical, she was written up as the most successful woman literature evangelist they had ever had.

The Gift that Seals the Deal

A number of months after Elza became a literature evangelist, Wladek made arrangements to go back to Ostrowo to visit her. He knew she was having surgery to correct her "lazy" eye that occasionally turned out—and he wanted to surprise her.

The trip, even by rail, was a long one and required changing trains with a three-hour layover. Wladek decided to sell some books instead of just wasting time. He ended up selling fifteen copies of William A. Spicer's book, *Our Day in the Light of Prophecy*, for a total of 225 zlotys. Elza would have had to work three weeks at Tschapka's to make that kind of money! With the profits from his sales, Wladek decided to buy Elza a beautiful brown leather case for 45 zlotys. It would be perfect for her to use in her literature evangelist work.

When Wladek arrived in Ostrowo, he decided that before visiting Elza in the hospital, he would make a "courtesy" call on Pauline and show her the expensive leather case to prove that he could support her daughter in style.

After showing Pauline the leather case, Wladek also casually mentioned the money he had made on the trip, which was impressive! "And when I went to seminary," he added, "I had more money in savings than any other student from Poland because I was such a successful literature evangelist. Right now, I get a salary of 200 zlotys a month from the church, and in addition, I usually make over 300 zlotys a month from selling books. Plus, I live frugally. I pay 30 zlotys a month for room and board and am putting approximately 400 zlotys a month in the bank, so I have a healthy savings account of over 2000 zlotys."

Pauline was indeed impressed. "You will make a good husband for my daughter. She deserves someone who can support her financially."

"Oh! And by the way," Pauline said with sudden insight, "I'd like to be able to purchase more products for my retail business. Would it be possible for me to get a small loan from you? That way, you would be earning more interest on your money."

"Of course," Wladek agreed. The money was exchanged, and Wladek left his soon-to-be mother-in-law's house with the blessing he wanted. The small loan for her business was well worth the goodwill it generated. And the evidence of his financial worth would undoubtedly continue to soften Pauline's heart toward him as her future son-in-law. He needed all the family support he could get to win the love and commitment of his soon-to-be bride.

At the hospital, Elza was happy to see Wladek and surprised at the expensive leather case he gave her. Now that she had made the decision to marry him, she felt herself actually falling in love. It wasn't the heart throbbing love she had once dreamed she would experience, but it was a growing gentle kind of love built on respect—the kind of love that it takes to sustain a marriage through good times and bad, through pleasures and disappointments, the kind of love that is built on commitment and not emotion. She felt at peace as she realized this was exactly the kind of love it takes to build a stable family unit where children are welcomed, loved, and nurtured. Although she still had doubts, she began looking forward to August 2, 1931, which was the date they had set for their wedding.

The Wedding

Wladek and Elza were engaged for almost two years but only saw each other four times after Wladek was transferred 300 kilometers away. Traveling that distance was impractical. Poland was suffering from a major depression, and times were difficult.

Because many people in Ostrowo were against Elza marrying Wladek, making mean comments and writing threats, the couple decided to get married in Bielsko-Biala, which was 300 kilometers west of Ostrowo. There was another reason for not getting married in Elza's hometown. Elza didn't appreciate the way Brother Cunitz, the local conference president, had treated Wladek by moving him so far away when he had just started courting her, so she didn't want him to marry them. She knew that if they got married outside the district where he was president, he wouldn't be expected to marry them. Bielsko-Biala was where the Seventh-day Adventist Polish Mission School was located.

They were married on Friday, July 31, at the city hall for the required civil ceremony. Then on Sunday, August 2, 1931, they had a beautiful church wedding where the thoughtful members had decorated the sanctuary with red roses and white carnations. Wladek was 36, and Elza was 28 years old.

The morning of the wedding, Elza woke up with a heavy feeling in the pit of her stomach. This should be the happiest day of her life, but instead, she felt she had been manipulated into this relationship, and rather than excited anticipation, she was resentful. She mourned the loss of her childhood fantasy of marrying the man of her dreams, and she wept bitter tears.

After a good cry, she wiped her eyes, took a deep breath, and prayed, "God, You have chosen this man for my husband. He is Your servant and I will always respect that, but I don't love him right now as he deserves to be loved. Work a miracle in my heart and help me to love the man You have chosen for me. Help me to be a good wife and honor and respect him—as I am about to pledge myself to him and become his wife. Give me peace and the assurance that You know what is best for me. Thank You for the way You have led me in the past, and please remind me each day of my life with Wladek that You will continue to lead us in the way we should go. Amen."

Then, once again wiping away her tears, she gazed out the window. Inspired by the beauty of the tree-studded mountains, she made the words of Psalm 121 her own, whispering, "I will lift up my eyes to the hills. Where does my help come from? *My help comes from the Lord.*"

It was a lovely service. Pastor A. Luedtke, who was a professor at the Polish Union Mission School, performed the wedding ceremony, and his wife planned the music. She played the organ as the service started and led a choir that sang two songs. One song was called "On the Road to Love." Elza loved the words, "Jesus, go ahead on the road of life…" That was her greatest desire—her prayer!

In his message, Pastor Luedtke mentioned that God established marriage in paradise and how beautiful and important it was. He talked about the responsibilities of a husband to his wife and a wife to her husband. The service ended with another musical number.

For the reception, the church members served a dinner in a church member's home that lasted all evening. Elza's mother made a delicious chicken noodle soup. Then, in addition to the main course, they served fruit salad and fancy cookies.

After the dinner, Wladek and Elza went to a church member's home where they spent their first night together. The following morning, they went on an outing with the church members into the beautiful Beskid Mountains near Bielsco. They had a wonderful time. Even Elza's mother, Pauline, and her brother, Emil, who were the only family members at the wedding, went along and enjoyed themselves. Then, the next day, everyone, including the newlyweds, left for "home."

Chapter 7

Together—at Last!

(August 1931–1932)

Marriage in the 1930s, especially for the working class of Poland, was the beginning of a lifelong commitment to reality, not necessarily a fulfillment of the couples' romantic childhood fantasies. Actually, after only seeing each other four times in the last two years, the weeks and months after the Kuzma wedding were a time for Wladek and Elza to discover exactly who they had married—for better or worse—and to accept their lifetime decision. Hopefully, they would each choose to show enough compassion and acceptance for their partner so that their verbal marriage commitment would last through a lifetime of ups and downs, triumphs and tragedies, miracles and misunderstandings.

Wladek and Elza had never "played" together. They had no hobbies, no sports, and no really close friends or family. In fact, they didn't have a lot in common outside of their commitment to put God first and totally trust that He had their backs—and always would.

Their only meaningful time together was work related. They both thrived on the thrill of selling religious books and presenting Bible truth to others. So, after their wedding, that's what they chose to do.

Saved by an Angel

For the next few weeks, Elza and Wladek lived with Pauline in the little family farmhouse in Ostrowo. Every day, they took their bikes out to the surrounding towns and villages to sell books, Bibles, and health magazines. And yes, time also healed the bitter conflict in town over Elza's baptism and the accusation that the Adventist Church stole Ostrowo's Sunday school teacher!

One day, in a strong Catholic region on the outskirts of the town of Pleszew (about 33 kilometers north of Ostrowo) Wladek went one way on his bicycle, and Elza went the other. They had made arrangements to meet each other at a certain time back at the railroad station.

Elza faithfully knocked on doors. Most people, if they weren't interested, politely declined her canvass, so she was shocked when a man came out into the yard and actually threatened her, "If you don't immediately leave, I'll stab you with this pitchfork!"

Stunned at the threat of violence, she quickly said, "I'm leaving," and jumped on her bike and rode away as fast as she could peddle. It wasn't long, however, before the man who initially threatened her caught up with her and began screaming, "If you don't get out of here, I'll turn everyone against you. And you'll be sorry!" The confrontation gained the attention of some neighbors who gathered around. They must have been the man's friends because they sided with him and began yelling at Elza, "Leave. Go, Go! You'll get hurt if you don't get out of here." Elza was frightened and began praying.

Suddenly, a stranger on a bicycle rode up and stopped beside Elza. He looked at the situation and asked the crowd, "What do you want from this good woman?" When no one answered, he said to Elza, "Don't be afraid; I'll take you wherever you want to go."

"The railway station will be fine," Elza replied in a shaky voice. Without any resistance from the crowd, he rode beside Elza all the way to the train station. When they arrived, Elza turned around to thank the man, but he had vanished without a word.

On the train ride home, Elza told Wladek about the man who had protected her by riding next to her all the way to the station. That reminded him about an "angel" experience that one of his literature evangelist friends had when selling books. The man came to a wide river that had overflowed the banks and he couldn't get across. To reach his destination, the man needed to get to the other side of the river which was impossible without a boat—and there was none to be seen. As he stood on the bank praying, a man in a boat suddenly appeared from nowhere and asked him if he needed a ride across the river. When the boat got to the other side, and the literature evangelist stepped onto dry land, the boat and the man disappeared. After hearing this story, Elza was quite sure that she had just experienced her own "guardian angel" encounter.

After a month, the couple moved to Dzialdowo, where Wladek had been a Bible worker for almost two years. For their first home, they had rented a small apartment from some German people. Even though Wladek had worked hard in the area for two years, he was unable to get much interest started. Catholicism was so strong in this area that he was shunned.

When Wladek and Elza married, the Seventh-day Adventist Polish Union administrators recognized that this couple was going to be an amazing ministry team. They were exceptional literature evangelists who were fluent in both Polish and German. They loved giving Bible studies, even though Elza left most of the Bible study work to her husband. When he gave sermons or evangelistic presentations in Polish, she would translate for the German-speaking listeners, meeting the needs of both language groups at the same time. They were an ideal couple to generate interest and organize new churches. That's why, a month later, Wladek and Elza were transferred to Brodnica, where, hopefully, the residents would be more receptive to the Bible message.

Truth Revealed

A few months after the wedding, Elza ran into Georg Czembor at a church convention. After a pleasant greeting, Georg mentioned, "I've always felt sad about how things ended with us. But when Wladek told me you were engaged to him, I felt it was improper to continue our friendship."

"What?" Elza exclaimed in shock. "Surely that isn't true! I can't believe Wladek would tell a lie in order to get me to marry him! At that point in our relationship, Wladek and I hadn't even talked about marriage!" Then she admitted as she looked up at Georg, "I liked you, and when you didn't pursue me, my heart was broken. But I finally accepted that we would never be together, so I said yes to Wladek's proposal." She took a deep, shuddering breath. "But now, I'm OK with the way things worked out." Then she quickly turned away so Georg couldn't see the tears begin to form in her eyes.

> *Surely that isn't true! I can't believe Wladek would tell a lie in order to get me to marry him!*

For the next few days, Elza found it difficult to believe that Wladek had lied in order to keep Georg from courting her. She had once felt such an attraction to Georg—and now that she was married to someone else, it was too late! She tried to comfort herself that at least now she understood how much of a gentleman Georg had been to back away from having a relationship with her because he thought she belonged to someone else. "How could Wladek have done this to her?" she questioned. She even blamed God, "Why did You allow Wladek to tell such a cruel lie?"

Soon, however, she came to the realization that God knew what He was doing, and pining away for something impossible was not God's will for her life. So she forgave her husband, whom she had grown to love, and buried her disappointment deep within her soul. Once again, she dedicated her life to God, believing He knew what was best for her. In time, her attraction to Georg turned into a healthy, meaningful friendship.

Shortly after this encounter, Georg Czembor married a nurse from a respected family who lived in Lubeck in northern Germany. At first, Georg had reservations about marrying her, but his good friends and colleagues encouraged him. The two families (Kuzmas and Czembors) became friends when the Kuzmas moved to Warsaw in 1935. Georg's wife, Irena, a nurse, even helped with the birth of Elza's son, Jan, who was born in Warsaw in 1936.

By this time, the Czembors had a son named Georg and a daughter. But their marriage was not happy and they later divorced.

Georg and Elza remained good friends. Both of them occasionally wondered how different life might have been if Wladek hadn't taken control of the situation and claimed Elza first. Because Brother Czembor had a son the same age as Elza's second daughter, Krysia, Elza once commented, "Wouldn't it be ironic if our children would marry!" But it was not to be. When the war ended in 1945, Brother Czembor moved to East Germany, which was under communist control. He chose to stay there even after the Berlin Wall came down. A number of years later, Elza received a telegram from one of her friends giving her the sad news that her friend Georg (now known as Wilhelm) had passed away.

CHAPTER 8

Brodnica: Working Together in Ministry

(1931–1933)

In 1931, Brodnica was a beautiful trade route town in the Polish Corridor[17] with a population of approximately 8,500 people, but it had no Adventists. The town was on the Drweca River with lovely lakes and waterways to the north, making it a popular vacation destination for locals as well as European visitors. But beauty can be deceiving!

Moving to Brodnica in 1931 was like moving into a hornet's nest. The strong Catholic influence, plus the growing conflict between the Polish and the German people (who were being influenced by the Nazis as they prepared the way for Hitler to fulfill his promise to retake the Polish Corridor), made the work extremely difficult. The Nazi mistreatment of Jews had already begun. Because most of the residents thought Adventists were Jewish because they kept the "Jewish" Sabbath, they shunned the Kuzmas rather than risk Nazi harassment. All this tension and conflict among the different ethnic groups was beginning to escalate when Elza and Wladek moved to Brodnica.

Couple Ministry

Wladek and Elza were excited about moving to Brodnica and beginning their ministry together. Wanting to make their first home as comfortable as possible, Elza asked her brother, Alfred, to ship them the expensive furniture she had purchased when working for Tschapka and making a good salary (a solid oak headboard and highboys with glass doors, and a two-door wardrobe with four sections). Having something they actually

---

[17] The Polish Corridor was a strip of land transferred by treaty from defeated Germany to Poland after World War I. It provided access to the Baltic Sea.

owned made Elza feel a little more secure even though the world around them was chaotic.

The political turmoil in Brodnica was intensifying, but it didn't stop this mission-minded couple from working hard for souls. They both sold books full time until a year later (1932) when their first child was born, and then Elza only sold books during her baby's nap times.

The last month before Elza quit full-time work, she made 400 zlotys, which was probably due to Wladek's genius idea: Instead of riding a bicycle, he arranged for his pregnant wife to have a "taxi" horse carriage with a driver to take her to the larger farms, some over 3000 hectors. People gave her special consideration because she was expecting; sometimes, they fed her dinner or sent her home with fruit. But no matter how hard they both worked, winning souls among the dominantly Catholic population was almost impossible!

Their First Baby

On Monday morning, July 18, 1932, Elza was out selling books at a judge's house when she went into labor. In her rush to get back home, she forgot her gloves. Three days later, the judge returned the gloves to Elza's apartment, thinking he would be able to see her baby, but she was still in labor—and it was getting more painful and dangerous all the time. The midwife tried everything she could think of to hasten the baby's birth, but *the baby just refused to come.* In desperation, the midwife exclaimed, "I feel like tying a rope around the baby and pulling it out!" She knew it was a crazy idea, so she continued encouraging Elza to push!

Thankfully, that morning, Elza's fifteen-year-old sister, Truda arrived from Ostrowo. She quickly assessed the situation and realized that something was wrong. Elza was getting pale and turning blue. The midwife was there, but obviously this birth was more challenging than the midwife's knowledge or experience could handle.

The midwife tried everything she could think of to hasten the baby's birth, but the baby just refused to come.

Truda was desperate. "I've got to find a doctor," she exclaimed to Elza, "or I'm afraid you're going to die!" Truda quickly made sure the midwife wouldn't leave, and then, between labor pains, Elza tried to give her sister directions to the closest doctor. Truda then dashed off to find help. But this was almost impossible since many people assumed that because the

Kuzmas worshipped on Saturday, they were Jewish. People were scared that they could be reported to the authorities if they associated with them. After being turned down by a number of medically trained people, Truda, in desperation, ran to the hospital. Surely, the medical staff would help! But instead, they tried to turn her away. **"Who is the doctor in charge?"** Truda yelled. A number of the nurses pointed to a man rushing down the hall in the opposite direction! Truda screamed, **"Doctor, if you don't come immediately, my sister will die! She has been trying to give birth to a baby for three days."** She then grabbed his arm and wouldn't let go. **"Please, please! Come help my sister!"** Finally, the doctor took compassion on the frightened teenager.

"Where is she?" he demanded as he grabbed his medical bag. Truda led him at a frantic pace down the road to Elza's apartment.

After he examined Elza, the doctor gave her a shot and put warm pads on her tummy, and things progressed. Within a couple of hours, the baby was delivered safely. The doctor then stitched up the episiotomy and charged 20 zlotys for his time and expertise. Truda followed him to the door and thanked him again, "You saved my sister's life—and the baby's! Thank you. Thank you!"

> *Doctor, if you don't come immediately, my sister will die! She has been trying to give birth for three days.*

And where was Wladek when all this was going on? Well, it wasn't really his fault that he wasn't home. He had asked Elza early Monday morning, "When do you think the baby will come?"

"Oh, not for a week or so," she replied.

He sat there for a minute, considering seriously what he should do. "Well then," he said, trying to make a decision, "if it's going to be that long, maybe I should go out selling books for a few more days. It would be a waste of time just to sit around here waiting. Besides, birthing is women's work. I'd probably just be in the way!"

"Go!" Elza said. "I'll be fine, especially with Truda coming on Wednesday."

So, planning to be home at least by the weekend, off Wladek went with two bulging leather cases hanging on his bicycle handlebars.

On Wednesday morning, however, as Wladek was selling books about twelve kilometers from Brodnica, he had a strong impression that he should immediately go home. *Something was wrong!* He turned around and peddled as fast as he could. He got home shortly after 2:30 in the afternoon.

The doctor had gone, and the midwife was just finishing cleaning up the baby and was about to leave. Wladek was shocked to learn that his wife had been in labor from shortly after he left on Monday until just a few minutes before he arrived!

"Congratulations, Mr. Kuzma," the midwife greeted him with an impish smile and a twinkle in her mischievous eye, "You have a son!"

Wladek was overjoyed by the news and had no idea the midwife was joking. When he went in to see Elza, the baby was wrapped in a blanket. He started kissing the baby, saying, "My son! My son!"

"No," Elza corrected him, "It's a girl!"

He looked shocked but quickly recovered, saying, "She's so beautiful. Look how pink she is." He would have liked a son—most Polish fathers in that era felt that way—but it really didn't matter to him. He was thrilled to have a daughter. They named her Danuta Eleonora (in English, Donna Eleanor), and they called her Danusia—a term of endearment.

Elza was exhausted. The challenging birth made her recovery difficult. She limped on the side where she had received the shot for almost half a year, and every time she gave birth she again suffered major pain in that region.

Time to Move On

When Danusia was a year old and Elza was pregnant with her second child, the President of the Adventist Polish Union sent his secretary/treasurer, a special friend of Wladek's, to check on the family. Brother Will stayed with them and had time to observe firsthand the conflict between the Germans and the Polish that was escalating as Germans flooded into that region. He also saw how difficult the work was because the Catholic population was so prejudiced against the Sabbath-keeping Adventists.

The more the two men talked together, the more they were impressed that it was time for the Kuzmas to move on. The president suggested that Leszno would be a good place because the small Adventist Church group in the town needed a pastor. Plus, it would give the young couple some fellow believers with whom they could associate. Hopefully, in Leszno their efforts to win souls would be more fruitful.

The literature evangelist was the first person of the Adventist ministry team to go into unentered territory to generate interest in the Bible. As soon as there were enough church members, a regular pastor would be sent to shepherd the group, and the literature evangelist would move on. With a sigh of resignation, Elza realized that this was only the first of many moves she and Wladek would make in the years ahead. She should have been excited to leave the conflicts in Brodnica behind, but instead, she was sad. They had come with such high expectations. They both had worked so hard, and now they were leaving with seemingly nothing to show for their effort. "Lord," Elza prayed as she began packing, "We'll go wherever you want us to go, but please prepare the way so our ministry in Leszno will be more fruitful." And He did!

CHAPTER 9

Leszno: Love and Soul Success

(1932-1935)

The Kuzma story continues in Leszno, a small town in Southern Poland 80 kilometers south of Poznan and about the same distance west of Ostrowo. It was in a beautiful lowland area where lakes were abundant. In the middle of Leszno's marketplace was the famous town hall that was first built when the town was established in 1547 during the Golden Age of the Leszczynski Family, who owned the land at the time, then was rebuilt after each of the two fires that destroyed the town during the centuries. On the top of the town hall's tall clock tower was the golden-crowned eagle, the emblem of the Polish nation which had been mounted there a year before the Kuzmas arrived.

Leszno had a history of Protestant influence. Not long after the town was founded, a community of Bohemian Protestants called Unity of the Brethren and some Protestant Silesia weavers moved there. Soon other Protestants arrived, and the town became known for its tolerance toward different faiths—that is, until the Nazi invasion.

The Jews had a lot to do with the establishment of the town. At one time in the eighteenth century, almost 5000 Jews were contributing to its economy with their many craft guilds. They started leaving, however, when Leszno was annexed to Prussia at the end of the eighteenth century. There was another exodus after the Polish uprising of 1918–1919 when the Treaty of Versailles returned Leszno to Poland, and the population was forced to get Polish citizenship. Soon, there were only a few hundred Jews left. When the Nazis invaded in 1939, most of the Poles, as well as the Jews, were killed. The remaining Jews were sent to die in the Warsaw Ghetto.

In 1932, when Elza and Wladek arrived with all their belongings behind them in a horse drawn cart, they were impressed with the beautiful churches in Leszno. They prayed that the people would be more tolerant of the Adventist message than they had been in Brodnica, even though most of the churches were Catholic; throughout the ages, they had been built by artisans of different faiths. Leszno was also the home of one of the oldest Jewish synagogues in Poland.

As Wladek and Elza admired the different styles of architecture, they wondered, *would Leszno accept the Seventh-day Adventist message? Would there someday be an Adventist Church structure for the small group of Adventist believers?* Leszno was a refreshing change for the Kuzmas, and they looked forward to God blessing them with many souls.

Baby Danusia was a year old, and Elza was pregnant with her second child when they began looking for a suitable place to rent. They had no idea the search would be so difficult. When they mentioned their housing problem to the Ostapowicz family, who were members of the Adventist congregation in Leszno, the Ostapowiczs said they had three houses. They lived in one, a son lived in another, but the third was vacant. They offered to rent the second story of the third house to the Kuzmas and allow them to use the first level as a church and lecture hall. The house was yellow with flower boxes in the windows. It was a dream come true for Elza.

The Ostapowicz family was a highly esteemed noble family in the community. They spoke both Russian and Ukrainian in addition to Polish. They had thirteen children (twelve boys and a girl). The boys were all good looking, educated, and financially secure. Most of their sons were in the Polish military and held various positions: officers, lieutenants, captains, or majors. One son was an architect, and one was a university student who would be joining the army when he graduated.

The Ostapowicz family grew to love the Kuzmas. Mr. Ostapowicz was a retired superintendent of the railroad. His wife, Maria, was always kind to Elza. As baby Danusia started toddling around outside, Maria watched her to make sure she wouldn't get into trouble while Maria's young daughter enjoyed playing with her.

An Affair of the Heart

The Ostapowicz's son, Mieczek, was the same age as Elza (about 31). Since he was a university student living at home, he was around a lot, so he and Elza enjoyed talking.

On nice days, Elza left the bedroom windows open for fresh air. When Mieczek walked by, he sometimes threw pebbles through the open windows to get Elza's attention. Once, Elza commented to his mother, "I wonder why there are stones on my bed?" Then they both started laughing as they realized this was Mieczek's teasing way of letting Elza know he was home. He made Elza feel special by doing unique things like standing at attention when she walked by.

Mieczek sometimes made excuses to come upstairs to deliver packages or give messages to the Kuzma family so he and Elza could enjoy a stimulating conversation. He was cultured and educated, and the two of them soon became good friends.

Once, after overhearing a quarrel between Elza and Wladek, Mieczek asked her, "How can you stand being married to this person? You have such a sensitive and lovely soul." He could sense that Elza and her husband, although committed to each other, didn't have the emotional connection he had with Elza.

Because of his work, Wladek was sometimes out of town three or four days at a time, and Mieczek, although sensitive to the fact that Elza was married, kept her from being lonely with his creativity, like surprising her with lines of poetry or creative ideas worth exploring. He wrote notes of appreciation and encouragement to her. Since what he wrote wasn't passionate, it didn't seem inappropriate to either of them but rather helped to fill an empty space in Elza's soul. Elza admitted she looked forward to his visits and their meaningful conversations.

As the weeks and months went by, Elza, not having a close girlfriend to confide in, began to feel a soul connection with Mieczek stronger than anything she had ever experienced before—including what she had with Georg Czembor. With Georg, it was a crush—intense but short lived. But with Mieczek, it was much deeper—like a soulmate. It was almost addictive. To function, she needed his attention, his listening ear, his perspective. It made her get up in the morning with a lilt in her step and a song on her lips.

> *He could sense that Elza and her husband didn't have the emotional connection he had with Elza.*

Elza's relationship with Mieczek was an affair of the heart—not physical. It made Elza feel alive and emotionally energized to be admired by someone. She was a very attractive woman with a charming personality and men responded to her. Since her husband was gone so much and had difficulty meeting her need to share concepts, ideas, and feelings, she was drawn to someone who would take the time to really get to know her. They never went out together. There was never any inappropriate behavior between them. However, one time, after hearing Elza and her husband argue, Mieczek told her, "When I'm done with my military career, I'm going to come and take you away." Then they laughed. They both knew that this was not going to happen, but it did make Elza feel good that someone understood her situation and how hungry she was for meaningful friendships and deep philosophical conversations.

Wladek wasn't blind to Elza's attraction to Mieczek. Sometimes, when Wladek and Elza argued, he tried to win by saying hurtful things like, "You've pined after Czembor, and now when I'm gone, you have Mieczek. Who knows how many others you've had!" These words were a low blow to Elza. They hurt her deeply. How could Wladek say things that made Elza feel he didn't trust her? She had both male and female friends. And she dearly loved Mieczek as a friend, but her loyalty and commitment was to her husband. How could she make him understand?

For the most part, Wladek did his best to be a good husband, but like many men, he really didn't know how to meet his wife's emotional needs. He did what he thought was important: worked hard, made a good living for the family, was successful and respected in his career, and he tried to show Elza he loved her by occasionally bringing her gifts but it wasn't enough. What she really needed was his time—his undivided attention resulting in an emotional bond that would prove his forever love for her.

And then there was that LIE! When tension arose between Wladek and Elza, Wladek often wished that he hadn't told the lie that sealed Elza's fate and forced her to accept his marriage proposal. He now realized it would have been better if he had just let God work things out. Love grows best in an atmosphere of freedom—and the bitter fact was that Elza had been manipulated into marrying him by not knowing the truth about Georg's withdrawal of attention. But it was too late now, and his falsehood would forever be a thorn in their relationship.

Elza, on the other hand, had strong opinions which at times made their relationship challenging. She was smart—probably smarter in some ways than her husband. She was also a multi-talented businessperson. When she sold books, she sometimes outsold him. In fact, she felt she could probably do as well as or better than Wladek in many things—although she never expressed this thought. She didn't want to compete—that was not her motive for doing the things she did—it just happened that way—and her sharp tongue of criticism that she had inherited from her mother didn't help their relationship.

As much as Elza disliked her own mother's dictatorial ways, there were times when she realized she was much more like Pauline than she wanted to be. It was as if she was programmed to take control and tell her husband what to do, for that was the role model of a wife her mother had given her.

When Wladek and Elza disagreed, she rarely gave in. Wladek soon learned that the only way to win was to either say hurtful things to put her down and humiliate her or to go silent and retreat. More often than not, he just packed his case with books and went out to sell more. Withdrawing from problems left a void in their relationship, which intensified Elza's need to share her feelings with someone who cared and showed understanding.

How should a married woman respond when her emotional needs are met by someone other than her husband? Elza was scared when she experienced strong feelings for Mieczek, but she also felt that it was his attention that kept her alive. Staying home with two babies was not a role model Elza understood. Without thinking, Wladek praised Elza for her success in selling literature and winning souls, but being a good mother was just expected and not something to be praised.

With Mieczek, however, she felt special just being herself. It didn't take Mieczek long before he realized he was an important part of Elza's life, and he often said, "You must get very lonely when you are raising the children primarily on your own." He was a great listener and understood a woman's emotional needs and it's hard not to fall in love with that!

Mieczek brought Elza red roses when she had her second child, Krysia. He not only came to see Elza and the new baby but also to seek Elza's blessing. He had decided to ask a teacher's daughter, Marisha, to marry him, and he wanted to know if Elza thought she would be a good wife for him.

"Yes, she's perfect," Elza replied. "Not only is she very pretty, but she's an only child with many advantages. Plus, she plays the piano beautifully." Marisha was not yet a Seventh-day Adventist, so she asked Wladek when he would hold Bible meetings so she could come. This impressed him, and Wladek told Mrs. Ostapowicz, "I don't think there is a better girl for Mieczek." By the time the wedding date was set, the Kuzmas had moved to Warsaw, so the couple had their wedding in Warsaw so the Kuzmas could attend.

One day, when the Kuzmas were still living in Warsaw, Mieczek came to tell Elza that he was being called into active duty in the military. That was the last time she saw him. He died in 1939. His parents were told that he was captured by the Nazi Germans during the invasion of Poland, taken to the forest, and killed. Elza grieved when she heard the news. His friendship was a gift to her that would never die—important enough that for memory's sake, she put a picture of him, dressed in his officer's uniform, in the Kuzma family album. Mrs. Ostapowicz lost three of her sons in this manner.

Wladek's Ministry in Leszno

Wladek not only sold books in Leszno and the surrounding area but also served as the pastor of the Leszno congregation. In addition, he was the evangelist for the area. He preached four times a week: Wednesday, Friday, Sabbath, and Sunday. While in Leszno, he gave over 250 presentations—all different. The lecture hall downstairs was always full. To meet the needs of both Polish and German people, Wladek would speak in Polish, and Elza would translate into German. The longest meetings were held on Sunday mornings when Danusia was napping. On weekdays, when Danusia slept, Elza went out selling books, just as she had done in Brodnica, making 20 to 40 zlotys each day and praying to find people interested in Bible studies. This was her routine—until her second child was born.

She and Wladek made a very effective ministry team and had success in Leszno. Not only did Elza sell books, but she was actively involved in visitation. She made additional contacts with those who bought books, hoping that after reading the books, they might be interested in studying the Bible. She also made home visits to the people who came to the meetings. She felt it was important to get better acquainted with these people and to answer their questions on a personal basis.

But their success in sharing Christ with believers wasn't without opposition. One day, Wladek handed out a pamphlet that announced that he would speak on the subject, "What happened in heaven in 1844?" One of the announcements got into the hands of the Catholic priest, who sent thirty theology students to the meeting. They joked that they had come to see if Wladyslaw Kuzma was in heaven in 1844! At the end of the meeting, one of the Ostopowiez boys, Speczek (the architect), followed the students to hear what they were saying. They commented, "He doesn't know what he's talking about because he didn't say anything about seeing St. Mary in heaven." Obviously, these men didn't come back to the meetings.

One of the Ostapowicz boys was a very educated major in the army. He did not attend church regularly, but his mother convinced him to come and hear one of Pastor Kuzma's presentations. He came, but Wladek didn't realize he was in the audience. After Wladek heard he was there, he said to Mrs. Ostopowiez, "Please tell me the next time you are inviting someone as educated as your son so I will know how to present the material. I simplify my presentations for uneducated people so they will be able to understand. Still, for those who are educated, I want to make sure I present something that stimulates them."

Mrs. Ostapowicz also invited a Catholic priest to come and listen to the "evangelical lay preacher." The priest came. Afterward, when she asked the priest why the Catholics taught things that weren't in the Bible, and he couldn't answer her, she got frustrated and shook the priest vigorously by the collar, "Show me from the Bible where it says that the priesthood was established in the New Testament." The priest's only response was, "You are a false church!" He immediately left the meeting and refused to attend again.

Dramatically Making a Point

At times, Wladek was known to use drama to make important points. Here's an example: One day, he heard a strong voice say to him, "Go visit Mrs. Marschalek." She was a very poor church member with six children. He recognized this nudge as the voice of God, so he immediately went to her house. When he arrived, he found a Catholic nun was harassing her by trying to pull her Bible out of her hands. When she saw her pastor, she immediately yelled, "This Catholic sister is trying to take away the Bible that you gave me because she doesn't want me to be a Seventh-day Adventist."

"Why do you call her 'sister'?" he asked. "She's not a sister. She's a representative of the devil." At this point, Wladek shouted, "Give me a broom. I'll beat her up." This shocked both women, and they stopped struggling.

He then turned to the Catholic nun, saying, "I can't believe a person who wants to serve God would try to take away someone's Bible. What kind of service do you think you were providing? You would be of greater service to God if you would just milk cows rather than try to confuse people by taking away their Bibles. After all, the Bible *is* God's Word."

Then he turned to Mrs. Marschalek and asked, "Now, where is your broom?" When he went to get the broom, the nun started to run. Wladek chased her all the way back to her church, and she never again tried to take someone's Bible away.

In another situation, Wladek was preparing a mother and her daughter for baptism. When the woman's son, who was a major in the Polish army, found out that they wanted to join the Adventist Church, he threw them out of the house. Wladek went to visit them and gave them the book *The Great Controversy between Christ and Satan* by Ellen G. White, with the warning, "Don't let the priest take this book away from you. Somehow, the priest learned about the gift, and he asked how far they had read in the book. When he found out they had almost finished it, the Catholic priest was afraid. He and one of his women parishioners then tried to take the book away, but the mother refused to let them have it. When Wladek heard what the priest and woman tried to do, he cursed them.

Winning Souls

The priests were always trying to counter Wladek's preaching, which pointed out the errors in Catholic dogma. Because the Bible was always on Wladek's side, their main defense was simply to argue the position that the Catholic Church was the ONLY true church. One priest did this by arousing the anger of as many church women as possible and encouraging them to argue with Wladek. But instead of their accusations hurting Wladek, more and more people began listening to the Seventh-day Adventist message. When the priest realized this method wasn't working, he wrote a letter to Krakow requesting that the Catholic Church bishop send someone to counteract Wladek's efforts.

The "missionary" priests came, and for ten days, they preached against Wladek and his message. Speczek Ostapowicz (the architect) happened to be in the audience and heard one priest ask, "Do any of you know where the "sezcarza" (sectarians) are living?" Then he answered his own question with the comment, "underneath the tail of an ass!" Speczek was shocked to hear the priest being so crude, and he spoke up, "You should be ashamed of yourself for saying such things." Then Speczek walked out—and a number of others followed.

Mrs. Lehman was a lovely lady. Wladek went to their home to visit her and her children. Mrs. Lehman said, "I'm so glad you have come. The Adventist preacher before you was a former policeman and couldn't explain things as clearly as you."

When the Lehman boys wanted to get baptized, people were critical. They will probably drop out of the church because they don't understand much about life. When Wladek heard this, he arranged a meeting for those interested in church membership and invited the four Lehman boys in particular. He explained, "As church members, we all need to work to share the gospel with others, just like the Apostle Paul." Wladek knew that the Lehman boys were very musical. Two played the violin, one played the trumpet, and all four of them sang—plus, they all had bicycles. So Wladek gave them some German *Signs of the Times* magazines and told them to first sing and play for the people and then encourage them to buy a magazine.

The boys liked the idea, so they rode off on their bicycles with their instruments and magazines. When they came to the Catholic Church parsonage where the priest lived, they started playing and singing. The priest and the maid came out of the house and said, "Play some more."

They enjoyed the music very much. They had no idea the boys were singing Adventist songs! The priest even threw down some money to have them keep singing. The music touched the people's hearts, and then the boys were able to sell the magazines. The women appreciated the boys so much that they gave them cakes, bread, and eggs. In this way, the boys could make enough money to provide food for their family. They always appreciated that Brother Kuzma took the time to teach them how they could be like the Apostle Paul, spreading the gospel while at the same time making enough money for their living expenses.

During the two years that the Kuzmas were in Leszno, fifteen people accepted Bible truth and became Seventh-day Adventists. These included the following: six members of the Lehman family (mother, daughter, and four sons), a rough looking policeman, Mrs. Marschalek, and Sister Schferovna who was a refined lady and midwife who became a good friend of the Kuzma family—and was somewhat interested in Mieczek. She was only in Leszno about a year—long enough to help deliver Elza's second baby—and then she moved to Warsaw, where she continued her friendship with the Kuzmas and was able to help Elza in the delivery of their third baby.

Both Wladek and Elza worked hard preparing people for baptism. When they were ready, President R.J. Cunitz, now from the South Polish Conference office in Krakow, came and conducted the baptism. (Oh, yes. By then, both Wladek and Elza had forgiven President Cunitz for sending Wladek 300 kilometers away when Wladek had just begun to court Elza!)

Krysia's Birth

Krystyna Bieruta was born on a Sunday at noon, June 17, 1934. The Kuzma family and friends called her Krysia. Her middle name was the Polish version of Ruth. So, in English her name would be Christine Ruth. The time of her birth was special because there was a military installation nearby, and the soldiers in the military band were marching by their home and singing at the exact same time when Krysia was born.

Compared to Danusia's birth, this one was easy. Wladek was home this time and although he had hoped for a boy, he was very happy with his second daughter. He bonded immediately with Krysia and they had a very close relationship throughout life. While Danusia was mama's little girl, Krysia was her tata's. Elza breastfed Krysia and had plenty of milk because she insisted on buying the very best food—apples, oranges, and other fruits—for herself and her family. She even had enough milk to breastfeed one of Mrs. Marschalek's babies when Mrs. Marschalek was not able to do so. Elza's thoughtfulness was one of the things that encouraged Mrs. Marschalek to be baptized and join the church.

When Krysia was born, Danusia was extremely jealous. It was *not* love at first sight. Elza often said, "Danusia, you need to thank Jesus for your sister. Otherwise, you would be all by yourself, and it would be very lonely." But this made no sense to Danusia. She saw the new baby as competition and sometimes even threw pots and pans into the baby's crib where Krysia was sleeping.

One day, when Danusia was two and a half, she walked away from the house to watch some soldiers marching and singing along the street. Suddenly, she saw a chimney sweep dressed all in black and carrying a black broom. She began screaming hysterically because she thought she had seen the devil. She came running home yelling, "Mama, the devil's coming! The devil's coming!" Elza held her close, trying to calm her. "Don't be afraid," she said, and then she tried to explain to her about the work of a chimney sweep.

The only real negative for the Kuzma family in Leszno was that Wladek had to be away from home so much—and neither he nor Elza liked that. He tried to make up for his absence by bringing home tasty apples, oranges, and other treats for the family, but nothing really made up for not spending time with them. When he was gone, Elza helped with Sabbath School and worked with the young people, but when Wladek was home, he was in charge.

Moving On

Wladek and Elza had a successful ministry in Leszno. Not only had they brought fifteen souls to Christ, but their success at selling literature was amazing. One time, in just three months, they sold 2,350 zlotys worth of books and magazines. Wladek reported this to Georg Czembor, who at this time was the new Polish Union Secretary working under President Theofil Babienco. Brother Czembor then exclaimed to the president, "Have you ever seen that much money being made in three months in literature evangelism work?"

"Never," admitted Brother Babienco. "Who is this Kuzma?"

Brother Czembor replied, "He is a good worker and has gained many souls."

Brother Babienco looked interested, "I want you to write a letter to him and ask Brother Kuzma to come to Warsaw and report to me. I want a good literature evangelist in Warsaw to be the Publishing Secretary and to train ten literature evangelists for the Warsaw area."

It was 1935, and time to move on to new territory and challenges. God's timing is always perfect. God knew what was ahead for the people in Leszno and mercifully moved the Kuzma family to a safer environment, a place where their skills were desperately needed, a place that Wladek often referred to as the "golden apple of opportunity," the capital city of Poland: Warsaw!

Although the Kuzmas were not in Leszno at the time of the German occupation of Poland in September 1939, many of their Leszno friends and church members experienced major persecution (as did the Slavic Poles throughout Poland) by fellow Poles who were of German descent. The plan of identifying the Polish leaders and intelligentsia and annihilating them was conceived by the Nazis in May of 1939 and called "Operation Tannenberg."

In Leszno, Polish Germans who sympathized with Hitler armed themselves with grenades, revolvers, rifles, and machine guns and attacked their fellow Polish citizens. These attacks were incited by a group of Nazi German Einsatzkommandos who were headquartered in Leszno. The mission was to kill Jews, the intellectual elite among the Polish citizens, and anyone who voiced objections to German rule. Neighbor turned against neighbor; consumer against merchant; clergy against parishioner. It was almost impossible to know whom to trust! Wladek could have very likely been in the group that was killed had the family stayed in the small town of Leszno where they were well known.

But this is getting ahead of the story. It is enough to say the winds of impending war were just beginning to blow in Leszno as the Kuzmas once again packed their belongings and, with growing anticipation, moved to Warsaw, where the headquarters of the Polish Adventist work was located. Their ministry efforts would be multiplied by training others to be successful literature evangelists like themselves. God's timing is always perfect.

Chapter 10

Warsaw: Golden Apple of Opportunity

(1935-1937)

In 1935, Wladek was asked to join the Polish Adventist Headquarters administrative staff in Warsaw. It was quite a promotion! He was happy that his literature evangelist skills had been recognized, and he was given the opportunity to multiply his influence by training others. The problem was that doing the work he loved required travel, and with two beautiful preschool daughters and his wife expecting again, he didn't look forward to being away.

The job also required local responsibilities, such as coordinating the annual Ingathering campaign of three Warsaw churches, which meant gathering funds from the public to help humanitarian causes. Plus, he was expected to preach when there was a vacancy—which basically meant that every Sabbath he was home he was preaching at a local church! In addition, he continued his own literature evangelism work, selling Christian books, finding interests, holding Bible studies, and preparing individuals for baptism. Wladek was a tireless and skilled worker for God. He was so successful with Ingathering and the literature evangelism program that in one year, he was able to double the yearly income of the Union. Elza was proud of her husband's accomplishments.

The Polish Union President Babienco was especially pleased with how the literature evangelism work prospered under Wladek's leadership. He had a way of encouraging his workers, especially the women, to get started at nine o'clock in the morning and be eager and enthusiastic—and look like beautiful Christians—not "ladies of the night." With Wladek's guidance, their sales improved significantly.

Living in a Fishbowl

The Adventist headquarters on #9 Tumska Street in Warsaw had been renovated into three upstairs apartments for worker's families—with the lower level serving as offices, a church, and a meeting hall.

Elza and Wladek lived in one of the apartments, which meant they were living in a fishbowl next to two other Adventist families, one of which was Elza's one-time romantic interest, Georg Czembor, and his wife and children! The Kuzmas had very little privacy. Everyone knew when they were coming or going. Their neighbors could hear what was said through open windows or, if the volume was high enough, through the walls! It was a full-time job for Elza to take care of the apartment and the children—and keep the noise level down.

The Birth of Janek

Wladek was 41 years old when Jan Miroslov Waldemar Kuzma, his first son, was born in Warsaw at 6 a.m., April 24, 1936. They named him Jan after Wladek's father and his oldest brother who died at six years of age. But during Jan's growing years, everyone called him Janek.

Georg Czembor's wife, Irena, a nurse, came to help, as did their friend, Sister Schferovna, the midwife who had helped with Krysia's birth in Leszno.

When Wladek heard he had a son, he was ecstatic. He loved his daughters, but as a Polish man, nothing was more important than having a boy! He shouted the good news to all the neighbors and then rushed to Brother Czembor's apartment, exclaiming, "I have a son!" Georg had a boy first and was very proud of the fact. Now it was Wladek's turn to experience a Polish father's pride in producing a male heir!

> **Both parents were horrified to think that he could have been killed or seriously injured!**

Danusia was a curious four-year-old, so she was taken to Elder Lute's house during the birthing time to play with his two daughters. Later, when they brought her home, Sister Schferovna told her, "You have a brother."

"Oh," she said, "Where did he come from?"

"The stork dropped him, and he landed on the upper shelf of the linen closet."

This information didn't make sense, so Danusia asked, "But there is no hole there. How was he dropped just in the right spot so he could come into the house?"

The explanation left Danusia rather puzzled. But it was not polite for a child to question grownups. Danusia was fifteen when she found out the truth. She was discussing birth with her friends at school and mentioned the "stork" scenario. When her friends told her about birth, she confronted her parents, "The girls made fun of me because I was so stupid that I didn't know how babies were born. I'll never forgive you for deceiving me! How can I ever face my friends again?"

Elza's milk was slow to come in, so baby Janek wasn't interested in taking the breast. Wladek decided he would do something to help and bought a five gallon milk can full of honey! *Why so much?* In a magazine from Paris, Wladek had read that honey on the nipple would not only help babies take the nipple but would keep them quiet.

On the first Sabbath after Janek was born, *before the honey arrived*, Brother Czembor was halfway through his sermon when he stopped and looked up at the ceiling, asking, "Why is that baby crying so much?" The honey was Wladek's solution. Janek soon became addicted and wouldn't suck unless the nipple was honey-coated. Unfortunately, Wladek hadn't read how bad honey was for a child's teeth, and a few years later, Janek's baby teeth rotted away!

When Georg Czembor first saw Janek, he exclaimed, "Look at his eyes. Doesn't he look intelligent? He's such a smart looking boy." At that time, Brother Czembor was preparing to travel to the United States to attend the Seventh-day Adventist General Conference session of 1936, held at the Exposition Auditorium in San Francisco, California." So, as he looked at Janek, he said, "Young man, I'm getting old. I want you to take my place in the United States attending important meetings," and then he pinched Janek's cheeks.

Living in a fishbowl meant Wladek and Elza had to be constantly on guard not to make a foolish mistake because if they did, everyone would know. One time, when Janek was a year and a half old, Wladek sat him on the wide kitchen windowsill to get some fresh air. A few minutes later, Wladek was distracted. At that same moment, Janek lost his balance and fell forward into the kitchen—about a three-foot drop—but both parents were horrified to think that he could have just as easily fallen backward out the two-story window and been killed or seriously injured! After a few accusations were thrown, Elza calmed herself, and praised God for protecting Janek and that none of the neighbors were aware of what just happened!

Next to the ground floor's back entrance was a spacious fenced area with a patio, garden, and grass, which was a safe place for the children to play. One time, when Janek was sleeping outside in his buggy, a stranger climbed over the six-foot fence and scaled the wall of the building, got into their apartment through their open bedroom window, and stole some money. By the time the theft was discovered, the robber was long gone. But it frightened Elza to realize they were living in the middle of a big city—and not even living on the second story surrounded by a high fence could keep them safe from intruders.

The positive part of living in a close Adventist community was that when her husband was out of town, Elza was not really alone. In an emergency, there was always someone she could call upon. This fact was not lost on Wladek—having an old flame of his wife's living so close!

With a family of three little ones, Elza needed help, especially since they had no washing machine, and she had to do all the cooking, baking and cleaning herself. To assist with these duties, Elza hired a young girl whom she trained to cook and care for the house and occasionally help with the children. Elza, however, never left her alone with the children because she feared they might be kidnapped. Even though it was three years before the German occupation when the kidnapping of Polish children became common, it was already rumored that Polish children were being taken from their families and placed in homes in Germany to be reared as German citizens.

Elza didn't like the big city, but Wladek reveled in it. Warsaw was a beautiful city with streets lined with linden trees and landscaped yards. Plus, the Kuzmas lived close to a number of historical sites. The family loved listening to the free concerts near Frederick Chopin's statue commemorating his birthplace. Once, the family went by train to visit King Jan III's palace, gardens, and museum at Wilanow Park. The problem was these opportunities were extremely rare because of Wladek's hectic work schedule.

Warsaw was what Wladek described as a golden apple for literature evangelism work. For three years, including the time he spent in Warsaw, Wladek sold more books than any other literature evangelist in Poland.

During the same time, membership in the Adventist Church in Warsaw grew 100 percent, and Wladek was recognized for contributing to this growth. Although he sold Christian books and Bibles, his greatest success was selling the German magazine *The Signs of the Times* and getting addresses for Bible studies. He would then hold Bible studies among those interested and get the people ready to be baptized by an ordained pastor. One would think that with the amazing success Wladek had when working for the Polish Union in Warsaw, he would want to stay there forever, but God seemed to be urging him on to new challenges.

In 1937, there was an administrative shift in Warsaw. Georg Czembor was promoted to President of the Polish Union which meant that Wladek was now working for Georg—Elza's old flame! At the same time, Wladek's longtime pastoral friend, Brother Klute, took Czembor's place as President of the West Polish Conference. Because Brother Klute was now living and working next to Wladek, it gave them time to share their dreams for the advancement of the Adventist message. President Klute wanted Wladek's energy and zeal to work for him rather than the Union. He shared his plans with Wladek, "God has laid on my heart to bring the gospel to the most difficult cities in Poland—the towns that are dominated by Catholicism and where the residents tend to persecute anyone who threatens their belief system. He then went on to explain that he had two cities in mind: Plock[18] and Sierpc[19]—with Sierpc being the most challenging. "In order to reach those cities, I need the best missionary worker I can find. In other words." he said, "I need you, Wladek!"

What should Wladek do? For some reason, the Lord seemed to have put a burden on his heart for the town of Sierpc. He didn't understand why he felt that way because he had already worked in a number of regions where the Catholic influence had made his work difficult. *Did he really want to take his family back into an environment where they might be the brunt of persecution?* Other cities had high concentrations of Catholics, but Sierpc was unique. It had a reputation for making life difficult for anyone with a different belief system—which made it tough for Protestants and Jews living there. Yet, in spite of this, Wladek felt God calling him in that direction.

There may have been other factors that influenced Wladek's decision. First, he didn't like having to spend so much time away from his family—especially with Georg Czembor living nearby! It was common knowledge that Georg and his wife were not very compatible, and Wladek guessed that their marriage might be in trouble. In addition, since Brother Czembor had just recently been promoted to the office of President of the Polish Union, it meant that if Wladek continued to work for the Polish Union, Georg would be his boss! Although Warsaw was a golden apple of opportunity, perhaps it would have been best for everyone if he and his family left town.

Wladek knew a move, however, would never work if Elza was against it. She was too strong of a woman and wasn't afraid to voice her opinion. Elza,

---

[18] pronounced "pwuhtsk"
[19] pronounced "shair-put"

however, was a small-town girl and really never felt comfortable living in the hustle and bustle of the capital city. Plus, she loved her privacy, and although their apartment in Warsaw was comfortable—it wasn't private. But more than that, Elza lived so close to God and believed so strongly that God was guiding her husband that it really never occurred to her to argue with the decision that Wladek and the church administrators were trying to make. If they agreed her little family should move to one of the most dangerous towns in Poland, she would make it work and just increase her prayer time to plead for God's guidance and protection.

Life with Wladek was not always comfortable. They didn't always agree. They had different needs, opinions, and habits that made living together a challenge. But there was one thing Elza never doubted. She never doubted that God was strong enough to get them through anything—including the evil and persecution they might face in Sierpce.

Leaving the capital city of Warsaw and moving to Sierpc meant going from the big, beautiful city with religious tolerance to go to the mission field of a small town of only 3000 people where Catholicism was the controlling force. It was like going from light to darkness, from peace to war, from sunshine to the eye of the storm.

Wladek told Elza, "I feel like God is leading us to Sierpc. I know this sounds irrational because we've experienced religious persecution before. What do you think we should do? It could turn out to be dangerous."

Elza replied, "Wladek, I won't argue with you about whether or not we should go. You're a man of God and if God is calling our family to Sierpc, I will not stand in your way. God has always taken care of us—and He can protect us even in Sierpc."

But what may have appeared to be an irrational decision would actually turn out to be a blessing. Only God knew that during the course of the upcoming war, approximately 84 percent of Warsaw would be destroyed by German and Russian mass bombings, heavy artillery fire, and a planned demolition campaign—and that hundreds of thousands of Warsaw's residents would be killed. By moving to a small town, they would escape much of the horror of World War II. God always knows best!

Chapter 11

Sierpc: Living in the Fire of Persecution

(1937–August, 1939)

A popular saying in Poland is, "If you're Polish, you're Catholic!" Even today, ninety-eight percent of babies born in Poland are baptized into the Catholic Church. Historically, the Roman Catholic faith was accepted in Poland in AD 966, when Poland was founded as a nation. By 1573, when the Warsaw Confederation passed laws that assured protection to various religious faiths, Catholicism was the dominant faith. The Reformation, which brought Protestantism to the rest of Europe and the Polish towns near the border of Germany, never had much of an effect on the rest of Poland, *especially not Sierpc*. The area was 125 kilometers northwest of Warsaw and completely controlled by the Roman Catholic Church,

Before moving to Sierpc, Wladek went by himself to check out the town. Although he felt called by God to go there, he had a strong foreboding that there would be trouble. It was common knowledge that a spiritual war was raging in Sierpc—a major controversy between Satan and Bible truth. Wladek was so concerned about this conflict that during his visit to Sierpc, he walked into a nearby wheat field, knelt down, and wept. "Oh, Lord God," he cried. "Show me what I should do. I have followed You all my life, but I now feel called to bring Your truth to this place whose leaders have cursed and threatened me. If I should come with a message that differs from the official church I know there will be trouble. If it were just me, I would give my life for Your work, but I now have a family for whom I am responsible. Lord, what do you want me to do? Give me clear directions; and if I should come here, give me strength to bear up under persecution; and may there be an abundant harvest of precious souls." As he prayed, Wladek became more and more convinced that God was calling him to this place and added, "And Lord, please protect my family. Amen."

When Wladek got back to Warsaw, he shared his reservations about Sierpc with his friend, Brother Klute. "Why don't I go visit Sierpc with you and we can decide together what would be best," he suggested. After their trip, President Klute agreed with Wladek that the work would be difficult, "but," he added, "not impossible! I'm very anxious to have the advent message spread to this dark territory, and I know that if anyone can do it, you can. I believe you are up to the challenge." So, with his friend's encouragement, Wladek rented the upstairs apartment in building #11 on Stodloni Street. It was large enough for his family's living quarters and it also had room where they could hold small meetings. As he signed the lease, he prayed the teacher who lived below them would not cause trouble. As it turned out, the teacher wasn't a problem, but many of the other neighbors were!

Baby Janek was a year old when the Kuzma family moved to Sierpc. As Wladek carried the heavy boxes up the stairs to their second-floor apartment, he remembered what had happened two years before when they had moved to Warsaw. He had asked a stranger to help him carry some boxes up to their second-story apartment and left him alone for a few minutes while he ran downstairs for some potatoes. When he returned about ten minutes later, the double window was open, and the man was gone—and so were most of the contents of the boxes, which included Elza's wedding dress. The thief must have thrown everything he wanted out the window and then climbed down himself! Wladek wasn't about to take the same chance with strangers in Sierpc. This time, he hired a trusted friend from Warsaw to transport their belongings on a horse drawn wagon, and he paid him to help carry everything upstairs—including a very heavy pump organ!

> *You should be afraid of Mr. Kuzma. He is a dangerous person. You should do everything possible to get rid of him.*

Persecution Begins

After getting his family settled, Wladek immediately started canvasing—and praying like he had never prayed before. Catholics dominated the town, and the priests would not be happy with the message of hope that he had come to share with the people. The only Protestant presence was a small Evangelical Church. But as it turned out, the pastor of that church wasn't in favor of anyone invading "his" territory either, especially not Adventists who followed Bible truth and kept the seventh-day Sabbath. So it wasn't long before Wladek felt caught, once more, in the middle of persecuting Christians. Unfortunately, Sierpc was even worse than their assignment in Brodnica.

One of the first families Wladek met in Sierpc was Mr. and Mrs. Kazimierz Kesicki, who were eventually baptized along with some of their family and friends. Wladek and Mrs. Kesicki met in an interesting way. As Wladek was walking toward the Kesicki house, gang members from the Catholic Church jumped out from two side streets, surrounded him, and started beating him up. Mrs. Kesicki interfered and frightened the hooligans enough to grab Wladek and hide him in her house. When the police came to investigate the incident, the gang members disappeared. The policeman pointed to Wladek and asked Mrs. Kesicki, "Why do you want to save a man like this?" She replied, "He is a human being, isn't he?" Not long after Wladek met Mr. and Mrs. Kesicki, he started Bible studies with a group of interested individuals who met in their home.

From Mrs. Kesicki, Wladek learned about Marta, her sixteen-year-old daughter. Marta wasn't in school and had no job, but she loved children. Because Wladek and Elza had just moved to Sierpc, they had not yet found anyone to help care for their little ones—and it was very important that they do so quickly because there were gypsies in the forests around Sierpc who wore long wraparound sarongs where they could easily hide stolen goods. Plus, it was rumored that they sometimes kidnapped young children.

For the next three years, Marta became the dearly beloved nanny for the Kuzma children and became an Adventist after taking Bible studies. Marta loved her time with the Kuzmas, and she often mentioned how much she learned from Elza about taking care of children, cooking, making sure food didn't spoil, and keeping the house clean and orderly.

One day, Wladek was canvassing in the countryside, about a kilometer from town. At one of the farmhouses, he met a woman with a Bible. Her name was Mrs. Wojenka. She mentioned that she was interested in the Bible but didn't understand it very well, so Wladek asked, "Would you like me to study the Bible with you? It sometimes helps to have a little direction." She was excited about learning more about the Bible, and they set a date for Friday. She invited three young Catholic men and some others to the meeting. Her kitchen was full! Wladek started sharing about the second coming of Christ and left a pamphlet with everyone. He then made arrangements to return the next Friday for another meeting.

As soon as the meeting was over, a Catholic man who had attended the meeting went to the local priest with the pamphlet. After quickly scanning the pamphlet, the priest said, "You should be afraid of Mr. Kuzma. He is a dangerous person." Then he advised his parishioners "You should do everything possible to get rid of him," so the man began to stir up controversy against Wladek.

When Wladek returned the next Friday, some of the people were so angry they were ready to harm him, especially when a man excited the crowd by yelling, "He's German. Let's kill him."

A woman standing nearby overheard this threat and went to the police and reported that a man had threatened to kill Mr. Kuzma." She then pleaded with the police to come and protect him.

The police replied, "We have a war going on with the Germans. If the authorities heard that someone from Sierpc killed a German, they would probably kill everyone in the village." So the policeman came to the next meeting and scared the people by asking them to show him their identification papers. He wrote down their names and addresses and acted as if he were going to turn them into the authorities. Then, to make sure Wladek arrived home safely, the policeman escorted him to his residence on Stodloni Street.

That incident scared the troublemakers. Wladek was praying the policeman's actions would silence the controversy, and he secretly went back the next Friday—and the next—to give more studies. Later, a number of these individuals were baptized.

Anti-Jewish Sentiment

The religious intolerance of the Polish people in Sierpc was not just against Seventh-day Adventists, who were sometimes confused with Jews. They were even more hostile to the small Jewish population of 300.

Many things were similar to the persecution that Wladek and Elza experienced in Brodnica. Rabble gangs carrying clubs and knives waited to attack Jews as they went to their places of worship, so it was too dangerous for them to go outside in the evening. The aim was to destroy the Jews of Sierpc economically, physically, and spiritually. Because of the hooligan network in Sierpc, the town became the hub of the new German political party called OZN, which was specifically organized to get rid of the Jews. The Jews tried to get the Polish authorities to do something about the persecution and stop the stream of hatred, but nothing came of it. The officials merely told the Jews, "Hitler is coming to destroy you. And every gentile in Sierpc has already decided which Jewish property he will plunder and which store or apartment would be his when the German army enters Sierpc."

Anti-Gypsy Sentiment

Sierpc also exhibited a strong Nazi anti-gypsy sentiment because there was a large group of nomadic Polska Roma people (gypsies) living in the surrounding forests. Although Elza had heard that the gypsies kidnapped children, she had a heart to help them when she could. Once a week, the city authorities allowed the gypsies to go house to house in Sierpc to beg. Elza prepared sandwiches or soup for them but made sure that baby Janek and the girls were hidden in another room during this time so they weren't in danger.

Sharing the Gospel in Dangerous Times

In the middle of this escalating hornet's nest of religious persecution, Wladek continued selling the German magazine, *The Signs of the Times*, gathering names and addresses of people interested in Bible studies, and arranging times for these studies.

The priest's harassment, however, was just beginning. He printed propaganda pamphlets against Wladek saying that Mr. Kuzma was a dropout and an enemy of the church, which also made him an enemy of the state. He then gave the pamphlets to young boys to hand out to the parishiners when they came to church.

The priest also paid some women in the church to spy on Wladek. One day, a woman went to the priest and told him that Mr. Kuzma was visiting people on a certain street. The priest called the police station and said, "This man is an enemy of the state, so you should take care of him. Since the priests in Poland had significant influence on city officials, the chief of police and one of his assistants went to where Wladek was said to be. Wladek was in a house and had his Bible open as he was explaining certain passages. His good friends saw the policemen coming and said, "Quickly, put your Bible under the feather bed."

A few moments later, the policemen knocked on the door and asked to enter. When they questioned Wladek he replied, "I have just come for a visit." The people didn't say anything against Wladek because he was friendly, and they enjoyed hearing what he had to say. The chief of police continued questioning him about what he was teaching from the Bible, and he replied, "I've come to share how to live a good Christian life."

Wladek knew the authorities were trying to scare him. He also knew the women in the Catholic Church were spying on him and had told the priest, who then called the police. So Wladek said, "In Poland, we have religious freedom. It says so in paragraphs 115 and 116 of the Polish

Constitution." That seemed to stop the interrogation, and the policeman left. But that wasn't the end. The women spies continued to report to the priest what Wladek was doing and the priest continued calling the police.

Wladek was not intimidated and kept giving Bible studies. He returned regularly to Mrs. Wojenka's house. And she kept inviting interested people. Sometimes, she would invite Wladek and her friends to have something to eat. One day, when they were eating cake and discussing the Bible, the mayor heard about it. Later, he contacted Wladek and "invited" him to come to his home (which was also his office). Wladek knew that because the mayor was a widower, the priest frequently went to the mayor's house to play cards, socialize, and have a good time. So he suspected the priest had something to do with this meeting. Wladek earnestly prayed before he went. The mayor began, "Mr. Kuzma, I hear you had a meeting at Mrs. Wojenka's house."

"How did you learn about it, Mr. Mayor? Who told you?"

The mayor didn't answer.

"Mrs. Wojenka invited me to have something to eat. It wasn't a meeting." Wladek knew that to have an official meeting, he had to have a permit—which was impossible to get from the city officials. Since it wasn't an official meeting the mayor couldn't do anything. That was the end of the discussion but not the end of the harassment.

Wladek kept in touch with the church administrators in Warsaw and reported about the persecution he was experiencing. The President of the Polish Union, Georg Czembor, replied, "Where there is persecution, there are souls!" The church leaders encouraged Wladek and said they would continue to pray for him and the situation in Sierpc, but they didn't suggest that he and his family should leave. So, the persecution continued.

On one occasion, in the middle of a winter snowstorm, a mob started threatening Wladek with sticks and throwing rocks. The ground was covered with snow, and the mob was blocking the main road, so Wladek started running through a field carrying his case of books and magazines. The people followed. Suddenly, Wladek fell into a hole, and the snow caved in on top of him. He tried to get out, but the sides of the hole were too slick. There was nothing to do but pray as the people ran toward him. Fortunately, because of all the snow, they couldn't see what had happened to Wladek and ran past him. After they were gone, Wladek tried once again to climb out of the hole and, this time, managed quite easily. He walked home without any interference. Once again, God had protected him.

Getting Ready for the Sabbath

Friday afternoons in their second-story apartment in Sierpc was probably the busiest time of the week for the Kuzmas because it was bathtub day for the whole family, in addition to house cleaning and food preparation for the Sabbath. Because their bathroom didn't have an indoor tub with running hot water, the weekly ritual began with Wladek lugging into the kitchen a big metal washtub while Elza was heating water on the stove. After pouring the warm water into the tub, the baths started with the youngest to the oldest—ending with Elza and Wladek.

Two-year-old Janek and his sisters had just finished their baths, were dressed in pajamas, and told to play in the sitting room, allowing the parents some privacy. *And that's when it happened!*

Janek was swirling around on the pump organ's round stool next to the window. Around and around, he pushed himself. Faster and faster he twirled, while the girls were throwing a ball across the room. The ball bounced and went out the open window. Four-year-old Krysia ran down the steps and into the yard to retrieve her ball. As Janek stood up on the stool to watch his sister making silly actions down below, he lost his balance, fell backward, and hit the back of his head on the sharp edge of the organ. The cut was deep and long, and blood started running down his back.

Elza grabbed a towel to stop the bleeding, but it was obvious that Janek needed stitches. Wladek, halfway through his bath, jumped out of the tub, pulled on his trousers and jacket, grabbed Janek, and, holding the towel to his head to stop the bleeding, ran with him to the nearest doctor's office. But, the doctor refused to help because he considered the Kuzma family to be Jewish. Wladek ran to another doctor. Once again, the doctor refused service. At last, Wladek found a Jewish doctor who was willing to help, but by that time, the pressure applied to the wound had stopped the bleeding. However, the scar would remain a lifetime reminder for Janek not to stand up on round swirly stools! Luckily, his hair grew over the scar, and it "disappeared!"

Persecution of the Family

Not only was medical help denied to the Kuzma family, but the Catholic priest continued to stir up trouble by encouraging his parishioners to be mean and threatening. For example:

- University students threw a large snowball packed around a rock that broke the window and landed on Janek's bed. (Danusia started crying. "How are we going to get the window fixed? We'll freeze to death!")

- Neighbor kids tried interrupting meetings by throwing snowballs through windows and spitting in the girl's faces when they walked to the store.
- Children with sticks chased the kids, sicced their German Shephard dog on them and stole their toys.
- Kids called them names and chanted, "You're Jews 'cause you go to church on Saturday."
- Neighbors threw ashes out the window when they walked by.

Danusia once asked her folks, "Why are people mean to us because we love Jesus?" She was told, *"Ryby I dzieci glosu nie maja"* (Fish and children don't have a voice.) In other words, "Don't ask so many questions!"

Pauline, Elza's mother, visited in the summers of 1937 and 1938, and when she saw how the family was treated, she was afraid for their lives. "Please," she begged Elza and Wladek, "Talk to the conference office. You've got to get out of this dangerous place before someone is seriously hurt."

And so they both suffered in silence—and the gap between them grew!

Personal Tragedy

In the midst of religious persecution, the Kuzmas suffered a greater loss. Elza was five months pregnant. The whole family was excited—especially Krysia. One day, Elza needed to go to the market after a rainstorm. The fastest way was down a hill. On the slippery grass, Elza's feet went out from under her, and she rolled to the bottom. She had a few scratches but seemed fine. However, the internal damage caused her to lose the baby. It was a boy, which made the loss even more tragic.

When a baby or a fetus dies, whether or not it could have been prevented, the impact of that loss is significant. After the accident, Wladek knew Elza needed comfort, but instead, he blamed her, "Why didn't you take the road instead of the shortcut?" Her retort could have easily been, "If you would have been home, you could have gone for me, and it wouldn't have happened." Blame, however, only causes pain. Time would eventually cushion the sadness and regret, but what Elza needed was someone to hold her and let her mourn. Unfortunately, Wladek was harboring his own sorrow and he had no idea how to comfort his wife. He knew how to make money and financially support her, but he had no clue as to what he should do to help her heal emotionally. And so they both suffered in silence—and the gap between them grew!

From Persecution to Prison

Wladek and Elza kept praying that conditions would improve in Sierpc, but as 1938 turned into 1939, the tensions between the countries of Germany and Poland increased, and so did the religious persecution. By this time, not only the Catholic priest was persecuting them, but the pastor of the one Evangelical Church in town began to speak out. One day, the pastor died. The church people blamed Wladek by saying, "The pastor was scared to death about having Seventh-day Adventists in the town because he knew it would bring persecution."

Wladek and his family were in the eye of the storm. Everyone seemed to be turning against them. They felt hostility from the leaders and members of the Catholic Church and the Evangelical Church, the town officials, and the police. How much longer could this go on?

By the summer of 1939, conditions were unbearable. One day, Elza went to the neighborhood bakery. When she was coming home, one of the neighbors who was hired to watch over the property the Kuzmas were renting hit Elza over the head with a spade as she walked by. Luckily she had on a double leather hat, so the blow split her hat but not her head. When Elza wrote her mother about what had happened, Pauline wrote back, "Get out of there with the kids before someone gets killed. And get your husband moved as soon as possible!"

Through it all, Wladek continued to hold unofficial meetings giving Bible studies. The assistant chief of police was confused about Wladek's true purpose because his boss and the priest called Wladek an enemy of the state. The policeman finally decided to attend one of the "meetings" and privately asked Wladek, "Why don't we go for a walk in the forest so you can tell me about your ideas." After they talked, the man confessed, "Mr. Kuzma, I thought you were a political agitator, but now I know differently. Be very careful. We are living in serious times. I understand we need to get ready for Jesus's coming and be pure like Christ, but I'm afraid your message may get you seriously hurt." They prayed and sang together, and the man didn't bother him anymore. But his boss, the chief of police, was still being influenced by the priest who was pressuring him to arrest Wladek!

One day, Wladek wasn't feeling well and was lying in bed while Elza was out with the children. There was a loud knock on the door. It was the chief of police saying that he needed to talk with him. Wladek got up and met the man. The police chief said, "You are a German and need to move out of this area."

"No," replied Wladek, "I am a Polish citizen. I have come from Leszno, where I am registered, and have papers to prove it."

"But you are receiving German magazines called *The Signs of the Times.*"

"Yes," Wladek replied. "You see, I am a Polish citizen, but I also speak German, French, English, and Esperanto." That quieted the policeman for a moment. Wladek went on to explain, "These magazines aren't political. They are religious. The articles are about God, Jesus Christ, angels, heaven, and health."

Because of the priest's unrelenting pressure, the chief of police finally decided that the only way to get the priest to stop pestering him was to arrest Wladek and put him in jail. They put him in a cell with a German miller who was crying, Wladek spent the night reading his Bible to the man and comforting him. Wladek never found out what happened to the miller, but he considered this encounter another one of God's divine appointments.

When Elza got home and learned her husband was in jail, she came the next morning with Marta and the children and brought him some food. When the children saw their father behind bars, they started crying. The policeman asked, "Why did your wife bring the children?"

Wladek answered, "My wife came to see me because she and the children missed me. They wanted to know why I was arrested and what the police were doing with me."

After Elza visited the jail, she immediately went to the doctor who had become a good friend after he had saved Janek's life with hydrotherapy and other natural remedies when he was eighteen months old. Elza said, "They have locked up my husband because he has German magazines." Then she showed him Wladek's Polish citizenship papers.

The doctor then called the chief of police and asked, "Why did you lock up this man? I have his Polish papers in front of me. He is a Polish citizen and a Christian. I want you to unlock him immediately. If not, I will call the Ministry of Justice in Warsaw, and you will have trouble like you have never had before!" The authorities immediately released Wladek but put him under house arrest, hoping this would satisfy the priest. For three weeks, Wladek was not supposed to have visitors or leave his home.

Gold from the Fire

Wladek spent his time at home organizing his books, packing things, and basically getting ready to move. But he still had some soul-winning business he needed to do. At about eleven o'clock that first night, Wladek had the strong impression that he should go see the Jankofski family on the outskirts of Sierpc. Mr. Jankofski was a teacher and a religious man who kept the Sabbath in his own fashion. He was rather strange. Wladek had left him a religious book with pictures in it. The man didn't believe in religious pictures, so he left the book outside his door. There were four young farmer boys who came to his house, and Mr. Jankofski tried to explain the Sabbath to them. They believed what he said and enjoyed looking at the book with all the pictures. But they wanted more information.

Mr. Jankofski was interested in what Wladek was presenting because of a dream he had where everything was burning. He was told in the dream that the entire world would fall and burn up, but a man with important information for him would come. When Mr. Jankofski told Wladek the dream, they both recognized that Wladek was the man with the information he needed. Wladek also sold him the book by William Ambrose Spicer, *Our Time in the Light of Prophecy,* and started Bible studies with him and his wife, along with a few interested friends and the four farmer boys. Now, they only needed a few more meetings to have all the Bible information necessary to be ready for baptism.

Wladek was not going to let the fact that he was under house arrest keep him from delivering Bible truth to this family and his neighbors, even though talk of war was escalating and there were many Polish soldiers in town. So, during the three weeks of house arrest, Wladek, in the middle of the night, carefully went on foot through the grain fields to visit this family. If he went on the streets, he thought he might be caught and arrested again.

In July 1939, Wladek wrote to Pastor Dzik in Warsaw to come and baptize those who were ready. The pastor came, and an Adventist Church with fourteen precious souls was organized in Sierpc because of Wladek's work. When Pastor Dzik heard Wladek's story about the dangerous situation in Sierpc, he commented, "These members are the gold plucked from the fire!"

Mr. and Mrs. Wojenka and a couple of people who studied at their home were baptized, along with Mr. and Mrs. Kesicki, Marta, and a few of their friends. A number of the people baptized belonged to the Jankofski family or were their friends. The four farmer boys were not baptized at the time, but they hid the book that Wladek had given them so it would not be taken during the years Poland was under Nazi and communist occupation, and they continued to read it. Twenty years later, these men came to Sister Betzel, who lived in Plock, and wanted to know where there was a Seventh-day Adventist minister so they could get baptized. They explained that they had read the book that Wladek had given them, so they knew they needed to be baptized by immersion since they believed in Jesus! (By this time, Wladek and his family were already in the United States.)

A sad ending to this story is that Brother Jankofski, a highly educated teacher, and his wife had smoked so much of their lives that they were in ill health and partially blind when the Nazis invaded Poland. Because the Nazi mandate was to exterminate the unwanted Polish citizens—especially the intellectuals and the maimed—the Nazis shot both Brother Jankofski and his wife.

Planning to Move On

When Wladek told his friend, Pastor Dzik, how his family was being treated, the pastor shook his head, "You are standing in the fire of persecution. Maybe it's time to get out."

By this time, Wladek and Elza had lived in Sierpc for two years. At first, it had seemed like an adventurous idea to start an Adventist Church, but now, with that mission accomplished, Wladek began thinking about Jesus' words recorded in Matthew 10:14 as He sent his disciples on their first missionary trip, "And whoever will not receive you nor hear your words, when you depart from that house or city, shake off the dust from your feet." After reading the passage, Wladek approached Elza and finally admitted. "Perhaps it is time to shake off the dust of Sierpc from our feet!" She agreed.

In early August, when Wladek attended a church worker's meeting in Warsaw, he pressed the issue, "If it were just me, I'd be willing to endure the persecution in order to win more souls, but I have to make sure my family is safe, and I can no longer do that in Sierpc."

Wladek's friend from Ostrowo days, Brother Kosmowski, now ministering in Warsaw, said, "Be very careful, Brother, Sierpc is very dangerous. You should consider going to Plock." The conference officials knew that Sister Betzel, who lived in Plock, had been praying for twenty years for an Adventist pastor to go there. Plus, President Klute had Plock as another "unentered territory" on his list of where he wanted to plant Adventist Churches.

After some discussion, the church administrators voted that the Kuzma family should move to Plock, a larger city just 42 kilometers southeast of Sierpc. Even though the town was mostly Catholic, there were other Protestant churches and a large Jewish population of around 9000. Because of this diversity, they felt there would be less chance of persecution from the dominant church.

Marta was eager to move with them. She loved the Kuzma family, and the kids loved her. In fact, Janek was so bonded to Marta that he refused to go to sleep or eat without her! Plus, with the war approaching, it would be difficult for her to find other work. Poland did not allow their citizens to have Saturdays off. And working for Jews was no longer an option.

After the decision was final, Wladek calmly said to Elza, "I have a plan. I'll make the final moving arrangements, but it will take a few weeks. Since the kids are in constant danger here, why don't you and Marta take them by train to Rybnik to see your mother and the rest of your family for a little vacation? When everything is ready, hopefully by the end of the month, we'll meet at the train station in Plock."

Elza was thrilled. "Oh, Wladek, this makes me so happy. I've been praying for weeks that God would impress the church administration to move us before someone gets seriously hurt. And now, because almost all my family is in Rybnic helping Emil with the confectionary factory, we'll get to see everyone and also have a little vacation! I'm so excited!"

When Elza, Marta, and the children arrived in Rybnik, Uncle Emil and Uncle Alfred picked them up in company vans at the railroad station. What a reunion! Then, they were off to Zakopone (about a three and a half hour drive from Rybnik), the vacation paradise in the Tartar Mountains. They rented a cabin for a week of hiking on the beautiful forest trails and sunbathing beside the cool running streams.

It was a welcome reprieve from the stress of the constant conflict they had endured in Sierpc. Elza wrote to her husband, "I am so happy you sent us here. If we had not left when we did, I'm afraid the children may have been killed."

While Elza was vacationing with the children, Wladek was wrapping up the work in Sierpc and making arrangements to move the last week of August. All he needed now was a permit from the authorities in Plock (which included the mayor, priest, and police) to make sure the family wasn't bringing a negative element to the city—such as drinking, gambling, or gang violence. Wladek told the Plock officials he was moving to Plock to help people improve their health by teaching them principles for living a healthy lifestyle. He explained that he did this by selling Christian books like *The Great Controversy* and *Steps to Christ* by Ellen G. White.

After Wladek obtained the permit, he rented an apartment in a five-story building that would be central to where he would be selling books. He was excited about the possibilities Plock held for his family. Elza was thrilled. At last they would have a safe place to raise their family and spread Bible truth.

CHAPTER 12

Plock: Trapped in the War Zone

(August 31, 1939–1940)

Thursday, August 31, was a late summer day in Sierpc. The rented wagon arrived early to pick up the boxes Wladek had packed and some furniture. Now, as the horse lazily trotted toward Plock, Wladek let out a sigh of relief to be leaving behind the chaos of religious persecution his family had experienced.

He felt his soul respond to the beauty of the countryside—the grassy meadows dotted with wildflowers and the peaceful stands of trees. How lovely were the cultivated fields of szczaw (sometimes called sorrel), a sour tasting spinach-type green used in soup, the neat rows of sugar beets, and the tasseled corn ready for harvest. He had bicycled through this countryside before—but it never looked as peaceful as it did at this moment, especially the little villages with their picturesque churches with pointed steeples. He smiled as he noticed an old man next to a small pond leaning against his walking stick, watching a flock of ducks as if he hadn't a care in the world, while an old woman, maybe the man's wife, was leaning out the cottage's upstairs window shaking her bedding. At the end of this perfect day, he would meet Elza and the children at the train station and get them settled in their Plock apartment. Later, he would go back to Sierpc to collect the rest of their belongings.

What a great reunion when the kids jumped off the train and into Wladek's arms, bubbling over with news of all the things they had done with Mama's relatives in Rybnik and Zakopane.

"Oh, Wladek," Elza exclaimed, "It was a wonderful vacation. Thank you! Thank you! I'm rejuvenated and ready now for our new adventure in Plock!"

It was late when they arrived at the apartment Wladek had rented. "Let's just grab some quilts and pillows, get some sleep, and wait until morning to unpack," suggested Elza.

As soon as the kids' heads hit the pillows, they fell asleep next to Marta, their beloved nanny. Wladek and Elza took time to make up their bed, knelt, thanked God for bringing them safely to this peaceful place, and fell asleep in each other's arms.

Suddenly, the family was awakened. Explosions could be heard in every direction. The children began screaming in terror. At first, Wladek and Elza thought (as did most of the citizens of Plock) that what they were hearing was caused by Polish Air Force maneuvers. But as the sun came up over the horizon, they could see that the sky was filled with Nazi warplanes clearly marked with swastikas. They were dropping bombs on the city. Then, as the people ran out of their houses to see what was happening, the pilots dived and sprayed them with machine gun fire. *Tata-tata-tatata.*

> *Elza took one glance at the tracer bullets whizzing through the air and screamed, "Get down! We're being attacked!"*

The Kuzma's new home in Plock, which Wladek thought would be a safe haven, was in the middle of a war zone.

Elza took one glance at the tracer bullets whizzing through the air and screamed, "Kids, get away from the window! Get down! We're being attacked!" It was 6 a.m., September 1, 1939—the official time when World War II enveloped the Kuzma family in their new home in Plock and changed the entire course of their lives.

Events Leading Up to the War

For a year now, it was reported that Hitler's Nazi German Army had begun mobilizing for war, so the possibility of Germany invading Poland had become a major theme of conversation among Poles.

A year before on October 15, 1938, the Poles shook their heads in disbelief as German troops occupied the Sudetenland, which was a border portion of Czechoslovakia that was inhabited by over three million Sudeten

Germans who were sympathetic to Germany. Like dominoes, this caused the Czech government to capitulate to German demands.

On March 13, 1939, Germany announced "Anschluss," their annexation of Austria. Immediately after, on March 16, the Nazis took control of the rest of Czechoslovakia—all without firing a shot!

It was obvious that Poland was next on the Nazi's hit list, especially after Hitler's Reichstag (parliamentary) speech on January 30, 1939, when he boldly predicted that the Jews would be eliminated from Europe. (Hitler was obviously referring to Poland since there were more Jews in Poland than in any other European country.) The world, however, believed that the proud Polish people would not allow their country to be overrun by the Nazis like Sudetenland, Czechoslovakia, and Austria. *The Polish would fight!*

What no one expected was that this war would be significantly different from previous wars, that the accepted rules of war would be ignored, that every Pole would be considered the enemy, that there would be no mercy toward civilians, and that there would be no humanitarian code of decency concerning the treatment of the prisoners of war. Hitler's ultimate objective was the annihilation of every Polish man, woman, and child—with major emphasis on the eradication of the Jewish population by outright murder!

After Hitler's January 1939 parliamentary speech, Wladek and Elza sensed that the invasion was imminent. They also knew the hostility toward them by the people and officials in Sierpc would mean that no one in that city would go out of their way to protect them. That's why they were eager to move. Hopefully, Plock would be a safer place to be when war came.

No one, however, expected the Germans to invade so quickly. Like the proverbial tale of the boy crying "wolf," the Polish people had heard about the threat of war for so long that on the morning of the first day of September at 4:45 a.m., when 2000 German tanks and over 1000 aircraft broke through the Polish defenses along the German/Polish border, they were shocked. And once the Nazis broke through the border, it was only an hour and fifteen minutes before bombs were dropping on Plock!

Although the Polish had an army of more than 700,000, it was unprepared for Germany's Blitzkrieg (lightning war) tactics that provided for the rapid advance of Nazi armored divisions across Poland. Within days the Nazis had almost completely destroyed the Polish Calvary, which made up a good part of the Polish military. The other surprise was the massive bombing raids that were used to break up Polish troop concentrations and destroy airports, trains and railroad stations, roads, and bridges so that the Nazis could kill large numbers of refugees crowding these transportation facilities. Aerial bombing of undefended cities, such as Plock, was used to break down civilian morale. In fact, on September 1, the German Luftwaffe (air force) bombed the city of Plock three different times, dropping over eighty bombs. Thirty people were officially reported as killed and over 100 wounded—but the actual numbers were probably higher.

Hitler's directive to his troops on the first day of the war was to murder as many of the Polish civilians as possible—men, women, and children. This was done by massive bombing in areas far removed from any other military activity—such as towns like Plock, where there was a large Jewish population.

As the Nazi front won territory, they captured thousands of Polish soldiers as well as Polish civilians. The Nazi military machine then moved on as special Nazi killing forces annihilated the POWs—military personnel and civilian men, women, and children. Nothing seemed to be able to stop this blitzkrieg of deceit, mayhem, carnage, murder, massacre, and suffering imposed on the Polish people.

Running for their Lives

Within minutes of the initial attack, the citizens of Plock were in panic mode. Shops were closed, and peasants who had come to the early morning Friday market rushed home.

Wladek and Elza realized their family was in grave danger of being bombed if they stayed in the five-story apartment complex in the center of town. "We have to get the children to safety. *But where?*"

They didn't know anyone in Plock—except for Mrs. Betzel, who was a kind, generous Adventist widow whose husband had died in The Great War. She and her three adult children lived near the airport on the outskirts of town. Wladek reasoned, "If we can get to the Betzels, they will probably know someplace where we can be safe until the fighting is over. But it was quite a distance—and the Kuzmas had no transportation.

"We'll just have to make a run for it," Wladek shouted above the explosions and machine gun fire. There was no time to deliberate. They hurriedly threw together a small satchel of clothing and some food and prayed for safety. Then Wladek, Elza, and Marta each grabbed a child and ran down the stairs and out into the early morning chaos toward the road that led out of town. This was NOT how they had intended to spend their first day in Plock!

It was a harrowing journey, especially for the children. At one point, they came upon three dead horses in the middle of the road. It looked as if the dive bombers used them for target practice. The planes flew so close to the ground that the two pilots could be seen; one was flying, and the other was shooting a machine gun.

Each time the family heard a plane approaching, the adults ran for the ditch by the side of the road and hid in the weeds with the kids under them, shielding them as best they could as the plane sprayed bullets down the crowded roadway. When the planes were gone, they crawled out of the ditch and continued their journey. At last, they could see Betzel's house. It was a miracle none of their family was killed in their mad dash to safety.

As it turned out, Mrs. Betzel had a brother whose family lived in the country. The next day, Elza, Marta, the children, Mrs. Betzel, and her grown daughters climbed into a horse drawn wagon to head to the farm. The wagon bed had been piled with loose hay, so if they encountered Nazi soldiers, the girls could hide. With no room for the men, Wladek and Mrs. Betzel's adult son hunkered down in a local barn until the bombing and the killing of civilians was over, and it was safe to return to the Betzel's home.

Meanwhile, on September 8, the Nazis' tanks and infantry marched into Plock and, within hours, took control, leaving a detail of German soldiers behind to maintain order while the rest of the troops moved eastward. As this was happening, other German troops attacked Poland from the north to take Danzig and the Baltic territory. At the same time, the third front advanced from the south through Krakow and then pushed north into Warsaw, surrounding and slaughtering anyone in their way. The strong resistance of the Poles in Warsaw delayed German victory until September 27, when the Poles "surrendered" after the Nazis army destroyed Warsaw—reducing that beautiful historic city to a pile of rubble. On October 6, the Germans annexed the Polish territories along Germany's eastern border, and the 1939 German occupation of Poland was complete.

The Underground Polish State

The Polish government, however, never formally surrendered. Instead, it went underground for the remainder of the occupation. It sabotaged trains and planes, blew up bridges, carried secret information, assassinated Nazi leaders, and basically bit the underbelly of the occupying forces in every way possible. Members of the resistance were often kept alive by brave Polish people who were aware of their activity and fed or sheltered them if underground activity was happening in the countryside or woods around certain villages. It is unknown how many Polish citizens suffered torture or death rather than betray the efforts of the Underground.

The Polish Underground State, which included the Armia Krajowa (Polish Army) with approximately a million Polish soldiers, also fought against Nazi domination on numerous fronts. By 1940, the headquarters of the Underground Polish State had moved to London, where it operated until the end of the war. It is estimated that hundreds of thousands of people were directly involved in the various agencies of the Underground.

The Involvement of the Soviet Russian Army

In September and October of 1939, the Russian army, according to their Hitler-Stalin non-aggression pact with Germany, occupied the eastern part of Poland. But instead of being a blessing, it was a curse. The Russians treated the Polish population with the same hatred and cruelty—and for some people, it was worse. They not only killed many Polish citizens, but they captured thousands and sent them to the Siberian gulags (labor camps), where the people were overworked and starved to death.

By June, 1941, the tables had switched. The Germans, now, instead of cooperating with the Russians in the occupation of Poland, began the conquest of the Soviet Union by invading Poland's eastern Russian-held territory and occupying all the rest of what used to be the nation of Poland, which for almost two years had been controlled by Russia. This move allowed Germany the freedom to continue killing the Jewish population while at the same time forcing many Christian Poles to support the German cause instead of the Soviets. They not only transported thousands of Poles to Germany and East Prussia to work in forced labor camps but also forced them to send needed supplies and food to Germany to support the war effort. This caused hardship and near starvation in many Polish families. But that's getting ahead of the story.

The Kuzma Story Continues

Eight days after the initial bombing, the fighting was over in the Plock region, and Mrs. Betzel's son brought Wladek back to the Betzels' house. Wladek immediately bicycled to Plock, only to discover that the apartment he had rented had been bombed. He found another place to live, even nicer than the first, on the third floor of a brick apartment building for 50 zlotys a month. He moved what was left of their belongings to #5 Tumska Street, not far from the Jewish quarter. Its central location made it a perfect place from which to sell books.

Wladek then went to the farm to get his family. How happy he was to find that everyone had survived. Elza had kept busy helping the farmer's wife. In a way, it was a nice reprieve for her to be away from the city and enjoy farm life—even though her family had to sleep on the floor. They thanked their hosts for giving them shelter during the bombing. The children sadly left behind the tiny yellow ducklings and chicks they had enjoyed. Reluctantly, they climbed onto the wagon with their parents, Mrs. Betzel, and her daughters, to return to the city. After a short visit at the Betzel's house, where Wladek reported the conditions in Plock since the military takeover, the Kuzma family went home to the new apartment that Wladek had rented.

A few days later, Mrs. Betzel helped Wladek find a farmer with a horse drawn wagon to move the rest of the Kuzma furniture and belongings from Sierpc to Plock. He and Elza left Plock with the wagon at 5 a.m. and arrived in Sierpc an hour later. Because they feared that their enemies might harm them if they were discovered, they packed up the wagon quickly and were ready to leave by a little after 7:00 a.m. The once beautiful pastoral landscape was now marred by bombed out buildings, slaughtered animals, and the bodies of Polish soldiers and peasants trying to escape.

The Rest of the Story

A few weeks later, after Wladek got his family settled in their new home, he went back to Sierpc to discover what had happened to the baptized church members. That's when he heard about the priest's confession. It happened on September 8 when German tanks rolled into Sierpc (just as they done in Plock) while the Polish army was quickly retreating. This resulted in a lot of shooting and bombing of the town and the surrounding woods by the Sierpienica River, where Polish soldiers and townspeople were hiding. The German bomber planes saw this group and started diving toward them with their machine guns blazing. That was when the people saw the priest kneeling down and heard him confessing his sins against Mr. Kuzma.

After the German occupation, many of the people of Sierpc who had at one time been on the priest's side now supported Wladek. They told the Germans, "The priest was hard on Mr. Kuzma, who had a German wife. He persecuted the innocent man and forced the police to arrest him and put him in jail."

And what happened to the priest? He was so afraid of the Nazis that he discarded his clerical robe, dressed in civilian clothing, and left town. After the war, it was rumored that he was selling milk and buttermilk in Warsaw.

If Wladek and Elza thought that by leaving Sierpc and moving to Plock, religious persecution would cease, they were wrong. Both cities were now under Nazi German control, which meant that *any* expression of religious belief was illegal, and the offending person could immediately be shot or hung, thrown in prison, tortured, or forced to suffer a slow death in a concentration camp. Plus, it was now illegal to sell Christian books and magazines. The work that once brought Wladek a sense of pride and accomplishment, as well as support for his family, could now bring him persecution and possibly death.

Chapter 13

Plock: Surviving Nazi Occupation

(1939-1944)

"The Princely Capital City of Plock"

If it hadn't been for the war, living in Plock would have been an amazing cultural experience for the Kuzma family. The city was one of the oldest in Poland and was located in a beautiful area—the Dobrzyn Lake District. From 1079 to 1138, it was the medieval capital of the region and an important center for science and art. It was called "The Princely Capital City of Plock," fortified with the Plock Castle built high on Tumskie Hill overlooking the Vistula River.

On October 8, 1939 Plock was incorporated into the Reich as part of West Prussia, and its name was changed to Schrottersburg. Almost immediately, the elite class of Polish teachers, scientists, professionals, and artists were killed. And many of the Slavic Poles (not just the Jews) were forced into German labor camps.

The Nazis' ultimate plan for Poland was simple: *Destroy the nation and all the people of Slavic ethnicity*. To do this, they divided German/Polish citizens into groups.

Group 1: *Ethnic Germans who had taken an active part in the struggle for the Germanization of Poland*. This group of Polish/Germans had the most privileges. Many Slavic Poles were shocked when they learned that some of their "German" neighbors had been spying on them for years. Through their help, the Nazis compiled lists of those they considered to be Polish leaders: intellectuals, teachers, professors, scientists, musicians, medical personnel and artists. Because of these lists, the Nazis were able to dispose of this educated class of approximately 68,000 within the first month of occupation.

If Wladek and Elza had remained in Sierpc, where they were known, their names could have been on the "extermination" list. But by moving at that critical time, no one in Plock knew them, which made it easier for Elza to claim her German heritage and go by her German maiden name, Gartz, rather than the Slavic name, Kuzma.

Group 2: *Ethnic Germans who had not taken an active part in the Germanization of Poland but had "preserved" their German characteristics.* Elza was in this group.

Group 3: *Individuals of alleged German stock who had become "Polonized" but whom, it was believed, could be won back to Germany.* This group also included *persons of non-German descent married to Germans* or members of non-Polish groups who were considered desirable for their political attitude and racial characteristics. Wladek fell into this category.

Group 4: *Persons of German stock who had become politically merged with the Poles.* This group, especially the Slavic Poles, were stateless and expendable. If Wladek had been single, he would have fallen into this group and very likely killed. They had to wear an identifying purple P on their clothing and abide by a curfew. They were banned from using public transportation or entering places where the sign "Entrance is forbidden to Poles, Jews, and Dogs" was hung, which included many churches, restaurants, and theaters. Shops owned by this group were taken over by Germans, and the prior owners were rarely compensated. Fortunately, the enforcement of the Nazi directives was dependent on local Nazi personnel, and some were not as cruel as others. The fortunate Poles could speak German, didn't have neighbors who would turn them in to the authorities, and could keep "out of sight." The Slavic Poles knew they had no rights and would have been instantly killed or brutally beaten and/or sent to a concentration camp if they spoke up. This is why the Nazis were able to mistreat so many "undesirable people" with no one interfering.

To further the Germanization of Poland, the Polish language was prohibited from being taught in elementary schools, and famous landmarks from streets to cities were changed to German names. During the occupation, food and other necessary supplies were scarce because the Germans first took what they needed for the war effort, leaving very little for the Polish people. The Nazis even took metal items such as pots, pans, cooking utensils and various tools. The Kuzma kids remember piles of "scrap" metal products on the street corners that Poles were forced to give up "for the war effort." The Nazis then issued coupons to the Poles for rationed items, such as clothing and shoes. Food staples like sugar, flour, butter, coffee, or meat were only available if you had food stamps, which were issued monthly. Poles were also given retraining cards because many of their jobs, factories, and farms had been taken over by the Germans, so retraining was essential.

Living on Tumska Street

When the Kuzma family returned to Plock after the September bombing, they moved into a comfortable third-floor apartment at #5 Tumska Street, one of the town's main streets. Because of the hatred of the Nazi German officials toward the Poles, Elza began using her maiden name, Gartz, because it was much more acceptable to the Nazis than the Slavic name, "Kuzma." When they were in public, Wladek became Wilhelm, which was a Germanic name.

Actually, in the years leading up to the Nazi invasion, Wladek saw the handwriting on the wall. His given name and nickname were about as Polish as one could get. With the idea of blending in as much as possible, he began using the name Wilhelm on such things as salary payments. Even his friends and coworkers at the Seventh-day Adventist Conference office started calling him Wilhelm while he was still working in Warsaw—a couple of years before the German occupation.

Because of Elza's German heritage, the family was able to make friends and avoid wearing the dreaded purple P, which identified them as Polish, which would cause others to either ostracize or take advantage of them. That's why the Kuzma kids have fond memories of their years in Plock. They never realized how privileged they were because of their mother's German heritage.

The apartment they were able to rent had an attractive courtyard where the children could play. Plus, it was a great place for Elza to socialize with the other families who lived there. Many of the residents worked for the German government and were probably associated with Nazi terrorists in some way—but no one asked.

Especially memorable to the kids was the time Elza was making plum jam ("*powidla*" in Polish) in the courtyard. She had two big pots standing on bricks over a fire with the thick sauce popping out of the pots. Residents of the apartment enjoyed watching the process—and being recipients of Elza's jam.

Since Elza was not yet working, she had time to enjoy making friends. She was savvy enough to understand what was happening to the Polish people, so because she was new to town, she introduced herself as a German woman who had married a Polish man. She played this role well and would present herself to the rot house (city hall) to play her German "card" and argue for the life of a Polish person whom the Gestapo had arrested. When a Polish woman dentist was arrested, Elza made certain the authorities heard about it. "How could you arrest a good woman who has a skill you or I may need in the future when we get a toothache?" Elza was persuasive and was able to get a number of Polish people released from prison and possibly death or at least saved from being sent to forced labor camps.

What a great central location for Elza's effervescent personality to shine! She took advantage of the opportunity to socialize with the German people living around her. One night, the German town officials had a gala event in the new theater next to their apartment complex, and Elza was invited. Wladek refused to attend because of his Polish heritage, and the event had something to do with the movie business, of which he disapproved. *But not Elza!* She had her long chestnut hair (which hadn't been cut for twenty years and hung down past her waist) braided in the back and twisted high on her head. She wore a long dress with sequins and a fur cape. She looked stunning! She easily socialized with military personnel as well as business people. The training she had received at Tschapka's Konditorei on associating with high society was extremely valuable. It was at affairs such as this that Elza was able to glean information that proved valuable in keeping her family safe and making the friends she needed when requesting certain favors.

The location of their Tumska Street apartment was also valuable for Wladek—at least at first. It was surrounded by apartment complexes which made it a perfect place for selling books and magazines door-to-door. Plus, it was only a few blocks from the historic Plock Cathedral and the scenic Vistula River.

The only problem was that after a few months, the German officials liked the same location and moved their offices into the apartment complex across the street from where the Kuzmas lived. The Nazis just forced out the occupants and turned the apartment units into their headquarters, which included offices for the hated Secret Police called the Gestapo (the *Geheime Staatspolizei*) and the SS (the "*Schutzstaffel*" or "Shield Squadron" that was a major Nazi organization to protect the Fuhrer and harass the enemy). Both organizations were known to be ruthlessly cruel and had the authority to torture, imprison, and kill the Poles.

The Harsh Treatment of the Jews

The Kuzma's Tumska apartment was also close to the Jewish section of town. This meant that at times the children witnessed the Nazi mistreatment of Jews, like holding them at gunpoint and screaming obscenities at them. They saw them being shoved, hit with weapons, and knocked down. They also saw them being forced into Nazi cargo trucks (lorries) and driven away as their families and friends agonizingly screamed after them.

By October, a decree was given that forced all Jewish industries, businesses, and workshops in Plock to be taken over by German and German/Polish trustee directors/owners.

The Nazi regime made all the Jews wear a yellow Star of David so they could be easily identified. Soon after that, they began liquidating them. People were being rounded up and taken into the town square to be shot, and others were sent to concentration camps. The Jews now experienced daily terror, and it was not safe for them to be out walking on the streets. At any time, their homes could be invaded. For example, one night in October, the German soldiers and Poles of German origin plundered Jewish property. They herded hundreds of naked and barefooted men into the courtyard of the "Hotel d'Angleterre," where they were tormented the whole night. On another occasion, some Jews were taken to the nearby village of Jadziwia, where they were buried up to their necks and abandoned. Thankfully, local peasants found them and dug them out.

Within a month after the German occupation, the Nazis established a fenced Jewish ghetto in Plock, where they crowded approximately 7600 Jewish Plock residents and 3000 Jewish refugees (who had come to Plock thinking they would be safe). They put the Jews behind barbed wire so they could more easily persecute, terrorize, exploit, and round them up for extermination. Sometimes, ten or more Jews were forced to live in one room. The Plock ghetto was just one of over 1000 ghettos that the Nazis established in the cities and towns of Poland. The Plock ghetto only lasted eighteen months and was closed in February/March of 1941 with two massive exportations. Here is a description by Abraham Wein in the *Encyclopedia of Jewish Communities*, p. 358–372, of how the first deportation of 7000 Jews was carried out. "At 4 a.m. on February 21, SS soldiers broke into the ghetto clinic and ordered the inmates—ailing old people and derelicts—to leave in five minutes…they beat to death nearly half the patients. All the Jews of Plock were ordered to appear at dawn at the assembly point in Szeroka Street.

"Even before the Jews had awoken from their sleep, the voices of the Germans could be heard shouting 'Jews, outside!' The evacuation went ahead methodically, house by house at breakneck speed. Anyone hesitating was thrown down the stairs and hurried to the assembly place with the help of blows from iron bars, rifle butts, and truncheons. At the place, the Jews were lined up in rows of five and kept standing there until noon without food or drink. They were forbidden to sit down or to leave their places for natural reasons. Acts of brutality were widespread; many Jews were severely injured, and some died. Children were trampled to death in the uproar, women and ill people fainted, and some suffered strokes.

"More scenes of brutality unfolded themselves as the deportees were hustled onto the lorries. Those who had difficulty in clambering onto them, including the old, the weak, and the sick, were beaten unmercifully. Many were killed or suffocated (up to 200 souls were jammed into each lorry). On the lorry, there was an armed SS soldier, and acts of violence continued to take place during the journey.... Tens of people perished on the tortuous four-hour journey—or were left behind dead in Szeroka Street."

After the second deportation in March, the few remaining Jews were transported to either the ghetto or the concentration camp in Dzialdowo.

One of the unforgettable horrors that the Kuzma children remember from their early days in Plock was the hanging of ten Polish young men because one German soldier was killed. The slogan of the Nazis was grilled into their minds, "For each German life, ten Polish lives would be sacrificed." It was widely advertised that their bodies would be displayed over the weekend. Danusia was curious and asked her father about going to the event. Wladek, with great sorrow, replied, "No way! Sabbath is coming, and this is nothing for a child your age to see."

Dangers Facing Polish Children

In war torn Poland, Elza and Wladek were even more concerned for their children's safety than they had been before. It wasn't a secret that the Nazis were kidnapping Polish children. This was actually happening as early as 1936 when they were in Warsaw, but now with the Nazi occupation, it was common knowledge that thousands of children (statistics say over 50,000 from Germany's annexed countries) were taken from orphanages and foster homes or separated from their parents and taken into special Germanization programs.

If these kidnapped children passed the battery of racial, physical, and psychological tests, they were given new names, forbidden to speak Polish, and raised by German parents. If they were "not Aryan enough," they were sent either to orphanages, where they died for lack of food, or to concentration camps like Auschwitz, where many were killed by intercardiac injections of phenol. Few of these Polish children who survived the war were ever reunited with their Polish families.

As the months went on, Elza and Wladek also learned that if Polish women who were deported to Germany as forced laborers got pregnant, their babies were taken away. Or if the mothers before birth didn't look Aryan enough, many were forced to have abortions.

Shortly after Marta (the children's nanny) moved to Plock with the Kuzma family, she decided that although she loved her work and had learned so much from Elza, what she really wanted was to get married. This meant she needed to return to her hometown to be close to Henrick, the man she loved. So she left the Kuzma household and went back to Sierpc. *But not for long.* Because of the war, she and Henrick decided that marriage should wait. Marta spent the next five years working in Ostroda in West Prussia until the war was over in 1945. She then returned to Sierpc and married Henrick.

Hiding Berta

Elza began praying for a replacement for Marta. God answered her prayer in a most unusual way by impressing her to bring home a 26-year-old Jewish girl by the name of Berta—and her father, whom she had met when she first came to Plock and visited the fabric store they owned. A few weeks later, Elza learned that the Nazis had taken the store away from the family and put it under "German" management. She had admired Berta's sewing ability and missed seeing her when she went shopping.

One day Elza happened to notice that Berta and her father were among a group of Jews that had been detained in a Nazi raid. Elza, playing her "German citizen card," was impressed to intervene and negotiate their release.

Since everyone knew that it was an automatic death sentence if a German or Pole was caught harboring a Jew (or even feeding one), the officials obviously thought that after the Jews were released, the girl and her father would go back to the ghetto. It never occurred to the authorities that Elza would take them home with her! Elza knew, however, that sending them back to the Jewish quarter would have meant continued persecution and, eventually, death. So she did the unthinkable!

Berta's father only stayed for a couple of weeks. Wladek and Elza pled with him not to leave, but he felt he had to check on his wife and three other daughters, so he left, saying, "I'll return as soon as I can." But he never came back.

When Elza brought Berta home, Berta volunteered to not only care for the children but also to sew clothing and quilts for them. Plus, she made Elza a number of beautiful dresses, and she sewed enough children's clothing for a year!

Five-year-old Krysia had a special relationship with Berta. Since Krysia didn't yet know how to read, Berta would read pages of Wladek's books to her. Sometimes, while Berta was sewing, Krysia would sit on a stool next to her, grab little books from the shelf, and pretend to read. Berta went along with the stories that Krysia made up and would look down occasionally and say the words from the book for her. She was always very accepting of the children.

Berta sewed in the Kuzma's small pantry so she wouldn't be seen by neighbors. She never left the apartment. Three times while Berta was staying there, the Gestapo came to search the Kuzma apartment. The family hid her in the *"Szaffa"* (wardrobe) behind the clothes, and they put Janek's small bed in front of it. Thankfully, the Gestapo never found her.

After six months, Berta became obsessed with going back to the ghetto to find out what had happened to her family. Elza pled with her not to leave, reminding her that her father had never returned and she was afraid the same thing would happen to her. But Berta was determined. One day, Berta secretly left in the predawn hours. When the children awoke, they were very sad to discover she was missing.

After a few days, when Berta didn't return, Elza sent someone to find out what happened. They were told, "She was on her way back to where she was staying when she was picked up. We have no idea what happened to her." The best guess is that Berta and her father were victims of an edict by the Nazis that required the Judenrat[20] and the auxiliary Jewish police force to supply—*on a daily basis*—150 women aged sixteen to sixty for forced labor, along with whatever number of men the Germans demanded. Particularly horrible was the fact that the Judenrat and Jewish policemen who were forced to work for the SS were constantly beaten and tortured to make sure they obeyed. No Jew, not even the ones who were forced to help the Germans, escaped Nazi persecution.

Berta's disappearance made a major vacancy in the Kuzma's household. Once again, they needed someone to help care for the children. They asked their friends if they knew anyone. A man by the name of Rafanovich said he knew a young fourteen-year-old girl named Stasia who was very

---

[20] the Jewish Committee to oversee the ghetto

responsible and might make a good nanny. *And he was right!* Stasia was a perfect fit for the family. She was a pretty dark haired Polish girl who was excellent with children and willing to learn. The whole family loved her and she became like a daughter to Elza.

During the months the family lived in the apartment on Tumska, the children and Stasia had a great time playing near the cathedral and on the hill that sloped down to the river. The kids enjoyed wading or swimming in the shallow water near the shore. They also enjoyed taking walks through the gardens surrounding the cathedral or sitting on the benches enjoying the view. In the winter they made snow angels, and then after Christmas, when the Kuzma kids received a little wooden sled, they went sledding.

Selling Books and Holding Religious Meetings

Wladek's major life desire was to share Bible truth, so while living on Tumska Street in the early months of the occupation, he continued selling literature door-to-door. Sometimes, he canvassed the apartments close to where they lived, but as the Gestapo presence became more prominent, he spent more time canvassing in the country near Mrs. Betzel's house. He even occasionally stayed overnight since the less he traveled back and forth, the less attention would be drawn to his work.

Wladek reasoned that if he mainly sold the German magazine, *"Signs of the Times,"* it would be less likely that someone would report him. But a month or so after the Nazi occupation, he was stopped by a Gestapo agent.

"What are you selling?" he inquired.

"German magazines," Wladek replied as he handed a copy to the man.

After a quick glance, the policeman replied, "You can't sell these magazines!"

"Why not?" he questioned, "They're German and there are many articles about health and family relationships that will help people lead a better life."

"But there are also Christian articles, and Hitler has forbidden the propaganda of all religions. You must report to city hall."

Wladek knew that going to the city authorities and alerting them to his actions was *not* a good idea. He had heard that Hitler was so vicious against Seventh-day Adventists that just to get rid of their influence he had sent some as far away as Africa. So Wladek ignored the order. He also alerted the church officials in Warsaw of his situation.

For a number of months, Wladek still worked for the Seventh-day Adventist conference and received a paycheck, but soon everyone agreed that for his own safety—and the safety of his family—his job description had to change. He could no longer sell books and other religious literature door-to-door. He couldn't even knock on doors to find people interested in religion. And since it was illegal to hold religious meetings, the members could no longer worship in churches and had to meet secretly in homes. At first, the Adventist conference sent official pastors around to "shepherd" these home churches. But when the Nazis started enforcing their anti-religion laws, it was no longer safe. Even meeting in homes for Bible study, if caught, could be a one way ticket to a concentration camp.

Yet, the work of spreading the gospel must go on. So, the work of the Seventh-day Adventist Church went underground, and Wladek became an "unofficial" pastor of a number of home churches and Bible study groups.

Moving Again

The amazing thing is that the order concerning no religious meetings came at the same time the family was forced to move from the city apartment to a house in the country. God's timing is always perfect!

On April 27, 1940, eight months after the Kuzmas moved into the apartment on Tumska Street, Wladek was notified by the Germans that his family had one week to move out because Nazi officials were taking over their apartment. The Kuzmas had no choice. This time, they moved to the outskirts of town to the second-story apartment of a nice looking brick home, #27 on a street called "Third of May" or "#27, Ul Trzeciego Maja."

The house was much bigger than their Tumska apartment. It had a balcony where the family could sit and enjoy the fresh air and a living/dining room area with a big white tile stove that could heat the entire apartment. In addition, there was a big bedroom where the family slept and a room with a large desk and bookshelves with glass doors that Wladek used as a study. Stasia slept on a narrow bed in a wide closet-like room where she kept her clothing. Plus, there was an attic with plenty of storage and an area where Wladek could set up a "black market" mill where they could grind their grain into Ralston-type cereal. After he finished grinding the wheat, he would disassemble the mill so it could be hidden in case the Nazis decided to search their home and take it as part of their war effort scrap metal campaign.

The front yard was fenced with a large grass area where the children could play. Wladek set up a picnic table next to an old gnarled apple tree and planted a strawberry patch. To complete the landscaping, Wladek paid a relative of his friend, Rafinovich, to plant a flower garden. This little garden area became a special spot for family picnics or for spreading blankets on the grass and reading on Sabbath afternoons. There was also space for a small chicken coop.

When Wladek could no longer sell books, living in the country made it possible for him to make a little extra money by buying logs for 15 zlotys a kilo and cutting them up for kindling, which he sold for 250 zlotys.

What Wladek liked best about the house, however, was the orchard across the street, which appeared to be abandoned. The orchard was next to a dilapidated apartment building that housed forty-eight poor Polish families in one-room apartments. It was so rundown that Germans refused to live in the project.

The unused land next to the dilapidated apartment building was about the size of a hectare. Because no one was using the land, Wladek had the idea that it could be used for a garden where they could grow their own food. In addition, they could harvest produce from the orchard, which had 153 fruit trees: plums, apples, pears, and four giant walnut trees. Later, because there was still some vacant land, Wladek in 1943 had some of his shoe repair workers plant more pear trees. He was proud of "his" orchard and told the children, "This is your inheritance. These trees will still be bearing when you're grown and you have children of your own." During the first year in their "country" house, Wladek had shelves built in a storage room where he could put the apples and other produce from the orchard until Elza had time to process the fruit or he was able to sell it.

Elza knew their Polish neighbors were watching as Wladek planted "his" private garden next to the dilapidated housing. So, at harvest time, she generously shared the produce with them so they could benefit from her family's labor.

The Gestapo neighbors also saw what Wladek was doing with the land. They knew that the Kuzma family would never be allowed to legally own or lease land in Nazi-controlled Plock, so they made Wladek "give" them partial use of the property. Wladek was obviously caught in a power play and willingly gave them what they wanted rather than chance being eliminated!

For two years, the Kuzmas enjoyed the produce from their vegetable garden until the Nazis officially confiscated the land so they could grow wheat and potatoes for the state. Thankfully, however, they left the fruit trees. When Wladek was forced to leave Poland in 1945, one of the things he would miss most was what he called "his orchard"!

Adjusting to a world where you are stripped of your freedom is not easy. Before Plock, Wladek wore his Polish heritage as a badge of pride. Now, the only thing that kept him from wearing the yellow and purple "infamy" badge that other Polish men were forced to wear was the fact that his wife was German. And at any time, this, too, could be stripped away. Imagine what that does to a man's ego!

The second thing that defined Wladek Kuzma was his reputation as a master religious bookseller. Before Plock, he could enjoy being recognized as earning more money selling books in the Seventh-day Adventist Polish Union than anyone else. Now the work that he loved was illegal. Instead of his bookselling being a source of pride, it could cause him to be sent to a concentration camp where he would likely die.

Men of lesser faith would have been devastated. But read on and see how Wladek and his family adjusted to Nazi control and how God opened unexpected doors of opportunity, causing Wladek to exclaim, "Nothing is impossible with God!" (See Mark 10:27.)

Chapter 14

Plock: Living next to the Nazis

(1940–1945)

The Gestapo Neighbors

There seemed to be only one downside to Elza and Wladek's new home on "Third of May Street," and that was the Gestapo family who lived next door.

At first, this didn't seem like a problem because the Kuzma kids didn't realize just how dangerous the Gestapo could be. The first clue was when some of their neighbors began disappearing. Someone would ask, "We haven't seen the 'Stein' family today. Does anyone know if they are OK?"

Often, the answer was, "They were here yesterday. But the Gestapo came last night and took them away." And more than likely, it was the work of their neighbor or his buddies, dressed in their gray-green uniforms with their wide black leather belts, billed caps, shiny black boots, and jackets trimmed in silver braid.

The Gestapo family had two boys: Klaus was a little older than Danusia, and Horst was around Krysia's age. It wasn't long before the Kuzma kids discovered that to tangle with them was extremely dangerous. One day, Danusia was riding her new bicycle on the street in front of their house. Something must have happened that made Klaus angry, and in a fit of rage, he pushed Danusia and her bicycle to the ground.

At this point, Danusia completely forgot her father's lecture about not crossing the Gestapo kids and, without thinking, yelled, "Stop it, you German pig!" When the boy's parents heard Danusia's words, *all hell broke loose!* Knowing the danger of insulting a Nazi, Elza and Wladek marched their errant daughter over to the man's house and made her apologize. But, they feared an apology would not be enough and worried they might lose the lease on their home. Another neighbor, after hearing what happened, commented, "If she had just left off the German part and called the kid a pig, it would have probably been just an innocent argument between two neighbor kids!"

After Danusia got in trouble for name calling, the Kuzma kids tried hard not to offend the neighbor boys. But as the months went by, Klaus and Horst began to take advantage of the situation and started bullying them. The boys knew they were immune to punishment because people were afraid of their father.

> *The Gestapo father was livid and confronted "Wilhelm" with his son's story.*

One day, when Krysia was playing in her yard, Horst came over to play hide-and-seek. He trapped Krysia in the basement corridor and told her to pull down her panties so he could see what girls looked like. She refused. So he grabbed her and pulled her panties down. She pushed him away and ran inside and told her father what Horst had done. Horst knew he could get in trouble if the truth were known, so he ran home and told his father that Krysia had shown herself to him.

The Gestapo father was livid and confronted "Wilhelm" with his son's story. Even though "Wilhelm" believed his daughter, because he was Polish, if he told the man his son was lying, he could have been immediately shot or sent to a concentration camp. Instead, he made sure the neighbor knew Krysia had been spanked with a belt! The war caused many people to do things they normally wouldn't do—just to save their lives!

Attending School in Plock

The Nazis indoctrinated the children in German-occupied counties by controlling education. Once German schools were established in Poland, all children were required to attend, except Jewish, gypsy, or certain faiths such as Jehovah's Witness and Baha'i, who openly refused to support the Nazi agenda. Because Wladek wanted his children to learn to read and write Polish, he privately hired a Polish teacher—until it became too dangerous. Because German children were treated with more respect, the children were enrolled under their mother's German maiden name of Gartz. The girl's first names, Danusia and Krysia, were popular names in a number of European countries so they didn't need to be changed, but Janek was definitely Polish, so they called him Hans.

School went from 8 a.m. to 1 p.m. Monday through Friday. There were forty children in each classroom with a German teacher who had sworn loyalty to the Nazis. The "Gartz" kids were handicapped because all instruction was in German, and they had always spoken Polish. To make up for this deficiency, the girls were required to take extra German classes with a bilingual teacher. Krysia, however, still had a difficult time. Finally, it was decided that she should wait a year. That made Danusia happy because she didn't have to put up with her sister's crying. Danusia was known to lament, "If I didn't have to be responsible for my little sister, my life would be a lot easier." Krysia retorted, "Danusia should have been an only child!"

At first, the classrooms were meagerly equipped with just desks and a black chalkboard. In Danusia's second year, each child was given a small slate and a sponge to wipe it clean.

When the teacher walked into the room, you could hear a pin drop. The children immediately stood and said in unison, "Guten morgen, Lehrer[21]." The teacher would then snap to attention, do the Nazi salute saying, "Heil Hitler," and all the children would salute and say, "Heil Hitler," and continue quietly standing until they were told to sit down. The children weren't allowed to think for themselves. Instead, they were to be obedient followers. The curriculum included physical education because Hitler was determined to raise healthy German children. This also meant instead of ice cream, children got a spoonful of cod liver oil each day. The "Gartz" kids hated smelling like fish!

If children whispered to each other, they were called to the front of the class and punished by being hit with wooden rulers across the top of their fingers two times. For major infractions, they got up to ten whacks, had to wear a dunce hat, or were forced to kneel on pebbles with their hands in a circle drawn on the blackboard above their heads. The physical punishment was painful enough, but the shame of being punished in front of classmates made it far more severe.

When the children were finally given notebooks and pencils, it was extremely important that they stay within the lines and make the letters perfectly. Danusia dreaded making a mistake and then having to use an eraser and risk tearing the thin paper—a "mistake" for which she would be punished.

Since schools were the major platform for indoctrinating children with Nazi propaganda, the children were taught that in 1919 their "beloved" Fuhrer left his homeland of Austria, went to Munich, and joined a small nationalist group called the German Workers' Party, which eventually became the Nazi party with two main goals: first, to unite all Germanic people under one empire controlled by a strong central government and

---

[21] "Good morning, Teacher."

second, to regain the German territory taken away by the 1919 Treaty of Versailles. To facilitate this, Hitler peacefully took over Sudetenland, Austria, and Czechoslovakia, but on September 1, 1939, Germany had to go to war to win Poland and other resistant countries. The children were told, "The war is being fought to bring the world a new system of government, ethnic cleansing, and work-based economic prosperity, and this will soon be accomplished thanks to the brilliant Third Reich leader, Adolf Hitler."

What the children *weren't* taught is the rest of the story about Hitler's rise to power—the bullying and the killing of non-Germans by using people trained in terror tactics to gain power and control. Nor were they aware of the current suffering, persecution, and killing that was taking place under Hitler's ethnic cleansing dictatorship in Poland.

Polish parents knew that German teachers were asked to keep their eyes and ears open for information on families who were opposed to the Nazi government. Wladek and Elza warned their children not to answer personal questions. Instead, the children were to respond, "Why do you need to know?" After Elza started working for the railroad, they were told to say to the most persistent interrogators, "I don't know. Ask my mother. She works for the German railroad."

School Attendance on Sabbath

As the months went by, school attendance on Saturday became law. The threat of severe punishment for disobedience made it difficult for the Kuzma family. For a while, the parents kept their kids home, but when the authorities informed them that their children would be taken away if they didn't comply, they reconsidered. There was no doubt that the Nazis had such little regard for the lives of Polish children and their parents that they would not hesitate to carry out their threat.

One of their church members, Brother Koenig, not only defied the authorities by keeping his children home from school on Sabbath, but when he was asked to join a team of men to patrol the parameters of their village, he had replied, "I will walk around the village and do my part, but I will not carry a gun." Fed up with his insubordination, the Nazis immediately took him behind the barn and shot him. Obviously, Wladek and Elza did not want to put their children's lives in jeopardy! So, they decided that the kids should dress in their "Sabbath outfits" and show up for school. Then Elza would pick them up early so they could attend church. Somehow, this compromise satisfied the law and still allowed their children to worship with their family on Sabbath.

Music Lessons

Music was always very important to both Elza and Wladek. But unfortunately, although each of their kids loved music, none showed any interest in putting in the time and energy it took to learn to play an instrument. Danusia started lessons on the pump organ but complained that it was too difficult to learn fingering while keeping her feet pumping the pedals. So, in 1941, Elza purchased an expensive piano from Danusia's music teacher, Professor Grabowski. Danusia took lessons for three years but constantly complained. Krysia loved music but refused to practice. Finally, the parents became like so many European upper-class families— they had musical instruments in their homes even though no one played.

Laundry Day and Other Household Tasks

In the spring and fall Danusia and Krysia had to wear school uniforms of navy skirts and white blouses. In the winter, when the weather was bitter cold, the girls wore one piece baggy overalls, which they hated, but at least their legs kept warm. When Janek started school, he wore navy trousers and a white shirt. The kids had to be very careful so their uniforms wouldn't get dirty because one outfit was all they had to wear for the entire week.

One Sabbath morning, Janek was the first one dressed and went out on the balcony to wait in the warm sunshine for the rest of his family. It had rained the night before, and there was a black, pitch-like substance in the cracks on the balcony. Jan's toy fell into a small crawl space, and without thinking, he got down on his knees to look for it. This resulted in getting black goop on his clean Sabbath clothes. Wladek and Elza nearly exploded.

Taking baths in Plock was slightly easier than in Sierpc because their house had a wood burning water heater for the tub in the bathroom. All you had to do was make sure you had enough wood and then fire up the heater an hour before you needed the hot water.

The Nazis and Religion

The Nazi objective was to systematically dismantle organized religion. Because the Polish people were primarily Catholic, the church now became a major target of persecution. The Nazis arrested leaders, exiled clergy, and closed churches, monasteries, and convents so quickly that by the end of 1939, eighty percent of the Catholic clergy in some areas had already been deported to concentration camps. The Evangelical Churches also suffered, as clergy were killed in Nazi purges or arrested and deported to concentration camps. Some Nazis felt Christianity could be "Nazified" into

"Positive Christianity" by renouncing its Jewish origins, the Old Testament, and the Apostle's Creed and bowing to Hitler as the new "messiah." Others believed that after the war, Hitler intended to simply eradicate Christianity in all German territory.

Because the Nazis were opposed to religion and the influence it could have on people, some minorities, such as Jehovah's Witnesses and the Baha'i faith, were banned, while others, such as the Salvation Army and Seventh-day Adventists went underground and met secretly in homes.

It has been said that God's timing is always perfect. And so it was with the Kuzma family being forced to move from Tumska Street, which was in the middle of the administrative offices of German Nazi officials, to the more remote location on the Third of May Street (Ul Trzeciego Maja). When Nazi eradication of religion became more severe, making all religious activity illegal, including home gatherings, it would have been impossible to avoid detection of their home religious activities in their "fish bowl" apartment on Tumska Street. But living on the outskirts of town made their religious activities much less noticeable, even with a Gestapo neighbor!

Worshipping God when "Church" was Illegal

The church members knew that at any time, they could experience the wrath of the Gestapo. It was a frightening situation, especially on Sabbath, because that is when the secret police would check to see what Seventh-day Adventists were doing and where they were going.

The first home church in Plock was at Mrs. Betzel's house. When the Kuzmas moved to the house across from the orchard, church services were held at their home. The living room was large enough to accommodate the members, and Elza didn't have to take the kids and food across town. It did, however, mean that they were meeting right under the watchful eye of their Gestapo neighbor!

Since assembling for worship was illegal, the members would act as if they were going to a social event. Sometimes, they brought packages tied with pretty bows or perhaps a cake or some other party food. Their Bibles were hidden in a bag. The "guests" would try not to arrive at the same time so their presence wouldn't be as noticeable. The curtains were pulled, and the members kept their voices low. When Wladek would preach, he would make it sound like a conversation instead of a sermon. Instead of singing, they would pull out their German hymnals and read the words together.

At any time, their services could be interrupted by two stern Gestapo agents knocking on the door. Immediately, the worshippers would hide their Bibles or songbooks on the secret shelf under the table that Wladek had designed and pull out cups and saucers to make it look as if they were having refreshments.

When they answered the door, a commanding voice would announce, "We've been informed that you're holding a meeting in this house, and we need to investigate."

"Oh, yes," the Sabbath-keepers would reply. "Come in. Would you like some cake?" Elza always baked a pound cake or strudel and served *getreide* (roasted grain) coffee, so it looked like they were having a social gathering.

For years the children remembered the terror they felt when they were having church and the Gestapo came by to search the house. It happened once at the Betzels and twice at their own home. Thankfully, the authorities never found anything that made them think it was a religious service. If they had, Wladek and the other grown-ups would likely have been taken away by the Gestapo, interrogated, and sent to a concentration camp.

Wladek's Undercover Work Gets Discovered

The danger of the Nazis discovering that there were people talking about Christianity to others was a very real threat. For example, one of the Seventh-day Adventist pastors, in addition to pastoring in East Prussia, also worked as a translator for the German court. Somehow, his religious work was discovered, and the authorities took him away. When that happened, "Wilhelm" Kuzma took over the man's pastoral duties. This meant that Wladek had to travel more than a half hour by train to get to one church on Sabbath morning and then speak at another in the afternoon, in addition to taking care of his home church in Plock.

One day a young Polish girl sent her tithe and offering addressed to a church administrator in Warsaw. Because the money went through the postal system, the Germans discovered it and began investigating why it had been sent. Months before, when the Nazis invaded Poland, the Adventist Church quickly abandoned the Polish Union office in Warsaw and established the General Government Conference under the Central European Division of the church structure, hoping to continue church business under this neutral name. Now the Nazis began to inquire, "What kind of a relationship did this Warsaw office have with Polish people? Why are Polish people sending them money?" That is when the Germans discovered that "Wilhelm" Kuzma was Polish—and, as a paid church worker, should have nothing to do with the religious work in East Prussia.

Within days, a Nazi official confronted Wladek in East Prussia. "You're Polish. You must go to the Gestapo offices in Plock and turn yourself in."

Wladek thought, *"How will they know if I go or not?"* But he knew it was no longer safe for him to do religious work in East Prussia. Plus, selling books in Plock was unwise. So, in 1942, the decision was made that for his safety, he could no longer work in an official capacity for the Seventh-day Adventist Church, which meant he would no longer get a paycheck.

What should he do? He chose to continue "shepherding" his Plock home church without pay. The war had destroyed his livelihood, which is hard on the man's ego and contributed to severly painful ulcers.

Elza Gets a Job

When the Germans occupied Poland, they needed "German" workers, so in the spring of 1940, they interviewed Elza "Gartz." Since she spoke German fluently, they wanted her to work at the railway station. But since Janek was only three years old, she argued that she couldn't leave him alone. The authorities, however, made it clear that she didn't have a choice.

Fortunately, it was just about this time that Stasia came to live with them. She was an answer to their prayers—and a wonderful addition to their family. So, with Stasia able to take care of the children and household, Elza consented to work.

When Elza told her supervisors that it was impossible for her to work on Saturdays because of her children, they reluctantly gave her Saturdays off. When they discovered she really wanted to worship on Saturday, they made her work a double shift on Sunday.

The job required working twelve hours a day Monday through Friday. She left her house on her bicycle at five in the morning to get to work on time, and often, she didn't get home until after supper. On Sundays, she worked from 6 a.m. until 10 p.m., so Wladek would sometimes bring her soup so she could have at least one hot meal. Having a German in this railroad position was vital since there was so much Nazi "business" going on, like unofficial Nazi trains with "unknown" cargo.

In spite of the many hours away from her family, Elza liked her job. The railway station was an interesting place to work and her position was an important one. She met many people. She answered the phone to receive vital information about when the trains were expected and when they actually arrived and were supposed to depart; she kept reports and sold tickets. Since so much of the Nazi activity came through the station, she was one of the first to hear the news about what was going on with the war in Europe.

In addition, she enjoyed dressing up and having her hair styled. She cut off her long braids, which required a lot of time, and enjoyed the benefits of short hair. She felt attractive wearing the pretty dresses that Berta had made for her. She had used her German heritage to her advantage in order to receive the best treatment possible during a time when she had few options.

Wladek did his best to fill in when Elza was delayed coming home. Fortunately, Stasia prepared all the meals. Bedtime was at 7:30 p.m., but when Wladek was in a good mood, he made bedtime special, like letting the kids munch on apple slices and walnuts, which he called "good brain food" while he would sit on the bed and say something like, "Tonight I am going to read you poetry from Adam Michiewcz about springtime." But by 8:00 p.m., it was lights out! When the children protested, he reminded them, "Sleep is good for you because that's when your brain develops!"

Hiding their Prosperity

Because of Elza's job at the railway station—and the savings from her husband's bookselling business—her family could afford many things that were unavailable to other Polish people, so the family was careful to keep their prosperity hidden. What would the neighbors think if they saw Elza's fine linen tablecloths, her crystal and china dishes, the big radio and oak bedroom set, a beautiful buffet, and piano?

Wladek had been a good provider. He could sell 60 to 80 zlotys worth of books in a couple of days—or a couple of weeks at the most. This was an amazing achievement in an era when eight zlotys would buy a cow or would pay a month's wage for a nanny, such as Marta or Stasia.

Wladek and Elza always dressed in stylish custom-made clothing. Because Elza's father and mother had special contacts with the textile industry, they were able to get silk, lace, and other expensive fabrics for bargain prices. For example, in 1943, Wladek was able to purchase a wine-red wool blend fabric and had beautiful coats with fancy buttons, fur-trimmed collars, and matching fur-trimmed hats custom-made for his girls. While living in Plock, both daughters had four or five different church outfits. Wearing beautiful clothes and having good quality shoes when the Polish neighbor children were dressed in rags and worn shoes because of the Nazi imposed rations made the Kuzma children feel privileged. They knew that God was watching out for their family—and they happily praised God for their mother making a good salary at the railroad when their dad could not.

Because the luxury of having a nanny was more than war-torn residents of Plock could afford, Stasia spent most of her time hidden from view. The family tried to mask their good fortune, but at the same time, when they saw a need, they generously helped others. Plus, they acknowledged the source of their prosperity and faithfully tithed.

Wladek was a good provider, but one thing he lacked was that he didn't know how to meet Elza's emotional needs; he didn't know how to be a good lover. Elza wanted unconditional acceptance and someone with whom she could share her feelings. Unfortunately, when Wladek abdicated this responsibility, she turned elsewhere.

Mitrichin Befriends Elza

Mitrichin was a German-speaking Ukrainian man whose job at the railway station was to receive and send packages. He made sure the contents matched what was listed on the boxes. Because he and Elza both worked for the train station, Mitrichin got to know and appreciate her. They enjoyed talking about stimulating topics such as politics. And he took it upon himself to occasionally accompany Elza home from work, especially after dark, to make sure she would arrive safely.

He also helped the family—especially when Wladek was away from home. He was an excellent accountant and helped Elza with bookkeeping. When coal was hard to come by, he somehow found a source and brought it to the family. But more important, he helped Elza feel special by listening to her and occasionally bringing her flowers. Wladek brought fruit and nuts for the family, but flowers seemed to him like a frivolous thing to buy during hard times.

Elza and the children liked Mitrichin, but Wladek questioned his intentions. He didn't appreciate another man showing his wife how special she was. Plus, living in occupied Poland was a scary business. You could never be sure who you could trust, and although there was never any evidence, Wladek sensed that there was something about him that was suspicious.

Unfortunately, Elza's friendship with Mitrichin soon became a bone of contention between Elza and her husband. A number of times, when they would shout at each other, the children overheard Tata accusing Mama of being a whore. The Polish word used was *"Kurva,"* which actually meant something even worse! Name calling rarely happened, but when it did, it cut Elza like a knife and severely wounded her heart. Wladek's irrational jealousy hurt Elza deeply and left her feeling unloved and rejected. Later, when Wladek cooled down and felt the sting of remorse, he begged Elza to forgive him for accusing her of unfaithfulness just because she had friends who were men. *Irrational jealousy is a grim foe to conquer.*

Wladek obviously felt insecure around men who admired his wife. If only he hadn't "tricked" Elza into marrying him. If only he had let God work things out instead of telling Georg Czembor they were engaged when they weren't. Wladek knew that Elza had agreed to marry him by default, not because she was head-over-heels in love with him. Now, years later, his deceit still caused a wrinkle in their relationship. She had grown to love her husband over the years, but not with the same intensity he loved her. She respected his love for God, his commitment to Bible truth, his care for the children, and his ability to provide for their family. But Wladek had no idea how to meet Elza's emotional needs. His accusations, his name calling, and his sometimes insane jealousy continued to erode their relationship at the very time when she needed his understanding and support the most—and he needed hers.

War often does strange things to people. Negative emotions (stress, uncertainty, distrust, and fear) can rear their ugly heads in relationships and magnify character defects—or they can bring about a change for the better. For Elza and Wladek war meant a tearing away of their purposeful work. It also exposed defects in their relationship that might have remained hidden in more peaceful times. But in spite of it all, they never doubted that God was in control. The war years and beyond would bring new challenges, new successes, new heartache—and separation.

Chapter 15

Plock: In Sickness and in Health

(1940–1944)

Surviving Role Reversals

After almost ten years of marriage, Wladek and Elza had grown comfortable in their relationship roles. Elza may not have married the most dashing "Prince Charming," but in the sphere of their friends and work associates where it really counted, Wladek was highly respected. And in turn, Elza respected him.

From Wladek's perspective, God had given him the ideal wife. If Elza hadn't been a capable housewife and mother and supported him in his ministerial work, how would he have been able to spend the necessary time away from home that it took him to become one of the most successful men in his line of work? But he may have admitted in private that, at times, he had wished she could have been a little less bossy!

A year after they married, it had been easy for Elza to slack off on doing the same work as Wladek, selling religious books—and divert her energy into raising their growing family. She saw this shift as God's will. If this transition had not occurred, her personality, natural skills, and success in selling books may have eventually overshadowed Wladek's achievement and chipped away at his feelings of personal value. Their work, however, never reached the competitive stage because neither saw it as "work" for work's sake. Selling religious books was basically doing what God wanted them to do.

From the outside looking in, it might have appeared God had put together the "perfect" family. Inside, however, was another story—at least when it came to understanding and meeting each other's emotional needs. But just because a marriage isn't perfect doesn't mean it isn't good! And one must admit, uncontrollable world events had much to do with the challenges that Wladek and Elza experienced.

The war did more than take away the freedom of religion for the Polish people; it turned Wladek's and Elza's roles as husband and wife upside down. For the first year or so after the German occupation, Wladek tried desperately to hold onto his job. It was not the money he cared about—although that was a welcome benefit. His job was his mission—His God-directed and ordained work, which gave him an internal feeling of value. Selling religious books and bringing the life-saving Gospel to others brought him not only deep personal satisfaction but also a valuable side effect: the respect of his colleagues and his wife. But by 1941, that option was over. Wladek and Elza's established marital roles shifted. She was employable because she was German—as a Slavic Pole, he was not! She was given the opportunity to bring home the paycheck. He was not! She had the satisfaction of doing an important work (even if it was for the Nazis). He did not!

Psychologically, something else shifted. The Nazi occupation of Poland had destroyed every opportunity for Wladek to express his Polish pride. Instead of his heritage bringing life and vibrancy to his soul, it brought the fear of persecution and death. Instead of being something he could proudly profess, it was something to fear or to hide. The only thing that was keeping his head above water psychologically and allowing his family's lifestyle to continue pretty much as it had before the war, were the benefits gifted to him through his wife's German heritage.

For a man's self worth—this role reversal could be devastating. For a marriage built on husband and wife fulfilling traditional roles, it could be fatal. Unless there was enough agape love—love for each other that God put into their hearts (not love built on behavior and the successful fulfillment of expected roles), the war could become not just physically threatening to their family—but psychologically threatening to their marriage.

The question was, *did Elza have enough love built up in her heart for her "God given" husband to love him even though he had no job? Or to love him through sickness or health—"until death do we part"?*

Wladek Gets Sick

Wladek had a long history of stomach trouble, but by the end of 1941, his ulcers started causing major pain. No doubt, this problem was aggravated by the stress he felt by not being able to sell religious literature. In addition, there was the constant threat of being caught by the Gestapo for holding secret Bible studies and church services in homes. He knew God would take care of him, but he did, at times, wonder what might happen if the Nazis discovered what he was doing.

Elza was frantic to find medical help for her ailing husband. By the early months of 1942, he was so sick that she feared he might die. She went to five different German doctors before getting permission from Dr. Niederehe for Wladek to be sent to the Berlin Hospital for treatment. The Berlin Hospital was an Adventist hospital in Zehlendorf, Germany, not too far from the Friedensau Mission Seminary where Wladek had trained as a Bible worker. She wanted him to go there because the hospital used natural remedies instead of surgery and strong medications.

As soon as Dr. Budnick, the administrator of the hospital, got word that governmental permission had been granted to Wladek, he arranged for an opening. Wladek and Elza left for Berlin that night on the train and arrived in Berlin first thing in the morning. An Adventist Church official (the Union Secretary) picked them up from the train station and took them directly to the hospital. As soon as Elza was certain her husband would be taken care of properly, she took the next train back to Plock so she wouldn't miss any more work than necessary.

> *Finally, he was discharged and was ready to go back to Poland and his underground work for God.*

Dr. Myer, the attending physician, explained to Wladek, "We don't use a knife like the Americans. We have a better method." They gave him special rest, hot and cold baths, good exercise, plenty of sleep, and hot compresses with steaming towels on his stomach—sometimes for an hour at a time. He was fed a wholesome diet and not allowed to have anything to eat that was sweetened with sugar. Using these natural remedies, Wladek made an amazing recovery.

As he was getting better, the church officials took Wladek to four different churches around Berlin to preach about his experiences. He felt fulfilled to be back "winning souls," even though it was now in Germany where the church work was given more freedom than in Poland. Finally, after six weeks, he was discharged from the Berlin Hospital and was ready to go back to Poland and his underground work for God. He had no idea, however, that in just a few weeks, he would be doing a different kind of "sole" work—making shoes!

From Bookseller to Cobbler

God works in mysterious ways. Before Wladek went to Berlin, he and Elza prayed earnestly about what God wanted him to do next since he could no longer be employed by the Seventh-day Adventist Church because of Nazi religious restrictions. Certainly, God must have some other work for him. But they never considered the possibility of Wladek actually going back to the work he was originally trained to do: making shoes. It wasn't until Elza was coming home from Berlin after leaving Wladek in the hospital that she realized why, years ago, God had Wladek take a cobbler apprenticeship. It was for such a time as this! Here's how it happened.

On the train ride back to Plock, Elza happened to sit beside a lady who was a secretary to a company that sold leather goods. As Elza was sharing her concerns about what her husband should do since he could no longer sell religious books and hold Bible studies, the woman asked, "Does your husband have a trade?"

"Why yes," she said. "When he was younger, he apprenticed as a shoemaker. That's what his father did and what his brothers are doing now."

"Really!" replied the surprised lady, "When he's well and comes back to Plock, he should go to see Mr. Vizquel, who is the German *"obermeister"*—the man in charge of all the shoemakers in the region. Your husband should register with that office and perhaps he can open up a shop."

Elza was delighted to learn about this possibility. As soon as Wladek got back to Plock, he made an appointment with Mr. Vizquel. When the man learned that he spoke both German and Polish, he said, "You don't have to begin as an apprentice; you can start as a supervisor. Perhaps you can have a big shop of fifteen to twenty workers because there is a great need in the country for more shoemakers." He then sent Wladek to city hall to obtain a license.

At the city hall he met a German-speaking Romanian who encouraged him to open up his own shop. Wladek liked the idea of working for himself and began looking for a good location. He found a building that had been a butcher shop. He leased it and began renovating. The licensing office at city hall even paid for the needed repairs to make the shoe factory operational. They wanted people usefully employed—and everyone needed shoes.

Once all the equipment was in place, Wladek hired eight trained workers, two students, and an accountant who used to be a teacher, and went into business making tall boots—including army boots. It wasn't long before his business had grown so much that he apprenticed a number of young people and was teaching them how to make boots. At the height of his business, he had fourteen workers.

Getting supplies was difficult in the middle of the war. Wladek ordered a catalog for shoemakers, where he found advertisements from various wholesalers in other countries who were selling leather bottoms and tops for less than he paid locally. One company from Vienna seemed to be an excellent source of raw leather materials. When he contacted the owner, he learned that the company had plenty of leather supplies but was having trouble finding shoemakers to buy their products. Wladek immediately recognized a good business opportunity. He needed leather supplies and the Viennese leather wholesalers needed meat (chicken, duck, and goose), butter, and other food supplies that were rationed in their country. It was illegal, however, to send these products to Austria when the German army needed them for the war effort. All Wladek had to figure out was how to get these rationed products to Vienna. And then it came to him: Elza's friend, Mitrichin, who just happened to be the railroad official whose job it was to approve the packages sent by rail. Now, it became clear why God brought Mitrichin into their lives, and instead of being jealous, Wladek praised God for Mitrichin's friendship with Elza.

Because Plock was a very prosperous farming area, Wladek had no trouble finding plenty of meat and butter. Although it was illegal to ship these items to Austria, it wasn't illegal to ship apples. So he purchased large basket-like containers, filled the bottom with meat and butter, and then covered the black market items with apples from the orchard across the street. Mitrichin would check each basket to see if it was filled with apples by inspecting the first few layers, making sure he never went to the bottom of the container. He then stamped his approval on the baskets and sent them off to Vienna.

Soon, Wladek had more than enough leather supplies —and his shoe factory thrived. His accountant knew a lot about business and taught Wladek how to take orders and keep accounts. Everyone seemed to need shoes—especially the army and the prosperous village farmers. Shoes were such an important commodity that Wladek could almost ask any price and the people would pay.

It wasn't long before the military heard about the quality of the boots that "Wilhelm's Shoe Shop" produced, and the orders to repair the soldier's boots came rolling in. Since "Wilhelm" spoke German, the military purchasing agents got to know him well and gave him all the business he could handle.

From Train Station to Cobbler Shop

The decision to have a baby in the middle of the war years was a calculated risk. If Elza had not fallen and lost a baby when they were living in Sierpc—that would have been the fulfillment of Krysia's dream of having a baby brother. But it was not to be. Now at nine years of age, Krysia's begging began to have an impact on her parents. "Maybe we should try," Elza confided to her husband, "even though the doctors told me that I shouldn't have another baby." Then, in August of 1943, the political climate of the war became a significant factor in the decision as to whether or not to risk another pregnancy.

Since July 9, 1941, the Nazis had been advancing on the Eastern Front toward the Soviet Union. Cities in Eastern Poland were being taken back from the Russians, and at that time, it looked as if the Nazi war machine couldn't be stopped. *Then winter came!* The winter of 1941 foiled the German attempt to surround and take Moscow. Then the winter of 1942 thwarted the Nazis from taking Stalingrad.

As 1942 turned into the winter of 1943, an interesting phenomenon could be observed on the country roads around Plock: Wagonloads of German families who had settled in Russia in the 1930s when Hitler first started talking about space in Poland and Russia for the Aryan population, were now heading back west toward Germany. Some had young children; some had older daughters, but none of these families had any sons twelve years of age or older! Living in Russia was no longer safe for them because of the westward advance of Soviet troops, and German boys were being taken for Russian military duty.

One day, when the Kuzma children were visiting the countryside, they watched as wagon after wagon went by. All were heading west. Then when the German military needed the road for their troops moving east, the wagons pulled off the road until the army passed—which sometimes took many hours. One particular ingenious wagon caught the kid's attention; there were two horses pulling the wagon and two cows tied in the back. A cage full of chickens was swinging from the bottom of the wagon, and people were sitting on boxes in the wagon or lying down on a feather bed. Why were all these families moving west?

By August of 1943, the German army was retreating westward as the Russian troops were at the border of Estonia and were marching quickly back toward Poland. *"What if the Nazis couldn't hold their line and the Russian soldiers marched into Poland, taking back the territory they had claimed as theirs when they made the Hitler-Stalin Pact of non-aggression* with Germany at the start of the war—a pact that Hitler never intended to keep?"

Everyone knew if this happened, the Germanized Polish people, like Elza, who had befriended the Nazis in return for special treatment, would be in great danger, not only from jealous Slavic Poles but from the Russian soldiers. It was common knowledge that the Russian soldiers were not only crude but extremely cruel. They were especially known for raping women captives. It was their way of paying back the Germans for invading Russia and killing so many of their people.

In the railway station where Elza worked, the talk was not "IF" the Russian army would reach Plock, but "WHEN." The handwriting was on the wall. Most felt that Germany was losing the war. Elza reasoned, "When the Russians march into Plock, being pregnant might save my life." She also knew that if Germany lost the war, it would be better if she didn't work for the Nazis as she had been doing at the railroad station since 1940.

In late 1943, the miracle happened; Elza got pregnant. She was spotting and went to see Dr. Niederehe. He said, "You will never have a baby working so hard." He gave her a special letter addressed to her supervisors that stated she could no longer work at the train station because of medical reasons. The Nazi view of the role of a German woman was that she should take care of her children and have more babies! Elza, being pregnant, was merely being a good German wife and mother. Her supervisors were cooperative when they understood why she was quitting, but they had to train two people to do the work that Elza had done for the last three years.

Elza was ready for a change. Not only was she pregnant, but her husband's business was doing so well that he needed her to help with the administration, which would make it possible for him to devote more time to making shoes. And so she went from the train station to the cobbler shop.

As a "German," Elza was able to negotiate with the Nazi military personnel more effectively than her Polish husband when it came to making contracts for shoes needed by the army. When she heard that certain of her Jewish friends, or the friends of their workers, had been detained by the Nazis, she traded souls for soles. Here's how she did it:

Nazi official: "We need your shop to make thirty pairs of boots for our soldiers."

Elza: "When do you need them?"

Nazi official: "It's a rush job. Our soldiers are desperate. We need them next week."

Elza: "Oh, I'm so sorry. It's impossible for us to meet that deadline. You see, some friends of our employees have been detained, and they are slated to be deported to concentration camps. Our workers are so sad and depressed they can hardly function—and our production levels are way down."

Nazi official: "But we need the boots and will pay you highly for your work."

Elza: "That won't change the problem…but if you could arrange for the release of these people, I'm quite sure we can make the deadline for you. Here's a list. As soon as they're free, let me know, and we'll put a rush on your order."

Nazi official: "I think this can be arranged!"

And so, as the factory administrator, Elza was able to get a number of Poles released through her negotiations. Plus, she was a savvy administrator, perhaps more so than her husband, and the shoemaking business continued to prosper.

*What a blessing Wladek's sickness turned out to be. If he had not suffered the pain, Elza would never have pushed for him to get medical treatment at the Berlin Hospital. If he hadn't gone to Berlin, she would have never been riding back on the train next to a woman whom God used to direct the family in a way that would not only restore Wladek's physical health but also revitalize his psychological health with the challenge of starting his own business. God **still** needed him. And in the end, God needed this amazing couple to once again work together.*

Chapter 16

Plock: Family, Challenges, and Celebrations

(1939–1945)

Family Dynamics

Danusia was her mama's girl. They had similar personalities and a close relationship. Elza often confided in her and expected more from Danusia than the others.

Krysia was more sensitive and often hurt by her mama's critical words. As a consequence, Krysia feared new situations and was scared her mama might leave her. But from the moment Krysia was born, she captured her tata's heart. He rewarded her with special treats, and she basked in his attention.

Being the first boy, Janek had no doubt about his family status. He knew he was the most loved, most wanted, most gifted, and most important, whether it was true or not! From the time he was very young, Janek took a leadership role, especially when it came to relationships. He was aware that Danusia could hold her own: she knew her worth, enjoyed her own friends, and chose what she wanted to do rather than trying to fit in with her siblings. Janek accepted that but felt sorry for Krysia when Danusia rejected her. He tried to compensate by including Krysia in the rough and tumble play with his friends.

Janek also enjoyed making his mama happy. He listened to her, told her jokes, and made her laugh. The older he got, the more he helped her care for the other kids, especially when his father wasn't around. Both parents were proud of their son and thought he could do anything. The girls remember their tata saying, "Someday, my son will be president."

Parenting

Wladek and Elza were amazing Christians. They knew their Bible backward and forwards and could give a Bible study on any topic. They loved God supremely and had faith that God could do anything. When others gave up, they never doubted God's love or His guidance in their lives—and they passed this faith on to their children. They also inspired their children to become educated and built within them a drive for excellence, taking advantage of opportunities and serving others.

Wladek and Elza were basically good parents and disciplined using traditional early twentieth century European practices: Wladek had his leather strap and Elza her wooden spoon or perhaps a snap of a dish towel. Plus, they both had their faults. Wladek could be stubborn. When he made up his mind, reasoning with him was impossible. That's why Danusia once said, "It's a good thing God also gave us mothers." And Elza had her sharp tongue. Regardless, their children knew they were loved and generally accepted the punishment they received as justified.

Marriage Dynamics

However, as a couple, Wladek and Elza often had no idea how to solve their conflicts without inflicting emotional pain. Obviously, neither had good role models for marriage! As the years advanced, this insensitivity had an effect on the closeness of their relationship, even though it never killed their commitment to each other.

Elza's role model for a wife was her mother. Pauline raised her voice to a commanding pitch and stayed in control. Wladek preferred winning by making hurtful accusations and then controlling the situation by giving the silent treatment or walking away. He couldn't compete with his wife's tongue, so he chose to win by name calling, accusations, and withholding loving actions.

Janek watched his parents' conflicts, and as the boy in the family, he often blamed his father for walking out when his mother was hurting—instead of staying, solving the issue, and meeting her emotional needs. Arguments didn't happen often, but when they did, the kids felt anger, hurt, and rejection.

This is not to say that Wladek and Elza didn't have a fairly "decent" marriage. Showing love and respect for each other was just more difficult to express when Wladek was forced to give up the work of selling books and sharing Bible truth. In the early years, Elza showed her commitment to her husband by sending him off with a healthy lunch and expressing concern for his safety and success when he left to sell books. He showed her how much he loved her by working hard to provide for his family and in bringing home gifts—especially fresh fruit that was not easily acquired. In response, she showed her respect by taking good care of the house and the kids. He appreciated that.

And it wasn't as if Wladek and Elza couldn't express their tenderness toward each another. The kids remember times when they happily saw their parents loving on each other and their tata giving mama warm caresses and calling her "Elusia" or "Moja Elush (My Elush)," which were his pet names for her.

The problem was that Wladek didn't know how to consistently show Elza the love and attention she craved by taking time to really listen to her, by encouraging her to express herself, or by bringing her personal love gifts, like flowers or perfume. And she didn't know how to consistently show her love to him by voicing her respect and appreciation. Wladek admired Elza's strength of character. She was a decisive person, but at times, he needed a wife who was willing to respectfully discuss options and compromise. However, it was no secret that while she could be demanding, he could be unreasonable!

The kids also noticed another interesting difference in their parents. Elza portrayed a sense of control over her world. The kids saw her as courageous, brave, and willing to stand up for what she felt was right. She was savvy and exerted her will if the situation called for it. They felt safe in her presence. Their father was more timid—not when it came to sharing Bible truth—but when it came to reacting to situations outside his control. He had a kind heart and, if treated with respect, was willing to do anything for his family or friends. But at the same time, he feared things that might cause pain or misfortune. In various situations, he admonished the kids, "Be careful. Don't get hurt. Watch what you're doing. It could be dangerous." This difference in character may have been a reflection of what it meant to be Polish in the 1930s and 40s versus what it meant to be German. It's sometimes difficult to separate what might be a reaction to life circumstances versus what may have come from innate personality traits.

In spite of their sometimes dysfunctional relationship and different perspectives on life, Wladek and Elza always prayed for each other. They were deeply committed to their marriage and to God. They just didn't always know how to get along!

Danusia's Leg

It happened around sundown one day in May 1942. Danusia was playing hide-and-seek in the front yard with Krysia, Janek and some friends. In order to run faster Danusia took off her sandals and was running barefoot through a pile of sand when she stepped on a large piece of glass from a broken bottle. She knew her father's rule: "Always wear shoes outside," so she was afraid to tell her folks what had happened. Instead, she pulled out the glass from her heel, washed out the deep wound as best she could, and figured it would heal. After two or three days, however, her heel began to hurt so much that she could hardly step on it—but still, she wouldn't tell her folks. Having no idea about Danusia's injury, Elza decided that she and the children should take a walk to Lask[22], their favorite vacation area. But as they walked, Danusia's heel began to hurt so badly that she started tiptoeing.

"What's wrong with your foot?" her mother asked.

Danusia knew she couldn't keep the secret any longer, so she told her mother about stepping on the broken bottle.

Elza immediately inspected her daughter's foot and noticed a big round black wound on her heel. By this time, Danusia was in so much pain that she nearly fainted. Elza flagged down a passing horse cart and explained that her daughter's foot had been seriously injured, and they needed a ride back to Plock.

As soon as they got home, Elza took Danusia to the doctor. He cut out as much of the infection from her heel as possible, cleansed the wound carefully, and sent her home. But once again, the wound turned black. Elza rushed Danusia back to the hospital for more of the heel to be cut out. A few days later, Danusia felt sick with a fever and Elza noticed bright red streaks had started going up Danusia's leg. Elza now knew something was seriously wrong. She examined the wound and dressed it properly, but the next day, the infection was worse, so she took Danusia back to the hospital.

The doctor took one look and said, "The infection has spread. I'm admitting your daughter to the hospital. If we don't cut off her leg immediately, the infection will continue to go up her leg. If it goes above the knee, it will hit the heart, and she will die."

"No way! You are NOT cutting off my daughter's leg!" Elza exclaimed.

The doctor replied kindly but earnestly, "It's too late. You should have brought her in earlier!"

Elza reluctantly left Danusia in the hospital that night but told the doctor she would not allow him to cut off the leg. Not having any debilitating injuries was very important to Wladek. When he heard that

---

[22] Pronounced "wonsk"

the doctor suggested amputation, his first reaction was, "Who will marry a woman without a leg?" Elza knew there had to be another answer. She and Wladek began praying. Across the street from their house, in one of the dilapidated apartments, lived a young Polish medical student who was in his internship year. Elza was impressed to seek his advice.

He replied, "I am not yet a certified doctor, and I could get kicked out of medical school if anyone knows I have given you this advice, but you can save your daughter's leg—and her life—if you can stop the infection."

"How do we do that?" Elza inquired eagerly.

"First," he said, "you must take her out of the hospital. Then, have your husband get some pure spring water to cleanse the wound. Don't use city water because of the chlorine. Then you must get some healing earth called "*Heilerde*" for a compress. Mix the powdery earth with the pure spring water to make a paste. Then, find some wild Babkowe leaves (large green leaves with veins that look something like spinach). Put the mud paste on the leaves to make a compress and apply it to the wound. When the dirt gets hard that means it has absorbed as much pus as it can hold. Take off the compress and throw it away. Every day, cleanse the wound carefully with the pure spring water and apply a new compress."

> *I am not yet a certified doctor, and I could get kicked out of medical school if anyone knows I have given you this advice.*

Elza and Wladek did as the medical student suggested, and in three weeks the infection had stopped advancing.

"Now," the medical student said, "take your daughter back to the hospital and have the doctor make a couple of incisions in the wound and insert tubes for the pus to continue draining until the wound heals."

With hope in their hearts, the parents took Danusia back to the hospital and asked the doctors to insert the tubes. The doctors were shocked to see that Danusia was still alive. They exclaimed to Elza, "Du bist eine Hexa!" meaning "You are a witch!" But they did what the parents requested.

Danusia spent months in the hospital in a small children's bed in a ward with six older women. It was a long, painful process, starting with about a quart of puss draining daily from her leg. Danusia was in the hospital for so long that she was beginning to think her leg would never heal. In fact, she missed a year of school because of the infection. In the meantime, one of Danusia's school friends died from blood poisoning caused by a wound that wouldn't heal. Because penicillin was not readily available during wartime in Poland, it was not uncommon for infections to take a person's life.

After the wound quit draining, the doctors released Danusia from the hospital, but it was a long time before she could walk again. Her leg had been immobile for so long it wouldn't move. After intensive and painful physical therapy three times a week for months, she was at last able to walk again—miraculously without a limp. The scars where the cuts were made into her leg were a lasting reminder of two valuable lessons. First, obey your parents; second, don't keep secrets from them, even though you think you might be punished!

Sabbath Celebrations

Wladek and Elza tried to make every Sabbath special. Friday was a time of preparation. Elza or Stasia would cook something special on the wood stove, since they didn't have an oven. When Elza wanted to bake, she prepared the dough at home, and then she and her girls would go to the neighborhood bäckerei (bakery) to bake the bread, cake, or strudel. Sometimes in the winter when they were heating their house with the tiled stove in the living room, Elza would warm food or bake apples on a shelf inside the top of the stove.

At sundown Friday night, the family usually sang a song about how the Sabbath evening comes tenderly. Then Wladek would read his favorite Scripture, Psalm 92, *"It is good to give thanks to the* Lord, *and to sing praises to Your name, O Most High; To declare Your lovingkindness in the morning, and Your faithfulness every night...."* The chapter ended with, *"The righteous shall flourish like a palm tree, He shall grow like a cedar in Lebanon. Those who are planted in the house of the* Lord *shall flourish in the courts of our God. They shall still bear fruit in old age; they shall be fresh and flourishing, to declare that the* Lord *is upright; He is my rock, and there is no unrighteousness in Him"* (NKJV). After telling a Bible story or sharing a miracle that someone in the family experienced during the week, they ended their worship time with prayer.

When Sabbath morning dawned, they ate a special breakfast and prepared for church. After the service and a potluck meal, they sometimes took a walk in a nearby park where they could enjoy nature. Or they spread a blanket on a grassy spot under the old gnarled apple tree in their front yard and listened as Wladek read to them from his treasured library of religious books.

The Kuzma family closed the Sabbath with a simple praise song for children, *"Sfpiewjcie"* ("Children Sing" in English), and after prayer the family held hands and said together the weekly blessing, "Happy New Week."

The Blessings of a New Baby

Five days after D-Day—the day the American soldiers landed on the beaches of Normandy, signaling the beginning of the end of the war for Germany—Krysia (and the family) experienced a memorable day. On June 11, 1944, her baby brother, Jerzey Henrick Kuzma, was born. Her dream had come true. After a high-risk pregnancy, what a blessing for Elza to have a healthy baby boy! In English, he would be called "George Henry." But his family called him Jurek, which is the equivalent of "Georgie."

Elza's doctor was worried about this birth, so he wanted Elza to deliver in the hospital. At about 9:15 on a Sunday morning, in the middle of a terrible thunderstorm, baby Jurek made his appearance. Wladek was the only family member at the hospital for the birth, but as soon as he saw Elza and the baby and the doctor congratulated him on having a healthy son, he headed home to tell the rest of the family.

Stasia heard the news first and teasingly told Krysia the baby was a girl. Krysia was broken-hearted and began sobbing, "It can't be a girl! I prayed for a baby brother and I believed God would answer my prayer."

"God did," her father said, trying to comfort her. But she wouldn't believe him. She cried for three hours until they were able to get back to the hospital, and Elza showed Krysia his little *ptaszek*.

Being eight years younger than brother Janek, Jurek would forever be the beloved baby of the family. And because he was the last, his father at times affectionately called him Benjaminek, because Benjamin was the last son of the tribe of Jacob in the Old Testament—and was deeply loved by his father.

Vacation Time

Celebration time! The Kuzma family was complete, and it was summer and time for the Kuzma's annual vacation at beautiful Lask, about 9 kilometers south of Plock. The calm of the lake and sandy shore where the kids played in the water and built castles was so relaxing. Surrounding the lake was a beautiful pine tree forest and a meadow filled with blueberries, wild strawberries, and big tasty mushrooms. Breathing the fresh air and enjoying the warmth of the sunshine was a way of renewing one's spirits, and it allowed Elza to forget about the terrible war that was raging around them. In Lask she could enjoy just being a mom! Then, once a week, Wladek would take a bus to see his family in Lask, where they would enjoy a day of fun and relaxation. Elza's brother Emil once visited them while they were on vacation in Lask and commented, "Being there was like being in the arms of God."

The summer of 1944 was a time of celebration. Not only did a high-risk pregnancy end with a healthy baby boy, but Mama no longer had to work those long, grueling hours at the train station and be away from her children. Stasia had developed into a capable and much-beloved nanny. Tata had a thriving business without the threat of being sent to the concentration camp for illegally selling religious literature. Danusia's leg had healed and she was soon to become a teenager with the excitement of new friends and experiences. Krysia had her baby brother to cuddle. And Janek was excited about boating, swimming, exploring and hoping he would find a friend his age to play with at their favorite vacation place. *Who could ask for more?* No one expected that at the best time in their lives, the worst would happen. But it did!

Chapter 17

Escape from Nazi Forced Labor (Wladek's Story)

(1945)

The handwriting was on the wall. The Nazis had tried to conquer the world—and had failed. It was just a matter of time before Germany's fate was sealed. The Soviet Russian army, bolstered by Polish forces, was steadily moving westward, city-by-city recapturing German-occupied Polish land.

In July 1944, the Russian army was still some distance from Olsztyn (known as Allenstein during the German occupation), where a large number of German troops were stationed. The Nazis had exhausted their resources and desperately needed reinforcements to rebuild bombed railroad lines, roads and bridges, guard prisoners, carry messages and perform whatever other work the Germans needed to have done in order to sustain their military might. The answer was the forced subscription of Slavic Poles into their army.

Although Wladek was fifty years old and far too old to be drafted, he was not too old for Nazi forced labor—which was basically "slave labor." By the summer of 1944, the Germans had over 7.6 million foreign workers brought into their country by coercion, which made up one-fourth of their entire workforce. Still others were forced to work for their war effort in occupied countries. Wladek was one of those unfortunate ones. He was ripped away from his family, his occupation, and his freedom and forced to work for the Nazis! But first, let's go back to the story as it unfolded in Plock.

The Family Faces Separation

It was the middle of July 1944. Wladek had put in a busy day working at the shoe factory and had just come home to relax in a quiet house because his family was at their summer vacation destination in Lask. Suddenly, there was a sharp knock on the door. One look at the two Nazi officials holding an envelope made his heart skip a beat. *Something was wrong!*

"Good evening. Are you Mr. Wilhelm Kuzma?" a stern looking uniformed man asked.

"Yes, I'm Mr. Kuzma."

"We have an official summons from the Furher that your services are needed to support the great German army. You are to report for duty on July 31, 1944. You have two weeks to put your affairs in order."

"But my wife is German. And I have four small children. The baby is just a month old! And I'm fifty years old! Plus, I'm operating an important shoe factory that the Fuhrer needs to make boots for his soldiers. There must be some mistake."

"I'm sorry, Mr. Kuzma. You have no choice in the matter."

Wladek stood there speechless. This couldn't be happening. He was being forced to work for the Nazis!

He meekly took the envelope the officials held out to him and watched as the men did their "Heil Hitler" salute, clicked their heels, turned around, and walked away.

Dumbfounded, he opened the envelope and read the summons informing him that he was to be sent to a Nazi German military forced labor camp and was required to present himself to authorities in two weeks.

> *Dumbfounded, he read the summons informing him that he was to be sent to a Nazi military forced labor camp.*

Elza, Stasia, and the kids were enjoying their annual summer vacation in Lask. His first thought was to let them know immediately what was happening. Writing them would take time he didn't have, so the next morning, he rented a horse drawn cart and headed south on the road to Gostynin to deliver the message in person. His sudden "middle of the week" appearance at the Lask resort was quite a surprise.

The children were eager to show their tata the wildflowers they had picked and the little boat that they played in at the edge of the lake. Once the children were filled with their father's attention, they ran off to explore and left their parents alone. This gave Wladek time to make plans with Elza while he enjoyed holding his tiny five-week-old son, Jurek.

The children weren't told the seriousness of what was happening. They didn't really know how much their father had been protected for the last five years from the atrocities that happened to other Polish men because Wladek had married a German wife—and now that protection was being withdrawn. They only knew he had to go away and work for the German army. They didn't really understand what "forced labor" meant. They weren't told that he was likely to be sent on dangerous missions when the Germans didn't want to risk the life of one of their own soldiers or that he would be forced to work unmercifully long and hard hours and wouldn't have enough to eat or wouldn't be given medical attention if needed. All of which meant that there was a good chance that they would never see their father again.

They only knew that what was happening to their family was very serious. Why else had their folks immediately packed their belongings, and the family headed back to Plock in the middle of their vacation? Why else would their tata have hired a photographer and made them all get dressed up for an official family photograph before he was actually taken away? Why else had Tata, during their last family worship, read from Psalm 91 instead of Psalm 92, which was his favorite chapter? *"He who dwells in the secret place of the Most High shall abide under the shadow of the Almighty. I will say of the LORD, 'He is my refuge and my fortress; My God, in Him I will trust'.... A thousand may fall at your side, and ten thousand at your right hand; but it shall not come near you.... For He shall give His angels charge over you, to keep you in all your ways.... He shall call upon Me, and I will answer him; I will be with him in trouble; I will deliver him and honor him. With long life I will satisfy him, and show him My salvation."*

The Olsztyn Forced Labor Camp

On July 31, 1944, Wladek was subscripted into the East Prussian German Forced Labor Camp in Olsztyn. Because he was attached to the German army, he wore a German military uniform. He worked in a supportive role for the army, primarily digging trenches and, when necessary, carrying messages. He had no choice!

At first, letters went back and forth between Elza and Wladek but he never said much about the camp or how the Germans treated him. He probably wanted to spare Elza the grim details of the conditions under which he was forced to live.

At home, he was greatly missed. Elza worked hard to keep the home church going, taking care of the children, which now included a newborn baby, while at the same time keeping her husband's cobbler shop running smoothly. Her life as a "single" mother was not easy. Even Stasia wrote to Wladek saying, "What a tragedy that you had to leave the family. Everyone is crying because their father is gone. Poor Elza has to carry increased responsibility, not only caring for a new baby but keeping the shoe factory going. Every day, she has to travel a kilometer and a half to work. It's such a pity you're not here."

In September, as Elza learned about the advancing Russian troops, she had a strong impression that her husband might not be stationed in Olsztyn much longer. Afraid she might lose track of where he was and never see him again, she made plans to visit him. She decided to take the two boys, but when Krysia learned that she was to stay home with Stasia and her sister, she became hysterical. She was so afraid that something might happen to her mother that she clung to her and uncontrollably wept, "Please, don't leave me. I'm scared you won't come back. If you die, I want to die with you. Please take me." Finally, her mother changed her plans and also took Krysia. After a short visit, as they were saying their goodbyes, eight-year-old Janek turned and looked back toward his father and said with pleading eyes, "Tata don't forget us." His words nearly broke Wladek's heart. The last thing his children remember about their father was tears streaming down his face.

Elza's premonition was right. After her visit, Wladek's unit was moved south toward the Polish city of Dzialdowo—an area that Wladek knew well because that's where he had sold books throughout the surrounding countryside for two years before he got married. Moving south also meant he was closer to where his family lived in Plock. If only the army would just continue in that direction. But it was not to be.

The Long Walk to Freedom

On Thursday night, January 18, 1945[23], a German commander lieutenant announced to the soldiers and forced labor workers, "Be ready in one hour to move out. The Russians are only twelve kilometers away in Soldau (Dzialdowo in Polish). Our only chance of survival is to get back to our main army base near Olsztyn."

The commander then handed Wladek a special order and told him to deliver the message to headquarters ASAP. He was chosen as a runner because he was well acquainted with the countryside since he had been a

---

[23] On Thursday, January 18, 1945, after a major storm that wrapped East Prussia and northern Poland in a deep blanket of snow, Wladek's German army unit was attacked by the Russians, and he began his 1000-kilometer (about 620 miles) forced walk across East Prussia and the Polish Corridor into Germany. Earlier that same blustery cold day, a train with the cattle car carrying Elza and the children pulled out of the Plock train station and headed west toward Germany.

literature evangelist in that area for two years, right before he and Elza were married.

As much as Elza resented President Cunitz making what seemed to be an irrational decision to send Wladek away when Wladek had started courting her—and *300 kilometers away* when he could have just sent him to a nearby town to solve the conflict—God knew that being familiar with this territory would someday save Wladek's life. But that's getting ahead of the story.

Knowing the message was urgent, Wladek began running in the direction of the army's headquarters. But before he had gone far, the Russian soldiers invaded the camp. Wladek was close enough to see his commander get shot in the leg. Then, the Russians blew up the gasoline reserves, causing a massive explosion.

> *He waited, buried in the snow, until the surveillance plane was gone and the silence of the night returned.*

The night was freezing cold, and the ground was covered with snow. With the signed order in his hand, Wladek once again began running away from the inferno. Just then, he heard an enemy bomber plane coming toward him. He turned around and watched as the plane flew past. Then, it banked and started flying back in his direction. Realizing that he might be the target in the bright moonlight, he dug furiously in the snow, fell into the hole, covered himself with snow, and waited. The plane flew low. The noise of the motors rang in his ears, but it soon passed. Wladek was shaken. "That was too close," he said to himself. Immediately, he thought about God's promise in Psalm 91:4 to cover him with His feathers, and he whispered, "Thank You, Lord, for covering me with 'feathers' of snow."

Wladek hated the Russians. Being forced by the Nazis to work for the German army was bad enough, but the last thing he wanted was to be taken as a Russian prisoner of war. If that happened, he knew that he could quite likely be killed or end up in a Siberian gulag (prison) and would never again see his family. *"Forget about delivering the message!"* he thought to himself. *"It's too late!"* Instead, he decided to concentrate on saving his own life.

He waited, buried in the snow, until the surveillance plane was gone and the silence of the night returned. He then brushed the snow from his clothing and cautiously made his way back to where his unit had been. The camp was deserted. The German soldiers and forced laborers from his

Escape from Nazi Forced Labor (Wladek's Story) ❖ 153

unit had disappeared into the night with their wounded commander. There were no Russians in sight. From all appearances, it seemed as if the Russian soldiers had swooped in on his unit in a surprise attack and had taken everyone as prisoners. He shook his head in amazement as the realization hit him that the only thing that had saved him from the horror of being a Russian POW was the urgent message his commander had given him that forced him to run toward headquarters just minutes before the enemy had attacked.

Wladek picked up the duffle bag that held all his belongings and began walking through the snow—away from the advancing Russians and toward the main German army. That night, he forced himself to walk 27 kilometers until he found a barn where he could burrow into the straw and get some sleep. His bag was heavy and cumbersome. He knew that carrying it would slow him down considerably, so when the sun came up, he took out all the clothing and put on as much as possible. He then threw away the bag and some other stuff—including the German papers he had been issued when he was forced into the labor camp.

A few nights later, around midnight, as Wladek was sleeping in a barn with a couple of other forced labor workers and a group of soldiers who had gotten separated from the main army, he was awakened as the guard duty sergeant shouted, "The Russians are four kilometers away in Allenstein (Olsztyn), and they are shooting people. Everyone is dead—men, women and children."

Armed with that news, Wladek and the other forced labor workers, and the soldiers picked up their belongings, ran out of the barn, and started traveling west toward Hamburg, Germany—instead of north toward the Baltic Sea and Olsytyn where their army headquarters had been. They ran, walked, and slid for three hours by holding on to the tailgates of slow moving trucks as they plowed through the freshly fallen snow.

Wladek began noticing that a few of the Polish forced labor workers began to lag behind, and the Nazi soldiers paid no attention. *"Maybe,"* he thought, *"it's safer to travel on my own."*

He waited for a time until he could see some farmhouses in the distance, and then he let go of the truck, rolled into a ditch, dug in, and covered himself with snow. At any moment, he expected someone to yell that he was missing. But nothing! He waited until he could no longer hear the heavy engines of the trucks, then he got up, brushed off the snow, and slowly began walking away.

The next day he linked up with another Polish "forced labor" worker who had become lost from his German unit. They came to a house where the door was wide open. No one was there. When they turned on the lights to check out the place, they found cooked potatoes on the stove—which they devoured.

Leaving the house, they saw a small group of German soldiers who were running east. The other Polish man yelled after them, "We've lost our unit. Can we join you?" The soldiers took one look at the two older Polish men in their dirty German uniforms and replied, "We're young and are heading back to the front to fight the Russians. You guys are too old and will have a hard time keeping up with us, but you can try."

They traveled together for a short distance, but Wladek wasn't interested in heading toward the Russian front, so he intentionally lagged behind. He wanted to get as far away from the Russians as possible. Finally, he shouted, "I have to make a bathroom stop," and headed into the woods. He stayed away until the unit of soldiers and the other Polish worker got tired of waiting and moved on without him.

It was freezing cold, and the ground was covered with snow. Wladek had no blanket but wrapped himself in a coat and shivered away the night. The next day, he walked past a cemetery and saw eleven women out in the snow holding babies. He realized these babies had probably frozen to death, and the mothers were leaving them on the ground next to tombstones because it was impossible to dig graves in the frozen ground. He thought immediately of his own baby boy—just seven months old. *Where was he? Was he safe and warm? Or was he with his mother and his other children fleeing for their lives in the freezing cold of this gruesome Polish winter?* He prayed for them as he continued his own journey to freedom.

A few days later, he came upon another group of young German soldiers who were guarding some Polish/American prisoners from Hamtramck, Michigan. The prisoners were very nice and shared some chocolate, bread, and crackers with Wladek which was an incredible treat because he was starving. Since he was still in a Nazi uniform, the German soldiers in charge immediately handed him a rifle and decided that it would be his job to guard the prisoners that night.

Wladek was very tired and explained to the prisoners that he was Polish, not German, and then said, "I'm sleepy, and you're sleepy. Let's all get some rest." They agreed and lay down and slept all night. Even the German commander slept. No one attempted to run away.

The next day, as they made their way west toward the German border, they met another company of soldiers. The Nazi captain was such a fine man that Wladek thought he must have been a Christian. The captain said,

"I know we will lose the war. It's just a matter of time." As the captain moved on with his company, Wladek wished him God's blessing.

As the weeks went by, it became apparent to the soldiers that Germany had basically lost the war, and the Russian troops were advancing quickly. Wladek knew the consequences of being caught as a "soldier" in the German army, so he threw away the gun he had been given. He would have gotten rid of his uniform, too, if he had had anything else to wear.

By now, there was quite a group of retreating German soldiers, prisoners of war, and Polish forced labor workers all making their way through blizzard conditions toward Germany—hoping to keep ahead of Russian troops. No longer was there the discipline of Nazi army life. The men had only one goal—to reach the German border. Day after day, they trudged on. They were cold, exhausted, sick, and hungry, but that was far better than being Russian prisoners of war!

In the end, Wladek figured he had walked for over 100 days (fourteen and a half weeks) through blizzards, deep snow, and freezing weather across the corridor of northern Poland and into Germany. Each day, he had probably averaged about ten to twenty kilometers, meaning he had been forced to walk at least a thousand kilometers!

What Wladek didn't know is that the Nazis were determined to leave no one behind who could help the Russians and their allies with the war effort: forced laborers, POWs, or even their own German citizens. He was just one of thousands who were forced to take part in what has become known as "The March" or "The Great March West."

War records show there were more than 80,000 allied prisoners of war held in German military prison camps who were forced to march westward across East Prussia and Poland in extreme winter conditions between January and April 1945. It was later documented that January and February of that year were among the coldest winter months of the twentieth century in Europe, with blizzards and temperatures as low as –25 °C (–13 °F), and even until the middle of March, temperatures were well below 0 °C (32 °F).

On January 19, the Nazis started evacuating Auschwitz Concentration Camp to take as many prisoners as possible on the torturous "Death March" to the West, hoping that most would die from starvation or exposure and their bodies would be scattered along the way so the Allies when they recaptured the land, would have no idea how many people had been imprisoned in Auschwitz. They were doing this with other concentration camps as well.

At the same time, hundreds of thousands of German civilian refugees, most of them women and children (including Elza and the four children), were also making their way westward by train in frigid cattle cars and by foot in these hazardous weather conditions. No one who was German was to be left behind!

The POWs and concentration camp prisoners who were forced to march west slept in factories, churches, barns—and in the open. Food was scarce; some were forced to eat dogs, cats, and an occasional rat, or they nibbled on grass when it could be found. Those who had boots had a dilemma of what to do at night while they were sleeping. Should they take off their boots and take a chance they might not be able to get their frozen boots back on their swollen feet—or that their boots could get stolen? And if they left their wet boots on, there was a good chance they might suffer terrible pain from trench foot because their icy, wet feet never dried!

For the most part, Wladek traveled west with small groups of German soldiers trying to outrun the advancing enemy. Although he was a forced labor worker, he was wearing a German army uniform, which was a badge of safety among Germans—but a lethal target if spotted by the Russians and Poles. Knowing who to trust was a constant dilemma. At any time, he could be shot or captured by the enemy. That's why he traveled with his Polish citizenship papers in his pocket! And that's why he finally decided that it was safer to abandon the Nazi army altogether and travel alone, hiding in forests, sleeping in barns, and begging for food from farmers or kind villagers.

The End of the Trail

One of the towns Wladek walked through was the German town of Belgard, which, after the war when boundaries were shifted toward the west, became known as Bialogard, Poland. He stopped there to get some buns to eat. At the time, he had no idea where his family was or whether they were still alive. By now, the war was basically over, and he knew how dangerous it would be for Elza if she were captured by the Russian/Polish army because she had played her German nationality card for special favors during the war. Once again, he stopped and prayed for her and the children. (Months later, when Wladek was in the displaced person's camp in Wentorf, Germany, he would learn that Elza and the children were in Belgard around the same time he was there. *If only he had known!*)

Toward the end of March 1945, Wladek was close enough to Hamburg to see the explosions and fires caused by the British bombing of the German oil refineries and depots.

As Wladek got closer, he actually ran into some British soldiers.

"Who are you?" the soldiers demanded of Wladek since he was still in German uniform.

"I am a Polish prisoner. The Germans forced me to work for them. That's why I'm in this uniform."

"Okay," the soldiers replied. "We will only be here two or three days, and then we will take you to Hamburg."

"But I am a Polish citizen."

"Do you have papers?"

"Yes," he replied as he dug them out of his ragged pocket. "This proves that I am Polish." He was suddenly very thankful he had kept his Polish papers and thrown away the German ones!

The soldiers looked at his papers, nodded their heads, and said, "Okay, you are free."

"But, look," Wladek pleaded, "I am still dressed in a German uniform. What shall I do? I've been walking for weeks with barely enough food to keep me alive."

Since the British soldiers weren't in a position to help him and Hamburg was pretty much destroyed, Wladek got the idea of seeking help at the city hall of a small town close to Hamburg. "Are there any Seventh-day Adventist families in this town?" he asked the officials.

"Yes," they responded, and directed him to the home of an Adventist family. The family helped him get new clothes and let him stay with them until arrangements could be made for him to be processed into one of the displaced person's camps, which were rapidly being set up to house the refugees until they could be sent back to their homelands, or if that was unsafe, to another location.

On May 5, 1945, British tanks rolled into Hamburg, taking control of the city. On May 8, the war was officially over, and Germany unconditionally surrendered to the Allied forces.

After the war, Wladek was not only homeless but had lost his family. *Were they still alive?* The officials responsible for registering the refugees and finding a permanent place for them to live at first wanted to send Wladek back to Poland, which was now under communist Russian control. They could have done this almost immediately. But he made it clear that he would be in serious danger in Poland because he was involved in helping the Germans during the war. More importantly, he had vowed to never live under communist rule. He emphatically stated, "Under no circumstances will I ever go back!" His dream for his family was to live in a free country where they could worship God without being persecuted, and his children would have unlimited opportunities.

As a result, Wladek was sent to the Wentorf Camp for displaced persons, which was 32 kilometers east of Hamburg. It was there that he found Adventist friends from Poland (including the Hinc and Klutz families from Warsaw and two of the Lehman brothers from Leszno[24]) with whom he could fellowship and worship. And it was from there that he began the search for his own family.

Even in the toughest and most dismal situations, Wladek never gave up his dream to someday take his family to the United States of America, where they would have religious freedom, as well as the freedom to become anything God wanted them to be. But first, he had to find them. That's when God gave him a dream about five white geese flying around an evergreen tree and landing on its branches. The interpretation of that dream gave him the hope he needed to "wait patiently on the Lord" for the news that the five members of his family were still alive.

---

[24] The other two Lehman brothers were found by Elza to be living in Slavno, Poland.

Chapter 18

Trying to Outrun the Russian Front (Elza's Story)

(1945)

It's time to backtrack and pick up the story of Elza and the Kuzma children after visiting Wladek in the Nazi forced labor camp in East Prussia. The summer of 1944 had turned to autumn, and the children were enjoying picking the crispy red apples, succulent purple plums, and juicy yellow pears from the trees in "Tata's Orchard" across the street from their upstairs apartment on the outskirts of Plock.

"Tata would love these," Janek said, pointing to his basket of fruit, "Especially the yummy pears."

"Yes, everything would be perfect—if only Tata were here," Krysia sighed, "I miss him so much."

Their last memory of their father was when they were leaving the German army camp, looking back at him sadly and waving goodbye. Everyone was crying—even Tata. They had no idea if they would ever see each other again.

Soon, the kids were back in school, and October was fast turning into November as the cold, brisk winds stripped the trees and carpeted the ground with golden leaves. Before long, the ground would be white as winter wrapped Plock in its frigid arms. Elza read the signs around her. Not only was winter once more coming to Poland, but the Nazis had basically lost the war. It was only a matter of time until Russian[25] and Polish soldiers would be marching down the icy streets of their town.

---

[25] Technically, by 1944-45, what was referred to by Elza and other Polish citizens as the Russian Army was really the communistic army of the Soviet Union, which included fifteen countries and was headquartered in Russia. In the final stages of WWII, two of the Polish army units joined the Soviets in their effort to defeat Nazi Germany, but in general, the Polish maintained their own military identity.

For Elza, life had been fairly comfortable during the German occupation. She merely played the chameleon. Although she was a Polish citizen, her German heritage allowed her to be German when it was politically correct. She knew, however, that those days were numbered. Her Polish papers were ready for the day the Russian/Polish armies would invade Plock, and to be German would be a death sentence.

For weeks now, her German friends had been moving west into Germany, rather than chance being caught by the Russians. "Elza," they begged, "Don't wait too long. Leave while you have a chance. Once those cruel Russians get here, your life will be in danger. There are too many people who know you worked for the Nazis at the train station and made boots for Nazi soldiers. You're foolish to think they will take mercy on you just because you're nursing a baby."

Elza knew her friends were right. She had heard her Polish neighbor's threats. They had resented her privileged German status. She knew when Germany lost the war, her life and her children's would be in danger. Plus, her close friend, Wanda Hinc, who was also German and lived across the orchard from the Kuzmas during the war, had already left for Germany with her children, hoping to join her husband when he was released from the German forced labor camp near Hamburg.

But Wladek was last seen in northeastern Poland. If she ever wanted to see him again, traveling west toward Germany didn't make sense.

Elza felt as if she were facing the end of the world. In reality, it was the end of "her" world—at least the world she had known for the last five years. And as the snow began to fall, she remembered Jesus' words of warning in Matthew 24:19 and 20. "Pray that your flight may not be in winter...." and "Woe to those with nursing babies." She was doubly cursed. It was winter, and baby Jurek was only seven months old.

Yet, she hesitated to leave her warm, comfortable home in Plock—especially when she had nowhere to go. Her relatives were facing the same danger, but they lived in a border town of Rybnik, in the opposite direction of where she had last seen Wladek. If conditions got bad, it would be easy for them to cross the border into Germany. But what should she do?

It had been months since she had heard from Wladek. The last news from the Eastern Front was that the Russians had captured Olsztyn, where he had been stationed. For all she knew, he was either a Russian POW or dead. Her heart, however, told her he was still alive. And just maybe, if that were true, he would make his way back to Plock. If she left too soon, they would have no way of finding each other in the chaos of the war. So, while others who feared the Russians had left, she stayed behind.

The New Year dawned cold and gray, and she still lingered, hoping for a miracle. But she prepared for the impending westward trip by ordering six good sized crates to use for packing what she wanted to take with her when she was forced to leave. When the crates were delivered, she began filling them with canned goods, her husband's precious library books, and various other things she would need in the future. She was sad thinking of leaving behind her beautiful furniture and piano. But lives were far more important than things.

While Elza packed, she listened to her little contraband radio, which she had hidden under a pile of dirty laundry for the last five years. It was always tuned to the British Broadcasting Corporation (BBC), while her large Blaupunkt radio was tuned to legal programming produced by the Germans. Everyone knew that the Nazis only broadcast propaganda. To know what was really happening on the political front, under the threat of death, people tuned in to the British public broadcasting station. That's why Elza knew the Russians were coming even though it was denied by German radio. Plus, she knew what they were doing to women. Rape was everyone's biggest fear. Safety meant getting out of town before the conquering Russian army arrived.

It was common knowledge that if the Russians wanted something and you resisted, they thought nothing of killing you and taking it. If you had a gold tooth and they wanted the gold, they would knock it out of your mouth. They were even known to bite off fingers if they couldn't slip off someone's gold or diamond ring.

At the beginning of the week of January 13, Plock experienced a major snowstorm. "Lord, not now!" Elza sighed as she watched the snow piling up. The next day, Plock looked like a white winter wonderland, with the air so frigid it nearly took her breath away. "Lord, not today," She prayed. It's too cold for the children!" And then she heard something strange in the distance—the barking and howling of dogs. They barked all day and all the next night. Elza knew something was wrong, especially when the eastern sky lit up with the explosion of bombs. Then she heard the news report, "The Russian army is advancing to the Vistula River. Once they cross the bridge, they'll capture Plock, and it will be too late!" She then understood the barking. Dogs could hear the high, shrill sounds of the artillery shells exploding in the distance that human ears could not yet discern.

Escaping from Plock

On Wednesday, January 17, the official German announcement Elza had been expecting came: "Warning! The Soviet army is advancing. *All German citizens must leave town immediately.* A train is at the Plock station to take you to safety. It will depart later tonight. No German will be left behind to be captured by the Russians. Bring only what you can carry. This is a temporary evacuation. In a few days, the German army will push the enemy back, and you can return to your homes."

It was time to go—regardless of the frigid weather, the biting wind, and the icy snow! With God's protection and help, Elza knew she could shepherd her little family to safety, even though she was alone. She prayed for strength and courage. She reminded herself of Mark 10:27, "With man it is impossible, but not with God." She calmed her fears by remembering that God knew where her husband was. Even though he hadn't made it back to Plock, they could find each other and once more be together as a family.

Right now, her job was to run a few errands, which took her most of the morning hours. The kids kept looking out the window, wondering when Mama would return. The older children began to worry. They kept asking Stasia, "What time is it? Shouldn't Mama be here by now?"

> *It was time to go—regardless of the frigid weather, the biting wind, and the icy snow!*

The last thing Elza did before returning to their home across from Wladek's orchard was to contact the owner of the horse drawn wagon that she had arranged to take her family and their belongings to the train station and tell him to be at her house by 4 p.m. Then she rushed home, much to the relief of the children.

While waiting for the wagon Elza did the last of the packing. She stuffed the baby buggy mattress with zlotys (Polish money) and important papers such as her Polish marriage certificate, the children's birth certificates, and school papers. Then, beside the mattress, she put the things they would need for the trip: a bag of extra blankets, some food, and a few of her husband's treasured books, hoping that somehow in the weeks ahead they would find each other. Then she got the kids dressed in their warmest clothes, including at least two or three layers. Elza put on three outfits—not just for warmth but to save suitcase space. As soon as the wagon arrived, she and Stasia began loading. The last thing Elza did was put baby Jurek in his baby carriage and cover him with as many blankets as possible, and then she helped the other children into the wagon.

"What about the two crates in the front yard?" Stasia called.

"The wagon is full. We can't take a chance of being late. We must catch tonight's train because there may not be another. We'll just have to leave the crates." Then Elza added, "We love you and will be praying for your safety," as they all waved and blew kisses to their much loved nanny.

Stasia nodded her head in understanding, then her eyes filled with tears as she waved goodbye to the people who had been her family for the last five years. Elza would have loved to have taken her along, but it was not possible because this evacuation was only for those of German heritage. At nineteen years of age, Stasia was not afraid to stay behind and face the Russian/Polish invaders[26]. And if she needed help, her relatives lived nearby.

When they got to the station platform where the train for the refugees was waiting, Elza immediately realized this would be a torturous trip. There were no luxury passenger cars attached to the old steam engine, only some unheated cattle cars that the authorities were attempting to pack sixty or more people into each. This meant standing or sitting room only.

The train platform was filled with a crowd of frightened people pushing and jostling each other, hoping to board the train. Nazi officials carefully checked papers. When it was the Kuzma family's turn to load, the officials barked at Elza, "Get your kids on the train with their suitcases, and leave the crates and the baby carriage behind."

She straightened her shoulders, looked the dispatcher in the eye, and spoke in perfect German, "I am going to take the crates AND the baby carriage!"

"No, you're not," the man argued. The children cowered behind their mother.

"Yes, I am. I worked at this railroad station for four years. I gave Germany my best—and I'm not going to be taken advantage of now!"

Her stubbornness was holding up the departure of the train. The people who were already loaded began to yell at the official. "It's getting late. Get her on the train. Let her take the baby carriage if she wants."

Finally, the official realized he wasn't going to win. "Okay," he said, "Take the carriage—but leave the crates."

In the end, Elza was able to crowd her family, the baby carriage carrying little Jurek, and two of the crates into the freezing cattle car—along with their suitcases and a bag filled with bedding. She had to leave the other two crates behind on the train platform. As Elza looked around the smelly cattle car and shivered in the frigid night air, she thought, *"What a pathetic picture! There were no chairs or cushions on which to sit—just the dirty straw*

---

[26] Unfortunately, the beautiful nineteen-year-old Stasia was one of those the Russian soldiers abused when they marched into Plock.

covered floor—with approximately sixty strangers huddled together trying to keep warm. This was no way to transport people!" Finally, the doors of the cattle car clanged shut.

The railcar was crowded, and the air smelled putrid. People began to jostle each other for what little space there was. Elza instructed her children, "Don't let go of the baby carriage. No matter what happens, hold on tight!" It was freezing. And the kids were hungry. Elza gave them some bread and fruit she had packed for the trip. By now, they could hear the explosions of the artillery shells in the distance—and the people out on the train platform could see the eastern sky light up as the shells exploded.

Everyone was anxious to get going. Every minute they delayed meant that the feared Russian troops were that much closer. Yet hours went by. The children sat on the suitcases and finally curled up on the straw and fell asleep. But the train still didn't move!

"What's wrong?" the people started complaining. Finally, word came that the Russian army had bombed the tracks ahead, and they couldn't leave the station until they received word that the tracks had been repaired.

The Bitter Cold Train Ride to "Freedom"

It was past midnight—in the early morning hours of January 18—when the train slowly chugged out of the Plock railway station where Elza had spent so many hours working—dressed in her stylish outfits with her hair elegantly fashioned and where the railroad officials and her coworkers had respected her. Now she was a refugee, thrown into a cattle car full of cold, hungry, fearful, disgruntled, displaced people hoping to get out of the path of the enemy. Slowly, the swaying and rumble of the cars brought exhausted sleep to Elza as the blackness of the winter night enveloped her little family! The train headed northwest toward Torun. The people were warned that no lights could be lit because enemy planes would see the train and bomb it. They had no idea what their final destination would be. All they knew was that the Germans intended to keep "their" people from getting captured by the enemy.

Most were unaware that the official evacuation plan of the Germans had actually started in August of 1944 when they began taking people of German heritage out of the path of the advancing Soviet/Polish armies in East Prussia. As trains were available, evacuees were shipped west and then north toward the Baltic Sea. About 450,000 Germans fled East Prussia over the frozen Vistula Lagoon. They were then evacuated by ship from ports such as Danzig (Gdansk) or Gdingen (Gdynia) or ports further north such as Konigsberg (Kaliningrad) and Pillau (Beltiysk), the most westerly city in Russia).

For the German evacuees coming from the regions of central Poland (Pomerania), like Elza and the children, the main Baltic seaport destination was the town of Kolberg (Kolobrzeg), which Hitler had declared a "fortress." It became the center for sea-based evacuation of both civilians and the military. The people were then evacuated on ships to German seaport cities west of the Oder River or, after the war, to Denmark, where internment camps were set up by the Danes. Almost 2.2 million people were evacuated this way. (And about 14,000 drowned when the Allies sank their ships.)

This was the route that the officials had planned for Elza and the other families on the train chugging toward Torun. The problem was that even though Elza didn't know what the evacuation plan was, the Allies did, so this entire area had become a main target for their bombing raids.

The sun finally came up. As the metal wheels suddenly screeched to a halt, Elza tried to look around. *Where were they?* Once again, word spread, "The train has to wait for bombed out tracks to be repaired." It finally dawned on Elza that this would be a long, cold trip. And no one really knew where they would end up. This evacuation train wasn't a regularly scheduled train, so they not only had to put up with damaged tracks, but their train had to be shunted off onto sidetracks for the regular trains to pass.

As Elza and the children waited, the doors opened for the evacuees to get out, stretch their legs, and use the "bathroom facilities" in the snow. Men were ushered to one side of the train, women and children to the other.

As people began to grumble, officials served hot black coffee. It wasn't much, but anything warm was appreciated. The break gave Elza time to pick up baby Jurek and nurse him. She praised God that they had all made it through the first night, especially when she and the children watched a German soldier wrestle a frozen dead baby out of the arms of its mother. They were horrified as he walked to the edge of the forest and threw the dead baby into a snow bank while the terrified mother ran after him hysterically screaming. This shocking scene would be repeated again and again as the below-freezing conditions took its toll on defenseless babies—especially those who were bottle fed—because even if mothers had extra bottles of milk—they almost immediately froze and were useless. The two things that saved baby Jurek were first that Elza was still breastfeeding—which meant a continual supply of warm milk—and second, the well insulated baby carriage piled high with blankets. The war was cruel. And winter was brutal, especially for the tiniest ones.

Once again, Elza and the children thanked God that they were all safe and the blankets stuffed around Jurek in his carriage had kept him alive through the frigid night—even though it was so cold that Elza found Jurek's diaper was partly frozen when she started to change him. After a number of hours, the people were once more loaded into the cattle cars, and the train slowly proceeded down the repaired tracks to the next stop where they took on water, the tender was filled with coal, and the Red Cross served cabbage soup and dried bread to the starving people. During the next few days, there were long delays as the tracks were being repaired. On two different occasions, the evacuees had to be transferred to the cattle cars of different trains in order to avoid bombed out tracks.

Torun was a large railway center, but other than taking on fuel and water, the train moved on through the next night and turned north to the little town of Nakel (Polish: Naklo nad Notecia) on the river Notec. The train stopped at this important railway hub, and the Red Cross once again provided the refugees with warm cabbage soup and a slice of dry bread. Later that day, the train stopped in an open field to wait for bombed out tracks to be repaired while the German soldiers took the dead babies from the arms of their mothers and threw them into the snow. Elza and her children were blessed to have the warm baby carriage that protected baby Jurek from freezing to death.

Schneidemurhl (Polish: Pila)

When the tracks were repaired, the evacuees traveled on throughout the coldest winter in European history, stopping over and over again as bombed out tracks were repaired. One time, a bomb actually hit the train, and two damaged cars had to be removed. Once again, the tracks had to be repaired before the train could move. As the bombing intensified, the train began stopping during the night because a moving train was easier for the bombers to spot. Finally, they arrived at the largest town in northern Poland, Schneidemurhl (German) or Pila (Polish). It was an important railway hub. But because the tracks were bombed beyond the town, the railroad officials made everyone disembark and take their belongings. They were told the train would not run for a day or two until the tracks could be repaired. It was now late in the afternoon. Since there was no official place for the refugees to stay, like an inn or hotel, volunteers from the town offered housing.

The Kuzma family got off the train with the baby carriage, suitcases, bag of bedding, and their two crates. When a local Evangelical pastor saw them on the train platform, he invited their family—and a number of others—to stay at his home. He and his wife had two small children—and they, too, were in the process of packing to leave town as soon as possible, hoping to escape the advancing army.

The pastor made arrangements for the Kuzmas and all their belongings to be taken to his home, which was set back from the street. He pointed to the barn and said they could store their crates and luggage there if it wouldn't be needed in the next couple of days.

The house was crowded, but the owners were kind, and everyone was grateful to be out of the bitter cold. One of the first things the pastor's wife offered Elza was the bathroom where she could give her children hot baths. What a luxury!

The town of Schneidemurhl was in turmoil. The Russian troops were advancing so quickly that most of those with a German heritage were planning to leave as soon as the trains were running again.

The Kuzma family stayed in the pastor's house for three days. Each morning, Elza had worship with her children, where she shared a Bible verse and a blessing, and then asked the Lord for directions for the day. As the railroad tracks were repaired, announcements were made telling the townspeople it was time to leave. The pastor and his wife and children left on a train Saturday afternoon—along with most of the others.

Elza had a strong impression that she should not continue in the direction the others were fleeing. She had to make a decision.

Once again, Elza delayed. She had a strong impression that she should not continue in the direction the others were fleeing. She had to make a decision. *"Should she leave the comfort of this home—or should she stay? She knew that sooner or later, she and the children would be overtaken by the Russians regardless of what she did. Was this the time to stop running and face the enemy, or should she flee like all the others?*

That night, after the children were sleeping, she heard artillery shells exploding, so she knew the Russians were close. But as the sun rose, there was no sign of the army in town. "It appears the Germans have pushed the advancing army back," she said to her children as she gathered them around her. "I heard there is bread available in town. Since there is no sign of enemy soldiers yet, I'm going to leave you here in this warm house while I go and get something for us to eat." She gave strict instructions to Danusia to take good care of her sister and brothers, and then she put on her wraps and went out into the cold.

She hurried toward town and found the bread line. As she waited her turn, people questioned her, "You're German. Why aren't you on the train? The Russian front is moving closer, and it's not safe—especially for a woman to be caught by the enemy. You have no idea what those crude soldiers might do to you!"

Now Elza was frightened. *"What should she do?"* She began to cry out to the Lord, "Please help us. I don't know what to do!" When Elza had left the house that morning, Krysia was so afraid she would never see her mama again that she never left the window. Instead, she stood there for hours with her nose pressed against the glass, searching intently for the first glimpse of her mama returning. As Elza neared the house with her allotment of bread, Krysia threw on her coat, dashed outside, and ran into her mother's arms.

Just then, a very distinguishing looking gray haired German soldier riding in a Red Cross lorry with two other officials stopped beside them on the road next to the fence. He addressed Elza in a concerned voice, "You're German. Why are you still here? The situation is very dangerous."

"I don't know what to do," Elza replied. "I have four children—the youngest is just an infant in a carriage. And now the trains that were scheduled to take evacuees away from the front have already left town."

"There is still hope," the officer replied. "Hurry! Pack up your things and bring your children and your luggage out to the road. The German army is evacuating. I will be at the end of the convoy pulling out of town. If you are here, I promise I will have the Red Cross lorry pick you up."

"But I have a baby carriage—and I won't leave without it."

"We'll make room for it," the German officer assured her.

So Elza and the children quickly repacked their suitcases, put Jurek in his baby carriage, took the bag of bedding and put it on top of him, and in less than an hour, were pushing the buggy and the two crates out to the side of the road. They then sat down on their suitcases and waited for the German convoy. To pass the time and keep warm, they stomped their feet and clapped their hands to the rhythm of their favorite praise song, "Spevichi."

Before long, they saw the line of army lorries coming over the hill. As they passed, they could see that the canvas covered backs of the trucks were packed with Nazi soldiers holding rifles. They could easily tell there was no room for anyone else—especially not a family with a baby carriage. The children became concerned, "Mama, when is the kind soldier in the Red Cross lorry coming for us?"

"Just pray," Mama encouraged. "The man said he would be at the end of the convoy. And look, the lorries are still coming over the hill."

As the sun was beginning to set on the western horizon, they saw the last lorry of the convoy come over the hill. It drew closer and began to slow down as it neared the little family. The distinguished army officer jumped out and shouted, "Hurry! We've got to get you loaded quickly so we don't get separated from the rest of the convoy."

The children were excited and jumped into the lorry, one by one, the suitcases were handed to soldiers and Red Cross workers. Finally, the carriage with baby Jurek was shoved into the back.

Elza pointed, "What about the two crates?" she asked as they were hurrying her toward the lorry."

"Sorry," the kind officer said, shaking his head, "We don't have room. You'll just have to leave them here. We have to rush. The situation is very dangerous. We could get bombed by the enemy at any time. The more distance we can put between us and the Russians, the safer we'll be. As it is, we'll be driving tonight without headlights."

Reluctantly, Elza accepted the help of the men as they pulled her up into the lorry and quickly drove on, trying to catch up with the convoy. Elza looked back sadly through the opening in the canvas flap as the crates containing her husband's precious books faded from view. That was by far the biggest loss that Elza experienced in the war. Some were extremely valuable out of print Polish language books that could never be replaced. She had tried her best to keep what was most precious to her husband, but she had failed. All she could do was pray that God would lead some interested soul to find the books, read them, and become a believer.

They traveled all night. The next day, the convoy arrived at the train station in Koslin, Germany (Polish, Koszalin)[27], a town located on both sides of the Dziezecinka River about twelve kilometers south of the Baltic Sea. "Trains are still leaving for Belgard, Germany (Polish: Bialogard) and Kolberg, Germany (Polish: Kolobrzeg) from this station," the German Red Cross worker explained. "You should be safe now."

Once again, the pile of Kuzmas' belongings was stacked on the train platform. But now the pile was smaller. *"We may have had to leave our*

---

[27] I chose to use the German names for towns in German territory when the war ended because those are the names that Elza and the children knew. After the war, the Yalta Conference gave German land to Poland so Poland could access the Baltic Sea, and the names were changed back to their original Polish names.

things behind," Elza thought to herself, "*but at least the children are safe. We each have a suitcase, and baby Jurek has his carriage. We have much for which to be thankful.*"

With all the bombing that was happening in the northwest region of Poland, it was a miracle that the family had made it safely to Koslin. They were within the borders of Germany—they should be relatively safe from the Russians. *But now, where should they go?* They had two choices. They could take the train going south to Belgard, Germany, or take the train going east to the port at Kolberg, Germany, which was the official escape route that the Germans had set up to allow their people to travel by ship to safer German seaports west of the Oder River. The problem was Kolberg was also where the Germans had established an underground ammunition factory where hundreds of Polish citizens had been forced to work during the war, making it a prime target for the approaching Russian/Polish army.

Elza prayed, and the children prayed, but Elza still couldn't decide. Escape by the Baltic Sea sounded most reasonable, but it would take her further away from the safety of the German border. It would, however, mean she would be closer to where she had last heard from her husband. But that also meant she would be closer to the Russian enemy. *What should she do?*

Then it came to her. Why not cast lots like the Bible characters so often did when making a decision? She tore off two strips of paper. On one, she wrote "Belgard." On another, "Kolberg," and then she put them in Janek's hat. She told the children her idea. "I think we should let Janek choose one strip of paper. We will take the train to the city that is drawn." They prayed, and Janek closed his eyes and reached into the hat, hesitated, and then pulled out the paper on which was written "Belgard."

"God has answered our prayer," Elza told her children as she sighed in relief. "We will get on the train to Belgard."

It was close to midnight when they arrived at Belgard, nearly three weeks after they had left Plock. Hundreds of evacuees were milling around the train station. It was terribly cold. People were shivering. You could see their breath. A few benches were along the station's walls, but most people were sitting on the floor. Luggage was everywhere. Elza took one look at the mass of humanity that had been displaced from their homes and exclaimed, "Maybe we should have gone to the end of the line so we could have escaped by ship! How will we ever find somewhere to stay when there are so many homeless people?" Then, just as suddenly, she exclaimed, "God has a plan for us. He knows where we will be safe. He led us to Belgard, so there's no need to worry."

The children huddled together on the floor as Elza covered them with the quilts from the bedding bag. "The Red Cross is working as fast as possible to transport us evacuees to a church where we will be safe for the night. Until then, try to get some sleep," she told the children. "Tomorrow, God will help us find a place to stay." Then she prayed over them.

Around six o'clock the next morning, as Red Cross workers were serving hot chocolate to the evacuees who had spent the night in the unheated church, word spread through the crowd. The train to Kolberg, which was going in the opposite direction, had been bombed as it neared the city, and almost everyone had been killed. Although they mourned for the dead, it was also a time of praise and thanksgiving for Elza and the children, as they realized that, once again, God had protected them from certain death by directing them to take the train to Belgard. The long race to outrun the Russians had been won—but only for a short time.

Years later, Danusia summed up the experience of escaping from Plock in these words: "In Plock, we were still children. Once we left on the train in those cattle cars, our carefree childhood was over because of the responsibility each of us kids felt. Our biggest worry was the possibility of losing Mama. We had already lost our tata. Mama was now the only person in the world who could keep us together. She gave us courage, hope, and the assurance that God held our lives in His hands."

As Elza reflected on how God had led them to take the train to Belgard when the sensible thing would have been to accept the evacuation plan of the German authorities and continue to the Baltic Sea and the safety of a ship, she began to hum that old Martin Luther hymn she had learned as a teenager in the Ostrowo Evangelical Church, *"A mighty fortress is our God, a bulwark never failing; Our helper He, amid the flood of mortal ills prevailing."*

What next? Where in this crowded city would she find a place for her family to live? She had no idea, but with God as her "mighty fortress" against the enemy, she knew He would provide. What she didn't know was how often she would need to call upon Him in the days ahead when the enemy actually marched into the town.

CHAPTER 19

Belgard: Caught by the Communists
(1945)

The Nazi German government officials had fulfilled half of their promise to Elza and the other citizens of German heritage who had gotten on the cattle cars at the Plock train station; they had rescued them from the immediate danger of the advancing enemy troops and had transported them to a town in German territory where hopefully they would be safe. But they had failed to keep the second part of their promise. *They hadn't defeated the enemy so Elza and her children could return to their home in Plock.*

The longer Elza was on the cattle car train, the more she began to realize that sooner or later, the Russian/Polish troops would catch up, and she would have to deal with Soviet occupation. At the same time, she knew she was getting further away from where she had last seen her husband. Plus, they had not eaten much more than cabbage soup and stale bread for weeks. *Maybe it was time to stop running.*

God Provides

All during the war, Elza never lost her faith. As she woke her children in the unheated Belgard church next to the train station, she assured them, "God had provided for our family before, and He will do it again. Now, it's up to me to find the house God has for us here in Belgard. While I'm looking, your job is to stay together at the church. Danusia is in charge." Then she looked at Krysia and Janek. "You are to listen to her and obey her. Do you understand?" They nodded their heads.

She hated to leave her children, but she also knew they would be more comfortable huddled together in the church under the watchful eye of Red Cross workers than trying to keep up with her as she raced around town. She would start her search by asking church members for temporary housing. She knew they would be registered at the city hall. She took a deep breath, whispered a prayer, and inquired of the local Red Cross worker, "Sir, can you give me directions to the city hall?"

"It's in the center of town—just up the street," he pointed.

Elza then waved to her children, blew them kisses, and rushed out the door.

When she got to the city hall, she asked, "Are there any Seventh-day Adventists living in Belgard?"

"Yes," the secretary answered. I'm an Adventist and my father is the pastor of a small group of about twenty members. His name is Pastor Fleming.

Elza was amazed to find how quickly God was working. Elza then explained her situation, ending with, "I'm trying to locate a place to stay until the Red Cross finds permanent housing for me and my four children, and I wondered if a church member might help."

"I'm sure someone will take you in," the young woman cheerfully replied. "Here's the address of my parent's house, they should know. They live just a few blocks away."

When Pastor and Mrs. Fleming answered her knock, Elza once more explained her situation. The couple then looked at each other and responded, "You can stay with us."

"Oh, that would be wonderful! This is an answer to our prayers."

"Where are your children now?" Pastor Fleming asked.

"In the church next to the train station."

Pastor Fleming arranged for a horse carriage to take Elza back to the church to pick up the children and their belongings. Before the sun set that night, they were safe and warm in the pastor's home.

The Flemings had two grown daughters (Esther and Ruth) in their early twenties. Esther was married—and pregnant, but since her husband was actively fighting in the war, she had come back home to stay with her parents until his term of duty was over. (Sadly, only a few months later, Esther died giving birth.) Their younger daughter, Ruth, worked at city hall.

The girls willingly offered to share a room so there would be a room for the Kuzma family. That night, the soft feather beds and fluffy down-filled pillows made them feel as if they were floating on clouds. It was a heavenly feeling to their stiff, weary bodies.

"God really answered our prayer quickly, didn't He? Danusia said as she climbed into bed next to her siblings."

"Yes, He sure did! Let's say prayers and tell Him how thankful we are?" Elza suggested. And they did. Minutes later, they were sound asleep.

The next day, Elza contacted the International Red Cross office, who introduced them to a German Count and Countess who had offered to help with the refugee problem by dividing their home into apartments to make room for more families. Elza and the children were the first family they took in. "What a beautiful gray brick home," Danusia exclaimed. But Janik was more impressed with the von Bernick's limousine!

Countess von Bernick was tall, slender, and regal. But more importantly, she was kind and treated the kids as if they were her own grandchildren—even knitting each a pair of socks when she realized they didn't have a second pair. She also provided food for a number of days until Elza was able to purchase what they needed. When the Countess realized the Kuzma family didn't have any eating utensils, she broke up a beautiful set of silver tableware and gave two place settings to them.

The Russian Army was advancing, so the von Bernicks only stayed with the Kuzma family for a few weeks, and on March 2, 1945, three days before the front came through Belgard, they quickly packed up what they could carry and left the rest behind. The Kuzmas were sad to see them go, for they had grown to love them in the few short days they had been together.

Starting a Home Business

Elza's next challenge was to figure out how she could earn a living since their meager savings wouldn't last long. Elza noticed there were many German families, like the von Bernicks, who were leaving the city and needed to get rid of their belongings. At the same time, there were Polish families moving in who needed home furnishings. Because of the hard feelings and distrust between the two nationalities, the Germans wouldn't sell their belongings for a reasonable price to the Polish, and the Polish refused to pay exorbitant prices for German possessions.

Since Elza was a Polish citizen of German heritage and spoke both languages fluently, both sides trusted her. So she set up a small home business where she bought the things German people wanted to sell for an honest price, marked up the merchandise to a reasonable price, and sold them to Polish families. It was a genius idea—a win-win for everyone. And it was amazingly successful. Within a few weeks, the shelves were full of merchandise.

Elza and the children missed the von Bernicks, but they felt more at home with each passing day. They faithfully went to church each Sabbath at Pastor Fleming's, where they easily made new friends. Elza also met with various town officials and explained how she was helping Belgard's citizens to either sell or buy what they needed. Everyone seemed pleased Elza had found a way to support her family while at the same time helping others.

God had abundantly provided as He promised in Ephesians 3:20. But the war was still raging—and the Russian troops from which Elza had hoped to escape were now closing in on Belgard. This time, Elza chose to stay.

The Deadly Explosion

Mid-day, March 3, 1945, the dogs in the neighborhood started howling, just as they had when the Russian army was approaching Plock. Immediately, Elza realized the dogs were hearing the high pitched sound of the enemy's artillery shells. It wouldn't be long now until Belgard would become a killing zone.

The next day, the howling became more intense. Elza decided that staying in the second story of the von Bernick home would make her family an easy target for the advancing army, so she took some blankets and food and moved her family into the spidery, dirty potato cellar under the house.

Throughout the day, the intensity of the shelling increased. The ground shook with each explosion. "The fighting is coming closer," Mama explained, "but it will soon be over." The family huddled together, bundled up in their winter clothing with an old quilt thrown over them. Krysia and Janek tried to bury their heads under the quilt to muffle the scary sounds. Then, for no apparent reason, there was a lull in the shooting. At about this same time, baby Jurek started crying.

Maybe this break in the shelling would allow them to sneak back into the house to get something to drink and some more food and blankets.

Elza knew it was important that she stay hidden from the Russian soldiers since she didn't have the protection of a husband, and if she couldn't get Jurek back to sleep, his crying might expose their hiding place.

At about this same time, the children complained of being thirsty. "Maybe the attack is over for now," Elza whispered. The sun was setting, and twilight shadows were creeping in. Maybe this break in the shelling would allow them to sneak back into the house to get something to drink and some more food and blankets since she was quite certain they would be hiding under the house all night.

Finally, she made the fateful decision—they would leave the cellar just long enough to run around the house to the staircase leading up to the second floor, where they could get into their apartment and replenish their supplies. She explained her plan to the children and ended with, "It is very important when we go into the house, even though it's almost dark, that you pull all the shades and DON'T turn on a light. Our kitchen window faces the east, where the Russian soldiers have their tanks and guns. If they see a light in the window, they might think it is the enemy, aim at the window, and we could all get killed. Do you understand? *Don't turn on anything—not even the stove!*"

The children, their eyes wide with fright, silently nodded their heads. "Krysia, you go with Janek and see what you can find in the refrigerator for Jurek. Danusia, come with me and let's find some quilts to keep us warm. Then, we can get some more water and food. OK! Everyone ready? Let's go! Hurry!"

Janek obediently pulled down the shades in the kitchen and opened the refrigerator as Krysia held baby Jurek. "There's some cereal," she said. "Let's get that."

"But it's cold," Janek said. "We'll need to warm it."

"Yes, but Mama said not to turn on the stove."

Well, what about a candle? Janek thought. Without considering the fact that the flame of a candle would make unwanted light, Janek took a match from the matchbox, struck it, lit the candle, and started to hold it under the aluminum pan of cereal. Suddenly, just as Mama and Danusia came back into the kitchen, there was a terrible explosion. The whole family was knocked to the floor, even Krysia with baby Jurek in her arms.

When the dust cleared, the kids asked in shaky voices, "What happened?" The shards of glass from the broken window had flown all over the kitchen. It was a miracle no one was seriously hurt.

Then Mama noticed the candle in Janek's hand and immediately realized what had happened. "Did you light that candle?" she asked.

"Yes, I knew I shouldn't turn on the stove, but since the cereal was too cold for baby Jurek to eat…"

Mama nodded her head in understanding, "Just the flicker of that candle seen through the drawn shade was enough for the enemy to think soldiers were hiding here, so they shot an artillery shell at the window. There's an old Polish proverb that says, 'Man may shoot the bullet, but God can determine the destination.' We could have easily been killed, but God protected us!"

The kids were so scared they forgot all about how thirsty they were and dashed through the hallway to the door leading to the staircase, leaving Elza to pick up some food and a jug of water and quickly follow. Taking two steps at a time, they dashed down the stairs and around the house through the patches of snow and back into the dark, scary cellar just as the artillery shelling began in earnest and the sky lit up as if they were experiencing a severe lightning storm.

The kids cowered among the cobwebs as the fighting intensified. To calm their fears, Elza started softly singing until she saw two Nazi soldiers behind the house hurriedly taking off their uniforms and putting on civilian clothing. Later, they heard men whispering in German about escaping to the west as soon as the fighting stopped.

The noise of bursting artillery shells was frightening. The ground shook with each blast, but in spite of the fighting, the exhausted children finally went to sleep as Elza lay awake, cuddling her children like a mother hen and praying for their safety and for Wladek wherever he might be. Finally, exhausted with worry and wondering about what tomorrow would bring, she fitfully dozed.

It was early. Elza woke with a start as the kids began squirming and finally crawled out from under their covers. Everything was still. No barking dogs, no ratatat-tat of automatic rifles, no artillery shell blasts, no explosions from dropping bombs. Just silence.

For the Kuzma family, the war was over. There would be no more running—at least, that's what Elza thought.

Cautiously, the kids peered out the cellar door into the frosty backyard. The first thing they noticed were the sacks of food and the German "Wehrmacht" uniforms that the soldiers had left behind. Hopefully, they had escaped and would make it back to their families.

Rubble was everywhere as bombs had hit buildings and broken down walls. Then Elza noticed that the tall apartment building next to their house had been destroyed by explosives and was now a pile of rubble. Apparently, the shell meant for their kitchen window was aimed too high, went over their house, and hit the building next to them. Once again, she praised God for His protection.

"It looks like the war is over for us," Elza sighed. "The Nazi army must have retreated, and the Russians are now in control."

The family gathered their belongings and cautiously made their way to the staircase. As they glanced around, they could tell which homes were occupied and which were empty because the people who had stayed behind had hung out white flags of surrender made from sheets, towels, and even underwear. When Elza got back to her apartment, she, too, made a white flag from an old pillowcase tied to a broomstick and hung it out the window. Later, she decided that since her family was Polish, that it might be wise to fly the red and white Polish flag from their window. She found a red shirt and tied it above the white pillowcase to resemble the Polish flag. Later that day, a Polish soldier knocked on their apartment door. When she slowly opened it, he said, "The Polish army camp is just a couple blocks away, and I saw your flag." Then he asked, "Ahhh, Pani. Are you Polish?"

When Elza confirmed that, indeed, her family was Polish, he said, "I thought you might be when I saw your flag." He hesitated and then added, "But it's upside down! The red always goes on the bottom. It symbolizes the blood our people have spilled over the centuries, and the white is for the high ideal of freedom, which is so important to us."

Elza apologized for her mistake. "I put it up so quickly that I didn't even stop to think which way it went! I just wanted the army to know we were friendly."

They both laughed. As the soldier turned to go, Elza asked, "Where is the Russian army camp?"

"Oh, it's about a mile away—just outside the city limits."

Elza breathed a sigh of relief. "Good!" she exclaimed, "I've heard some terrible things about how they treat Polish women—and I'm afraid for my safety—and for my daughters."

"I understand," the man said, "Things are pretty chaotic right now—and it would be best to keep out of sight."

With a pleasant "*do widzenia*" and a friendly wave, the soldier turned and left. The amazing thing is that the man returned to their home regularly for the next six weeks, bringing the family food items like flour, sugar, oil, and powdered milk until the stores once more opened for business.

Exploring Belgard

After the fighting was over, Belgard was an exciting new experience for Janek. His sisters, especially Krysia, were afraid to venture out. But Janek loved adventure—and begged, "Please, Mama, just let me look around and see what I can find. I won't go far." By now, the rest of the family was cleaning up the mess caused by the exploding artillery shell, so permission was granted.

Once outside, Janek noticed two Russian soldiers walking down the middle of the street with rifles slung over their shoulders. They had smiles on their faces and appeared to be joking. They didn't look scary. They paid no attention to Janek. Evidence of war was all around him:

destroyed buildings, rubble, and broken glass. There were even a number of dead German soldiers. Janek immediately thought about his father in his German army uniform and turned over a few bodies to make sure they weren't his tata.

Then Janek noticed people walking in and out of stores and unoccupied houses, carrying food. His first thought was that they were stealing, until he overheard two people with their arms full of canned goods, saying, "It's going to be weeks—maybe longer—before the stores are open. Thankfully, people left their food behind for us when they left town."

That gave Janek an idea. Why not take some food for his family? He cautiously went into a store where the people were taking items off the shelves. He watched for a few minutes, then he went back to the place where he had seen a small abandoned wagon and "borrowed" it. He then went back inside the store, and began to fill the wagon.

As he left the store, he once more spotted the two dead soldiers. This time he noticed that each had a pack of cigarettes in the pocket of their uniforms. "I bet I can sell these to other soldiers. (A few days later, he took the confiscated cigarettes down to the Polish army camp and found that the soldiers were more than happy to trade food for his cigarettes.)

When Janek returned home, he parked the wagon behind a bush and dashed up the stairs. "Mama, Mama, I saw some Russian soldiers." He was just about to tell her about his wagonload of food when she turned toward him and asked in a worried tone, "How do you know they were Russian?"

"Because they looked different, and I couldn't understand what they were saying. If they were German or Polish, I'd know." That was enough for Elza. She quickly herded her children into their second-story home, shut the door, knelt down with them, and asked the Lord for His protection, claiming Psalm 91:11, "Lord, You kept us safe during the fighting, now, please keep Your promise and send Your angels to take charge over us and keep us safe from the dangers around us—especially the Russian soldiers." Then she added, "And Lord, please help me find a way to get the food we need to feed my family until the stores open again."

At that point, Janek interrupted the prayer. "Mama, you don't need to worry. Come see what I found." He grabbed her hand and headed down the stairs. He then pulled the wagonload of food out from under the bush.

"What?" she exclaimed. "Where did you get this?"

"Down the street," he pointed. "The stores and houses where nobody lives are open, and people are taking the food. I heard people say it would be weeks before stores open up again—so if we don't want to starve, we better get it now. I know if Tata were here, he'd bring it home. So I decided to bring some home. And tomorrow, I'll go back for more!"

For the longest time, Elza just stood there shaking her head in disbelief. "What a boy!" she exclaimed under her breath. "Eight years old and already providing for his family!"

That night, as Elza was trying to sleep, she began thinking about her husband—knowing that Janek was right. If Wladek were here, he would have brought food home. After all, he had been doing it for years. She wondered: *"Where is he, Lord? Did he survive the bitter cold winter? Was he captured by the Russians and is now languishing in some POW camp—or is he being forced to work in a Siberian gulag? Or is he dead?* Somehow, that last option didn't resonate with Elza. Wladek was a survivor. God had protected him too many times during his bookselling days just to let him die in this senseless war. *"He must be alive,"* she thought, *"But where? And how will we find each other?"*

For Elza and the children, the fighting was over on March 5, 1945, when Belgard surrendered. But it would be another two months (May 8, 1945) before the Soviet/Polish troops captured Berlin and forced Germany into an unconditional surrender. Then, on August 15, 1945, after the bombing of Hiroshima and Nagasaki, Japan surrendered, and the Second World War, the deadliest war in human history, involving more than 100 million people from over thirty countries, was over.

Unfortunately, the end of the war was not the end of the persecution and hardship for the Polish people, who were now forced to live under communist control and helplessly watched as the Soviets closed Poland's borders. The war may have been over, but Elza and the children were not yet "free!"

Chapter 20

Belgard: Post-War Survival

(1945)

Celebrating in the Midst of Chaos

War has a way of stripping away the security, stability, and routines that make families healthy, happy, and productive. War changes priorities. Instead of planning fun activities or enjoying family and friends, war often forces families to live in survival mode with only the basic necessities.

While living in Plock, Elza and Wladek did everything possible to provide a good life for their children and to keep their daily routines stable. So, on most days, the children forgot they were living in the middle of a war-torn world.

But near the end of the war, everything fell apart. Their father was taken away to a forced labor camp. Stasia, their nanny for the last five years, was ripped out of their lives at the same time they lost their home, their orchard, and almost everything they owned, except the baby carriage and a few suitcases. Next, there was that freezing cattle car train ride trying to outrun the enemy. Every time they heard bombers overhead, their hearts raced. Then, in horror, they watched railroad officials throwing dead babies into the snowbanks.

Finally, there was the Soviet/Russian takeover in Belgard—and the threat of what those "cruel Russians" would do to Mama or the girls. *How does a single parent hold everything together through this scary time of uncertainty?*

Routines like morning and evening worship, singing, and Bible stories helped. But Elza also determined that her family would celebrate special occasions regardless of where they were. For example, when baby Jurek had his first birthday in Belgard on June 11, they dressed him up in shorts and a nice shirt, put him in the middle of the table covered with a white cloth, and played the game "What will you be?" by placing twelve items in a circle around him. If he reached for the pencil, he would be a teacher; if money, he would be a businessman, a Bible, a preacher, and so on.

For birthdays, Elza would make sure there was cake or some special "celebration" food, and the children would find or make special gifts and wrap them in pretty paper. For Mother's Day, the children made breakfast and gave their mama little presents, like pretty rocks or a handmade card. The gift might be that they were on their best behavior and promised not to argue, or maybe they would memorize something from the Bible and say, "We learned Psalm 100 just for you."

School was a stabilizing factor. As soon as Polish schools were opened in Belgard, Janek and his sisters attended. But after five years of German school, they didn't even know how to sign their names in Polish. For example, men would sign "Kuzma," unmarried daughters "Kuzmowa," and married women "Kuzmowna." Needless to say, it was very confusing!

Perhaps the most important thing that Elza gave the children during this unstable period of their lives was hope. "God brought us to Belgard safely. God can protect us."

And when they faced uncertainty, Elza would repeat Isaiah 41:10, *"Fear not, for I am with you; Be not dismayed, for I am your God. I will strengthen you, Yes, I will help you, I will uphold you with My righteous right hand."*

With all the changes that Elza and the children had endured, Elza was hoping that Belgard would be where they could settle down, find friends, make a living, and she would be able to raise her children as a single mother if that was God's will for them. Or God could bring Wladek back to his family. She had to keep reminding herself, "With God, all things are possible!"

Janek Works for the Polish Soldiers

Janek loved challenges. And making money was one of them. After finding the cigarettes in the pockets of dead soldiers and trading them for food, another business opportunity opened—the need for a translator! Why? Belgard had once been German territory, so there were lots of German frauleins but not many Polish girls. The Polish soldiers wanted to get better acquainted, but most didn't know enough German to communicate well, so they hired Janek until the friendship between the couple progressed to such a point that translation was no longer necessary. In return, Janek brought all kinds of food supplies home to his family.

The Unexpected Visitor

All was peaceful for a couple of weeks. With Janek bringing in food and actively trading with the Polish soldiers, they had all the provisions they needed. Elza's store was meeting people's needs and bringing in a decent income. The bodies of dead soldiers had been taken away, the streets were slowly being cleared of rubble, and damaged buildings were being repaired. And the new communist town government was being established. All in all, it seemed that life after the war would go on pretty much as it had before.

It wasn't long, however, until this peaceful existence was shattered by a sharp knock on the door.

While the Kuzmas were living in Plock, what they feared most was the Gestapo, the Nazis' secret police. Now that they were under communist rule, the fear was a visit from the Soviet secret police, called the NKVD (pronounced "In-Ka-Vo-Day"). It was well known that even though the war was over in Belgard, these communist officials were still arresting Polish people and sending them to forced labor in the gulags (Russian forced labor camps) in Siberia, as they had done during the war.

It was estimated that the Russians deported to the gulags or killed 1,700,000 *non-Jewish* Poles between the time they occupied Poland in 1939 and June 11, 1941, when Germany attacked Russia. Then, as the German army attacked, the fleeing NKVD had no time to evacuate the Polish political prisoners, so thousands were killed in cold blood, tortured, crucified on prison doors, or left to die. One particularly cold-blooded killing happened in 1940 when 20,000 Polish officers were taken prisoner by the Russians and killed individually by a bullet in the neck at Katyn and at two other localities. Those who died were mostly Polish reserve officers who were the professional elite of the country. It was no wonder that just the name NKVD brought terror to the Polish people living in Belgard in 1945.

When Elza answered the knock and slowly opened the door, she was startled to see two fully uniformed NKVD officials standing there in their khaki gray jackets and royal blue pants tucked into hightop black boots—and blue visor hats banded in red. It was a frightening sight! Trying to mask her shock, she asked in a trembling voice, "What can I do for you?"

Since the Russians could not speak much Polish or German, they made some flimsy excuse in Russian that made Elza think they were looking for someone. Then, by their gestures, they made it clear that they intended to enter her house. She stepped away from the door, and they nodded to her as they came in and began looking around. The children were standing nearby. They were so scared that they were tongue-tied and stiff as wooden soldiers.

The men spent a lot of time looking at the items in Elza's "store," things that she had purchased from German citizens leaving town but had not yet sold. Because she had worked at the railway station in Plock, she had guessed that the Nazis, during the occupation of Poland, were shipping the treasurers of Poland to Germany, things like expensive antiques, famous artwork, and gold and silver objects. Now, she presumed that these Russian officials were planning to do the same—ship expensive treasures to Russia—like some of the items she had for sale. She had even seen a Soviet train on a sidetrack that she presumed was being loaded with "Polish" possessions. This mid-day visit was likely just an excuse to scout out potential booty. After a few minutes, they walked back to the door, politely said "Spa-Sl-ba," (thank you), and left.

Two things really bothered Elza about their visit.

The first was the reason they gave for looking around. They weren't looking for someone; they were looking for things they could steal. What tipped her off was the way one of the officials looked at her wristwatch. It was an expensive gold watch that Wladek had given her as a wedding gift. It was the only thing that she had left to remind her of her husband and she highly treasured it. Although she could not speak Russian, the look in the man's eyes when he saw the wristwatch was one of greed and she instinctually knew he would come back for it. So, after he left, she removed it from her wrist and hid it, replacing it with another, less expensive watch with no sentimental value.

Late that night, Elza's premonition came true. The NKVD officer came back in plain clothes—alone. As soon as he was inside, he drew his revolver, pointed to Elza's arm, and demanded in broken Russian/Polish that Elza give him her watch.

She immediately took the less expensive watch off and handed it to him. He looked at it carefully, then violently began to shake his head. "Nyet, Nyet," he exclaimed in Russian. With gestures, he made it plain that he knew the watch she had given him was not the one he wanted. Once more, he demanded in Russian, "Eurie, Eurie," and pointed to his wrist to indicate that he wanted the watch that he had seen earlier that day.

She shrugged her shoulders as if to say, "I gave you the watch," but she knew what he wanted. She began to look through the jewelry she had on her shelves and found another watch and held it out to him. He took one look and knew it was also an inferior watch. His anger was increasing. When she once again shrugged her shoulders, he pushed her up against the wall, pointed his revolver at her head, and basically said in broken Polish, "I'll kill you if you don't give me the watch I want."

Once more, Elza hesitated. The watch was a treasure from her husband. She really didn't want to give it up, but her bluff was wearing thin.

Suddenly, Krysia, who was watching the entire interplay, began to cry, "Mama, if you have the watch, give it to him," she pleaded. "I don't want you to die."

That broke Elza's resistance. Just a few days before, she had come across the bodies of two older people on the street. "What happened?" she questioned the bystanders. Their answer was, "They wouldn't give the Russian soldiers what they demanded, so they shot them." Certainly, Krysia was right. Her life, which meant being there to care for and protect her children, was far more important than a watch. Reluctantly, she went to Jurek's buggy, where she had hidden the watch, took it out, and gave it to the man.

> *Her life, which meant being there to care for and protect her children, was far more important than a watch.*

Without another word, he examined the watch and, convinced it was the one he wanted, walked toward the door and slammed it behind him. After locking the door, Elza gathered her children and prayed, "Thank you, Lord, for protecting us from harm."

The Makeover of Danusia and Krysia

The second thing that disturbed Elza was the way the NKVD officers looked at Danusia—and, to a lesser extent—Krysia. Danusia had celebrated her fourteenth birthday. She was a very attractive teenager who looked older than she actually was. Krysia was only eleven. Although soon to be twelve, she still looked more like a kid than a young lady. Her mother was concerned for her daughters' safety—but she felt Danusia was in more imminent danger.

Because of the stories Elza had heard about the brutality of the Russian soldiers—especially concerning their treatment of women, she determined to immediately do something about the looks of her daughters so they wouldn't be so attractive.

She gave Danusia an extreme makeover, smearing mud on her cheeks and arms, mussing up her hair, and "fattening" her up by stuffing extra clothing under her skirt. No longer was she a sexually desirable teenager that would tempt wanton men. She did the same for Krysia—but to a lesser extent. She was also determined to keep the girls inside, away from the soldiers, while Janek was free to roam through the streets.

Over and over again, Elza warned her children that even though things seemed peaceful, they were living in enemy territory. She especially made it clear that the Russian soldiers were known to do terrible things to teenage girls and women, so it was just safer not to have anything to do with them. The girls had seen the results of war and were content to basically stay at home where they were safe.

Trouble with the Russian Soldiers

Everything changed when the Red Cross assigned two other families to live in the extra rooms of the Baron von Bernick's house where the Kuzmas were staying. The authorities made it clear that the newcomers had their own rooms but needed to use the Kuzma kitchen and laundry facilities, which consisted of a tub, laundry soap, and scrub brushes.

The first family didn't stay but a week or two. It was an inconvenience to have to live with strangers, but Elza knew times were difficult. She was thankful that others had gone out of their way for her family when she and the children had nowhere to go, so she tried her best to be kind and helpful.

The problems started when the second family moved in. The new family consisted of a middle aged mother with a young seventeen-year-old daughter who had a nine-month-old baby. When they arrived, the baby was very sick, which was evident from the yellow pus coming out of the baby's eyes, nose, ears, and pubic area.

Elza knew that the baby's infections were severe, but there was no medical person to consult as to how this infection should be treated. Instead, she naively thought that with good hygiene and the continuous washing of the baby's infected areas, the disease would eventually go away, so she and Krysia, who loved babies more than anything in the world, became the sick baby's primary caretakers. They washed away the smelly discharges, bathed the baby, and kept the little one as clean as possible, but nothing they did completely cleared up the sores. Instead, Elza and Krysia, and tiny baby Jurek, unknowingly became infected. What a shock it was almost a year later when they learned the germs were in their bodies—even though dormant. It was just one more curse of war!

In talking with the family who had the baby, Elza soon learned that during the war, the daughter had been raped by soldiers, had gotten pregnant, and had given birth to the baby with no medical treatment. The worst part was that after the war, this young, vulnerable Polish girl had been discovered by the Russian soldiers who also forced themselves on her. The mother and daughter had hoped that by moving, these unwanted visits would stop, but the men had somehow discovered that she was living in the von Bernick's home—and the visits continued.

Shortly after the family moved in, there were five bad-mannered Russian soldiers who started to make regular visits to the von Bernick house to see this family. At first, they just visited the young mother. Then after a few weeks, in addition to seeing her, they demanded that Elza feed them and wash their clothes. The men were filthy and covered with lice. And they had no manners. One even washed his hands in the toilet bowl. Obviously, he had never before seen an indoor bathroom!

At first, Elza complied with their demands because she was afraid that if she stood up to these intruders, they would attack her or abuse her children. When their demands increased, she finally decided, "Enough is enough!" She knew what these men were doing was frowned upon by the conquering army commanders, and it was time to report them. She asked directions to the Russian army camp that was just outside the city limits, grabbed the dirty shirts and underwear that the soldiers had left behind for her to wash, and bravely walked into the camp and demanded to see the general—or whoever was in charge. When he appeared, she presented him with the dirty clothing and reported that five of his soldiers were visiting her home and taking sexual advantage of a young teenage girl who lived there. In addition, they were demanding that Elza feed them and do their laundry. The officer listened respectfully and said he would handle the situation.

Elza left, thinking the matter had been solved. She didn't see the soldiers for a couple of days—and then they appeared, making the same requests. This time, she didn't wait. She steeled herself for a showdown with the Russian general. He was surprised this was still happening. He then remembered that five of his soldiers had mysteriously disappeared from the camp, and he realized that they were the troublemakers. This time, the scoundrels were caught and punished, and they never again visited the von Bernick house.

Shortly after this incident, the family, with the young mother and baby, moved out.

Attacked

Dealing with the threat that the Russian soldiers imposed upon the population of Belgard—especially the women—was more frightening to Elza than facing the whole Russian army in the war zone! Protecting her daughters from this unwanted element of society became a constant concern.

Things came to a head late one night in May. There was a banging on the door of their apartment. The children had been asleep in their rooms for hours, and Elza was the only one awake. Elza tried to ignore the knock, but the pounding became louder and more persistent. It was accompanied by drunken curses from the man on the other side of the door. The intruder obviously wanted in, and from the words that he uttered, it was clear that no locked door was going to keep him out for long.

Elza began frantically looking for some weapon she could use to protect herself and her family from this intruder, but she had nothing. *What was she to do?* Suddenly, she heard the lock on the door give way, and before she knew it, he was upon her. He appeared to be Russian, but he spoke understandable Polish, demanding that he would kill her if she didn't allow him to have her daughter. He reeked of alcohol and filth. Elza struggled, but it was no use. He was stocky and strong and the more she fought him, the rougher he got with her.

Once more, he demanded her daughter, but Elza refused to give him any information. Instead, she kept repeating, "She isn't here. She isn't here."

His eyes became wilder, and his fists pummeled her face and body, causing excruciating pain. Finally, she realized that she was no match for his strength. Instead of fighting him, she would try reasoning. "My daughter's not here. Use me." She knew a sexual assault could wound her precious, vulnerable daughter for a lifetime, but she was strong and understood the consequences of war. If she could just live to take care of her children, she could overcome whatever was forced upon her—even rape. So, to save Danusia and possibly Krysia, she offered herself. This was not what the man expected.

He hesitated for a moment and then threw Elza to the floor and fell on her. Elza shut her eyes and her mind to the assault and began to groan in pain. Just at that moment, Krysia, awakened by the noise, appeared at the door. Seeing the man on top of her mama, she began to frantically scream, "Get off! Get off my mama." She was just about to kick him and scratch his face with her fingernails when he suddenly jumped up and ran for the door.

Elza quickly got up off the floor and went over to Krysia, who was hysterically crying. She hugged her until her sobs subsided, and then she once more tucked her daughter into bed. After making sure that her other three children were safely sleeping, Elza returned to her own room and cried herself to sleep. The incident was never again talked about. It was just one of the horrors of war—and best forgotten. They never saw the man again.

The Search Warrant

After Belgard fell to the Russians, Elza had expected the von Bernick's to return to their home since they had left most of their belongings. Now, three months after the war was over in Belgard and a month after Germany unconditionally surrendered to the Allies, the von Bernicks still had not returned. Elza was beginning to doubt they would ever return.

As much as Elza appreciated living in the von Bernick's house, she was constantly worried about the safety of her daughters. The house was too close to the train station and the army camps—both the Polish Camp, which was just down the street, and the Russian Camp on the outskirts of town. Surely, there was a suitable house in a safer location for her family. She began to search. In June, she found just the right place at #1 Army Polskiej Street. Now again came the hard work of transporting all of their belongings, plus the inventory Elza had accumulated in her store. Hopefully, this would be their last move.

By the end of summer, Elza had a thriving enterprise going on in the new location. In fact, she had so many customers and so much merchandise that she dedicated one entire room to her business. The shelves were loaded with all types of bedding, towels, clothing, pots and pans, crystal, silver, and tablecloths. There was even a huge grandfather clock! In addition, there was clothing of every shape and size and personal items such as jewelry and watches.

But for the kids, the best discovery of all was that this house had an attic filled with children's toys. They immediately began playing with a miniature kitchenette set that had a tiny oven with little black bricks that looked like coal. "I wonder if it really works," Janek questioned.

Krysia replied, "Let's find out!" Somehow, the kids found paper and a match. But when they lit the match and touched the paper and bricks, flames burst out of the play oven and frightened the kids so badly that they grabbed it and threw it out the window. It landed on the street very close to someone walking on the sidewalk. The person stopped, picked up the smoking toy oven, and decided to investigate. He knocked on the front door and asked, "Do you realize that someone in your attic is playing with fire?" When Elza heard what the kids had done, she promptly gave both of them more than a good lecture—like three lashes with a leather belt! She ended with a sound warning that if it were ever to happen again, their punishment would be even worse!

Two weeks later, Krysia's curiosity about the oven returned, and once more, she and Janek tried to light the little bricks. Again, the oven caught on fire. Once more, the kids got lashed by the belt and then the stove was confiscated. Mama even took the little play pots and pans, so Krysia wouldn't be tempted to try cooking the third time.

After a few weeks, a number of new home supply businesses opened in Belgard. The new owners had a difficult time competing with Elza's established business. Because of her Polish/German background and her willingness to deal fairly with everyone, her reputation spread rapidly, and her clientele had grown. The shopkeepers become jealous and disgruntled. They complained, "Why should this woman be allowed to come into our town and take away what should be our business?"

> *They finally tried to force Elza out of town by drawing up a petition against her.*

Discontent grew. They finally tried to force Elza out of town by drawing up a petition against her. Elza was aware of the controversy, but she knew she had done nothing wrong and was performing an important service. Plus, she had friends in city hall, so she didn't take the threat seriously.

The disgruntled store owners, however, refused to give up. In November, they finally persuaded the authorities, no doubt by offering a "lapowki" (bribe), that Elza's business was a threat to their town. To gain the information the police needed to move forward with the request of the business owners, a couple of police officers showed up on Elza's doorstep with a search warrant. "Why?" she asked, concerned for her family's safety.

"It has been reported that you have stolen forty army coats, so we need to search your house."

Elza rolled her eyes and shook her head. *What a ridiculous accusation.* "Forty army coats?" she repeated with a question in her voice. "Now, why would I ever want forty army coats?"

Since she had nothing to hide, she invited the officers in and allowed them to search her inventory. It was obvious these men were spies for the business owners who were demanding that she leave town. Since the police didn't find any army coats, she hoped the charges would be dropped.

Forced Out

A few days later, Elza was shocked when the policemen handed her a written warrant that she and her family were to leave Belgard in a week or she would be arrested. She pled with the police, but to no avail.

In Elza's mind, the whole controversy was a frivolous suit by a few disgruntled storeowners, and it would eventually go away, so she made no preparations to leave other than instructing Janek to start moving some of the inventory to the homes of friends and to a church member's barn, which required a train trip!

At the end of the week, the authorities came back. This time, they demanded that she and her family leave in twenty-four hours and take the first train out of town. Furthermore, she and her children would only be allowed to take two suitcases each.

"Impossible!" Elza exclaimed when she was given the summons. It was time that she went personally, along with her children, down to city hall to plead her case. She was hoping that if the authorities saw her children, they would be more understanding and allow her a few more weeks to settle her affairs. But instead of being understanding, they were angry she had ignored their first summons.

After some pleading, they finally give Elza three more days. When she started to object to the ruling, the official got angry and started shouting, "It won't help to argue. You're lucky to get three days after all the problems you have caused. The conditions remain the same. You can only take two suitcases for each of you. You must get on the first train leaving Belgard. AND you are barred for a year from returning. If you disobey this ruling, you will be arrested!"

It was quite evident to Elza that not only did they want her out of town, but they also wanted to confiscate the things she had in her house since there was no possible way she could liquate everything in three days!

When Elza returned home, she was discouraged. "Don't worry, Mama," Janek tried to console her, "we can take a lot with us in our suitcases ... and I'll try to take as much as I can to our friend's barn. It will be OK."

"Where will we go?" Danusia asked.

"The authorities will force us to get on the first train out of town. It might be going west toward Germany, or it might go east toward Slawno. Pastor Fleming mentioned to me a few weeks ago that the Lehmans, our good friends from Leszno, now live in Slawno and attend church there, so they might be able to help us until we can get settled. It would be nice to live close to friends. The problem is I can't contact them to let them know we might be coming. I guess we'll just have to leave it in the hands of the Lord. Right now, we need to start packing."

As fast as the family could pack up their possessions, Janek raced across town to deliver the boxes to various people. Somehow, he even managed to move the grandfather clock to a friend's barn. And every day for three days, a city official showed up at their house and authoritatively inquired, "Pani Kuzma! Are you packing?"

Three days later, the police were at their door to escort them to the train station. They each carried a small bedroll and two suitcases, stuffed full, yet they were leaving far more behind than they were taking with them. The last of their belongings Elza had sold to a merchant for a small agreed upon fee. But the man wasn't expected to come with the money until later that day. Elza would just have to go to the train station with the police and once she had purchased the tickets, if they had enough time, come back to meet the appointment with the buyer.

Elza and the girls tried to be brave, but tears slid down their cheeks. They had thought that Belgard would be the answer to their prayers of where they should live. They had hoped they could stay in the school they had started attending just a few short months ago. They even imagined that their father would somehow find them in Belgard. Elza had worked long hours to get her business going. What a disappointment it was to leave it all behind, knowing that she would have to start all over in some unknown town.

"Lord, guide us. Here it is winter again, and we have no home. When we get to the station, please have just the right train there to take us to the place you have prepared. And wherever that is, Lord, help Wladek to be able to find us!"

The Train Station Thief

When the family reached the train station, there was nobody to wave goodbye to them and no anticipation of soon seeing family and friends at their destination—wherever that might be. The station was crowded. The family put all their suitcases next to Jurek's buggy, and Mama instructed the older kids to watch over their things while she checked the train schedule and got tickets. What a relief to see that the next train was leaving for Slawno in two hours. She quickly purchased the tickets and showed them to the police officers as evidence that her family was indeed leaving. As soon as the officers saw the tickets, they assumed their job was over and left the station.

Elza raced over to the kids with the good news. "The next train leaving the station is heading for Slawno! Plus, I have enough time to run back to the house and get the money owed us for the inventory I'm leaving behind." She then turned to Danusia, "I need to leave you with baby Jurek to guard the suitcases. I'll take Krysia and Janek with me so they won't cause you any trouble. We won't be gone long."

Shortly after Elza and the two children hurried away, bedlam broke out on the platform. A man whom Danusia recognized as someone who had come to their home to make some purchases came over to her and started talking. She smiled, and they visited for a few minutes. Then he got a strange look on his face and furtively looked around as if to make sure no one was listening. Danusia thought he was going to ask her a question and didn't want anyone to hear. Instead, he suddenly turned toward Danusia, pushed her down to the ground, grabbed the two suitcases she had been sitting on, and started running away. Danusia jumped up and ran after the man, screaming, "Stop that thief. Catch that man!"

In the confusion on the platform, the thief bumped into someone and dropped one of the suitcases. But, by the time people realized what was happening, the man had disappeared into the crowd with the other suitcase.

When Elza arrived back at the station with Krysia and Janek, they found Danusia sitting on their suitcases beside Jurek's baby carriage with tears running down her cheeks. "What happened?" Elza knelt beside her and held her cold hands. After the story tumbled out, Elza stood up and exclaimed, "Well, we now have one less suitcase to carry!" Shaking her head, she sighed, "What more can happen to us?" Then she said with a smile, "Kuck in die sonne!" (Cook in the Sun), which basically means, "Look for a brighter day!" and quickly added, "And we still have each other. Our God in heaven is still in control!"

How much disappointment can the human heart take? Going to Slawno meant moving closer to Russia. Was that really God's plan when her soul yearned for freedom? When Elza finally had her precious children safely seated around her on the eastbound train, she sighed heavily, and a tear slid down her cheek.

CHAPTER 21

Slawno: The House with the Red Gate
(1945-1946)

Elza had been so busy during the last few weeks trying to get out of Belgard with as many of her possessions as possible that she had hardly taken any time to sleep, let alone reflect on what the future held.

Now, as she watched the skyline of Belgard fade into the distance, she began to think about the political situation in post-war Poland. The freedoms she had enjoyed as a German in Nazi-dominated Plock, and even Belgard, were being stripped away. The communists were taking over and bringing with them an even more coercive regime. The NKVD (Russian secret police) was operating in force, controlling the Polish Provisional Government that was set up to govern Poland. They also controlled the Polish military, the ports, the press, and the radio.

Communists were forcing people into compliance, taking land away from farmers and giving it to government controlled growers. Even Polish grown cattle were being shipped to Russia! They were forcing factory closures, like the Gartz family's business in Rybnik, and taking valuable equipment to Russia. They even controlled successful small business entrepreneurs, like Elza's home business, by forcing her to leave town and then confiscating her belongings.

This was not the "freedom" for which the brave Polish soldiers had fought. This was not the "freedom" that Elza had so earnestly hoped her children could enjoy. And instinctively, she knew that if her husband were still alive—he would never live under communist Russian domination. *Never!* Yet every day, the communist Polish borders became stronger, making it more difficult for her to leave. *What would become of her family?*

She had so hoped that, as she listened secretly to the BBC programs on her small clandestine radio, the participants in the Yalta Conference (who met on February 4-11, 1945) would decree a free Poland. Then she shook her head and said under her breath, "Poland has surely been dealt a death blow by that ailing American President Roosevelt—who basically has given Poland to the communists. *Life is NOT fair!*"

Communism was a godless philosophy. If her husband were here, there is no way he could do what he loved most—sell religious books and share Bible truth. He had suffered enough persecution in his life by going against the beliefs of the established churches in Poland. Going against a godless government could be far worse.

Elza had tried so hard to escape from this oppressive net of control, and now she could feel it strangling her, and she seemed helpless to do anything to prevent it. *"Lord, help me,"* she whispered. *"What should I do?"*

Living with the Lehmans

As the train neared Slawno[28], Elza took the small piece of folded paper out of her coat pocket and looked at the address. She thought, *"This is the first time in this crazy journey crisscrossing Poland that I've actually known where I was going. I just hope the Lehmans are still at this address and that they have room for my homeless family. I'm sure they will be shocked to see us on their doorstep. If only I could have told them we were coming—but I didn't know until I arrived at the train station where the next train would be going!"*

Then her mind flitted to one of the last times she had been with the Lehman boys in Lezno days—about the time Krysia was born. They were so poor that people brushed them off, thinking they had little chance of making a mark in this world. It was Wladek who had encouraged the boys to use their God given musical skills to play and sing hymns at people's homes and then offer the people a chance to buy some religious magazines. The boys had been amazingly successful and had been able to support their mom and themselves. Now, they were grown with families of their own. And throughout the years, they had been faithful to God and loyal members of the Seventh-day Adventist Church. What a testimony to God's power to change lives and open doors of possibility. How Elza looked forward to seeing them again. *"Would they be home? Would they have room to keep her family for a short time? Would they even remember her?"*

Actually, Elza wasn't sure if the Lehmans still lived in Slawno! If not, she had no other options. "But," she sighed, "God will provide—He always does."

---

[28] pronounced "swavno"

Suddenly, the train lurched and then stopped. Elza could see that the train had not yet reached the station. It was late at night, snowing hard, and the temperature was below freezing. They waited for the train to move up to the station platform so they could disembark. But it didn't! With Jurek's baby carriage and each person having two suitcases (minus the one stolen at the Belgard Train Station) Elza's first thought was that there was no way her little family could carry their belongings over the snow covered tracks to the station. But they had no choice. Somehow, with the help of some kind passengers and a crew member, the whole family and all their belongings were finally safe in the ice cold station. Once again, Elza thought, *"Why is it we are always 'escaping' in the middle of the winter?"*

> **"Won't the thief be surprised when he opens the suitcase," Janek laughed.**

Finding a warm place to stay at this late hour was impossible, so with another sigh, Elza spread a quilt on the floor, wrapped the kids in blankets, and they finally fell asleep. As soon as it was morning, Elza found a horse drawn taxi, loaded their belongings, and asked the driver to take them to the address of what she hoped was the Lehmans' house.

What a grand reunion it was when the two Lehman brothers[29] who lived there recognized Elza, their former pastor's wife, and her children. "Come in, Come in! What a wonderful surprise. We were told by Pastor Fleming that you and your family were attending his church in Belgard. What are you doing here?"

Over a cup of hot herbal tea sweetened with milk and honey, Elza told them a thumbnail version of what brought them to Slawno.

"Of course, you can stay with us until you find a place," they graciously offered. We don't have much room because so many people are living with us right now, but there is a warm room downstairs where the coal burning furnace is. We don't have extra beds—or bedding—so the only place to sleep is on the floor. But at least it's warm."

It was not until the next day when the children needed clean underwear and began opening all their suitcases that they realized the suitcase the man at the Belgard train station had stolen contained the children's underwear!

---

[29] What Elza didn't know at the time was that the other two Lehman brothers were in Germany in the same displaced person's camp as her husband, Wladek.

"Won't the thief be surprised when he opens the suitcase," Janek laughed, "and finds kids' underwear?"

"That should teach him a lesson," Danusia added.

"Yes, but Mama makes us change our underwear each day. What are we going to do now? Krysia questioned.

"I guess we'll get to see how long she can stand us in dirty underwear!" and they all laughed.

Slawno had a population of around 4000, with only a few stores, so Elza couldn't just go buy what they needed. So when she washed, it was an all day affair, trying to keep the kids in bed until their underwear dried! After a few miserable wash days, Elza said in frustration, "We cannot continue to live like this. We have to find a home!" But if she thought Belgard was a difficult city in which to find proper housing, Slawno was much worse. Day after day, Elza spent time searching from early morning to sundown. And day after day, she would drag herself home to her anxiously waiting children who asked, "Mama, did you find a home for us?"

And she would reply, "Not yet! But God has a special place for us. It will be the best house ever! We just have to be patient." Then, sometimes, she would add, "God is never a day late. We may wish He had something for us right now—but we can learn patience by waiting for His perfect timetable."

As the days went by, Elza was beginning to disbelieve her own words. "Please, Lord, let it be today that I find a place!" Discouragement was about ready to destroy the sparkle in her eye and the excitement in her voice that the kids loved so much about their mama. It wasn't that she disliked living with the Lehman's—they had been wonderful hosts—but every family needs a place of their own where they can put down roots—and perhaps even run around without underwear!

The Dream

One night, about ten days after Elza had been searching, she took extra time to walk and talk with the Lord about His timetable in finding a place for them. She then fell asleep, exhausted and empty. That's when she experienced the most wonderful dream. She saw herself walking across a vacant lot filled with patches of snow and rubble and suddenly spotted a house with a vivid red gate. She knew immediately this was the home that God had chosen for her family.

As soon as the sun came up, she woke the kids, fed them some breakfast, and announced in her lilting voice, "Kids, today I'm going to find a house where we can live. It's a beautiful little house with a red gate."

"Mama, how do you know?"

"Last night, God showed it to me in a dream. You will love it. So pray for me today that I will look in just the right place. God says if we trust in Him and wait patiently, He will give us the desires of our hearts. Well, I believe today is the day for His promise to be fulfilled in our lives."

"I hope it has a dog," Janek added. "I've always wanted a dog."

"Well, I don't know about that," Mama laughed as she put on her boots and heavy coat, tied a scarf around her head, and slipped her fingers into her warm gloves...and was off with a song in her heart.

Elza was hopeful as she began looking. "First, I have to find that vacant lot. Then I'll see the house across the street. *Where could it be?*" She searched all day, not even stopping to eat the bun and apple she had brought along for her lunch. "*Where is that empty lot? Where is the house with the red gate?*"

It was just about sunset. Her steps were not as buoyant as they had been when she started at the beginning of the day. But she hadn't given up! AND SUDDENLY, THERE IT WAS! Across a vacant lot, she saw a brilliant red gate glowing in the light of the setting sun. With a burst of energy, she sprinted through the empty lot and ran to the door on the side of the house. She was out of breath when she knocked, desperately praying that someone would answer.

An older man and his wife cautiously opened the door, "May we help you?" they asked as they caught the passion and eagerness in Elza's eyes.

"Oh, thank you for answering. I have a strange request, but I believe God has led me to your home. Last night, as I was praying for a house where my children and I could live, God showed me in a dream a house that looked just like yours. I've been searching for it all day. My husband was in a German forced labor camp when the war ended, and I don't know whether he is dead or alive, so my four young children and I are all alone trying to find a home here in Slawno. With so many houses destroyed in the war, it's been difficult. Here's my question. Can we stay in your home? Perhaps you have a spare room we could rent?"

To another person, in another time or place, the question may have been absurd. But this kind "retired" couple wasn't surprised. "Well," they said, as they looked questioning at each other, "we had three sons who have been lost in the war. We have learned that two were killed, but the third one was a prisoner of war in Russian territory. We have been thinking that instead of staying here and waiting for him to come home, we should go and try to find him. The one thing that was holding us back is that we had no one to take care of our house and Hexa, our German shepherd dog." (Hexa means "witch" in German.)

The next day, Elza brought her children over to see the "House with the Red Gate." They were thrilled. When Janek saw Hexa, it was love at first sight, even though one of Hexa's legs had been injured during the war, and she ran around on three. God had more than answered his prayers—a house AND a dog!

In less than a day, the German couple packed up the things they wanted to take with them, stored the rest in a big storage room, and were ready to leave. They gave Elza a few instructions and the key and were off to find their boy while Elza and her excited children moved into a perfect home for them. Danusia and Krysia shared a big double bed in one room. Mama and baby Jurek had the second, while Janek was given the living room sofa—where he slept with Hexa.

Hexa turned out to be an incredible companion for Janek. They were inseparable. On Christmas day, Janek and Hexa were out exploring when Hexa began sniffing under a bush. She then stuck her head into the branches and pulled out a 100 zloty bill. Janek had never seen that much money and was ecstatic. On another day, they came across a large rifle that was wrapped in clothing. *Wow! Just the thing with which to play cops and robbers*, thought Janek. But he was street smart enough to know that a large rifle could be dangerous. He carefully picked it up and, with Hexa by his side, made his way to the local police station and turned it in. Those were just a few of the adventures Janek had with his amazing dog! And even though she had only three legs, it didn't stop her from climbing over six-foot-high fences!

Government Harassment Begins

"Look at all these shelves," Elza exclaimed to her children as she opened the door to a large storage room. "It's the ideal place to store all the clothing and housewares I bought from the Germans who were leaving Poland. The problem is, it's all back in Belgard, with various families or in that old barn."

"I can get the stuff." shouted Janek. "I know the way. It's easy by train." And the amazing thing is, the next day, without getting permission from his mother, Janek caught the train to Belgard, went to the barn, and brought back a few packed suitcases.

When Elza learned what Janek had done, she exclaimed, "No way! There is *no way* I am going to allow a nine-year-old boy to take the train all the way to Belgard for our things." But Elza couldn't go—not with the responsibility of caring for baby Jurek. Plus, the authorities of Belgard had told her that it would be illegal for her to return to the city for a year. If caught, she would have probably been imprisoned or sent to Siberia.

Janek made one more trip to Belgard by himself, and then Danusia volunteered to go with him. "I can help Janek. I'm not afraid."

After much deliberation, Elza weakly nodded her approval, and her two brave adventurers set out on what turned out to be a number of exciting "expeditions" to salvage at least a few of their belongings. The only trouble they had was when they tried to retrieve two of Elza's suitcases from one of their "friends" and the lady refused to give Elza's things to the children.

"Oh, well," Janek shrugged his shoulders. "We have plenty of other stuff. You can just keep those old suitcases," and the matter was forgotten. Apparently, the woman was not a "friend" after all, but rather a spy for the Russian authorities.

Janek and his sister got quite experienced in getting the things from the barn to the railroad station and then getting help to load the items onto the train. Janek even figured out how to get the big grandfather clock to the station and talked a railroad official into helping him load it! It was amazing that no one ever asked the children for tickets.

Elza had provided the kids with enough coins for their fare, but Janek and Danusia decided that because they were young, they probably didn't need to pay. To avoid any encounter with the train officials, they blended in by choosing to sit by children from other families. Or they visited the bathroom. Or they just conveniently fell asleep. Elza had no idea what was going on.

After filling the shelves in the storage room, Elza once more started her business, and within days, she was buying and selling just as she had done in Belgard. She got new clients by going out on the street and telling others. Quickly, her inventory increased, and so did her customers.

Then, just like in Belgard, the government officials started to harass her.

Knock, Knock.

"Yes," Elza said in a kind voice when she came to the door and saw the Russian policemen. "What can I do for you?"

"We have had a report that you have 100 bicycles stored in this house, and we need to search."

"Come right in," Elza said with a smile. "In the last town, I was accused of stealing forty army coats. This time, a hundred bicycles! And where do you think I'm going to keep a hundred bicycles?" She had all her paperwork from Plock in order so she could prove to the authorities that she was a Polish citizen—and not German. (All the Germans were being sent back to Germany!) But the Russian police, the NKVD, were more interested in the little radio they found in Elza's bedroom than what was on her shelves.

"We heard you have been listening to the BBC news on your radio."

"Is that so?" Elza replied. "The radio doesn't work very well. Here, try it and see what you can get."

The truth was that Elza loved listening at night to BBC (British Broadcasting Corporation), the public news station, using a secret antenna she had hooked up. But after listening to the news, she detached the antenna which then made the reception lousy. The police turned the dial, trying to find BBC, but only got static and buzzing sounds. They soon gave up.

Once they left, she shook her head and sighed, "The Polish people fought so hard for freedom—and now all we get is this senseless interrogation about army coats, bicycles, and the BBC! If only we could have a democratic government that would allow us to make our own choices rather than having everything controlled by the authorities. *Maybe Wladek was right when he said he would never live under a communist government!*"

In the next few months, the authorities came three more times to inspect her possessions. Most of the time, their excuse was that they were looking for someone. Elza always invited them in and treated them with respect, regardless of how absurd their accusations were. And she noticed they always spent a lot of time looking at all the items she had for sale. Once more, just like in Belgard, she felt threatened by the officials' greed.

As it turned out, the Kuzma family was never able to retrieve all their belongings that they had left behind in the Belgard barn—or those items Elza had left with her "friends." It was time to forget the past and move on. But no one ever expected the way events actually unfolded in that little house with the red gate.

Elza and her little family were happy in Slawno. They had a wonderful church family, and Elza's business was doing well. She knew that if the authorities just left her alone, she could easily support her children until they were grown and would leave her nest. Also, because all German families had been forced to leave town, she was quite sure the couple who "owned" the house with the red gate would never be back. So, she began to put down roots. The older children started school, made friends, and began to think of Slawno as their permanent home. It was good to at last feel settled and not worry about being forced to leave.

In her heart, Elza knew her husband was probably alive, but the more weeks that went by without any word, the more she began to count her blessings and accept her current situation. It was peaceful not to have to deal with the tension and criticism that had grown to be a part of her relationship with Wladek. The children were happy, and they seldom talked about their father. They had settled into a healthy routine. They would survive. She had good memories of their early years together. But she knew she could raise her children by herself if that was God's plan.

Chapter 22

The News That Changed Everything
(1946)

On Sabbaths, the Adventist believers in Slawno met at the Lehmans' home for worship. Just after welcoming the 1946 New Year, the Kuzmas were greeted with incredible news. Elder Smyk, who was helping to shepherd their little home church, had attended the year end meetings in Warsaw, where an announcement was made that someone had heard on a Red Cross broadcast that Wladek Kuzma was alive in a displaced person's camp in Germany and was looking for his family. "If anyone knows where Elza and the children are now, please contact Red Cross Station 563 for more information."

At the same time, Wladek had written to the Warsaw Adventist Church asking the same question. Hearing the announcement, Elder Smyk spoke up, "Yes, yes! Elza and the children are alive. They're attending my church in Slawno." The letter was quickly handed to Elder Smyk. The first thing he did when arriving back at church in Slawno was to hand the precious letter to Elza.

It had been a year and a half since Elza had any word about Wladek. At first, she had prayed earnestly for this moment, hoping he was alive, but now that the war was over and she had been able to safely shepherd her children through the hostilities on her own and was making plenty of money to take care of the children, she had mixed feelings. Her head pounded with unanswered questions. It had been almost fifteen years since her husband had deceived her into marrying him. She had forgiven him, but every time he accused her of unfaithfulness or demeaned her, the hurt and heartache that his deception had caused her (knowing that he had stolen her one chance of having a passionate love relationship) simmered to the surface. It had been over a year since she had even thought about his lie. Would his presence in her life once again flood her life with junk from the past?

But even if she didn't harbor repressed anger, she knew what life was like with Wladek and she hated to go back to the conflict that had become a part of their relationship. She had to admit, she enjoyed not having to worry about getting along with someone who could be difficult!

Yet, for the sake of her children, being a complete family was important. They adored their father and needed him.

So many things had happened to both of them during the time that they had been separated. They may not have much in common anymore. She had taken a dominant leadership role with her children. She had so many questions:

- *Could she step back into a more traditional submissive role that was expected of Christian European wives, even though, at times, she didn't agree with her husband?*
- *Did they have enough love left to nurture each other, regardless of what may have happened to them?*
- *Would they be able to overlook the negatives, or would suspicion and accusations tear them apart? Was forgiveness and commitment still possible?*
- *Would Wladek try to meet her emotional needs, or would he accuse her of unfaithfulness—as he had done when he was jealous of the attention she received from other men?*
- *What about the attempted rape? Would her husband accept her unconditionally or blame her for being willing to compromise herself in order to save her children?*

In addition, *what about her appearance?* Since baby Jurek had been born, she had never been able to get back down to her previous weight—probably because she was still nursing her almost-two-year-old. But more than that, going through that awful post-war trauma when the Russians invaded—she had intentionally kept herself "fat" because it was the only way she knew to be protected from rape and sexual harassment. Wladek always admired her figure. *Would he accept the way she looked now? What was to happen to them?* "Oh Lord," she silently cried, "*What will become of us?*"

With a shaking hand, she reached for the letter that contained her husband's contact information. She closed her eyes and sighed, then put a smile on her face for the sake of her children and the watching church members.

There was rejoicing that day among the Slawno church members. They were happy for Elza and the children. So many people taken into forced labor hadn't returned. Wladek was one of the lucky ones. He was alive! It was a miracle!

That night, Elza wrote a letter to the address she had been given, stating that she and the children were alive. She then provided the address of their home in Slawno. After posting the letter, the wait began with the worry and the questions!

The Dream of the White Geese

To follow the story, it's important to go back to Wentorf, Germany, to the Wentorf Displaced Persons Camp, where Wladek was living, praying, and frantically searching for his family through whatever means possible. He had recently contacted the International Red Cross, which was the listing agency for missing persons. In radio broadcasts, they read off lists of names of people searching for their families throughout Germany and Eastern Europe. Hopefully, someone would hear his name and know where Elza and the children were living—if indeed they were alive. In addition, he had written to the Warsaw Seventh-day Adventist Church. Perhaps someone there would know where they were.

It was difficult to wait. Most of his Adventist friends and fellow pastors, who were also in the displaced person's camp, had already found their families. Days and weeks went by, and he heard nothing. It was easy to get discouraged and he began to think that he would never again see his family.

Then, one night, he had a dream that he clearly remembered when he awoke. He was acquainted with these kinds of dreams. It was like the dream he had about the book salesman who had Bibles and the one about Christ handing him pieces of bread and saying, "Feed my people," which was the dream where he felt Christ was calling him to be a religious bookseller. *But what did this new dream mean?*

The next morning, when Wladek saw Pastor Hinc and a couple of the other pastor friends in camp, he told them, "Last night I had a strange dream. I saw a beautiful, tall, evergreen tree. There were five white geese flying around the tree and then they all lit on the branches of the tree. What do you think it means?"

After some discussion, the consensus was, "You will soon hear that your wife and four children are alive," Hope was renewed in his heart when he heard their prediction. And sure enough, when the mail was delivered there was the letter from Elza giving him the address of her home in Slawno—the house with the red gate.

Wladek's Letter Arrives

With a trembling hand, Wladek pulled out a piece of paper, an envelope, and a pen. He first addressed the envelope. "Pani Elza Kuzma...." And then wrote this short note:

"I just received your letter. What good news that you and the children are all alive. I have been praying daily for you. I am safe in the Wentorf Displaced Person's Camp in Germany. I have a dream that we can all go to the United States. Please find a way to come to Wentorf. Tell the children I love them. Your husband, Wladek."

After posting the letter, the wait began.

When Elza read Wladek's letter, she shook her head. It was an emotional relief to know her husband was alive, but his request was unreasonable. How was it possible for her and the children to escape from communist Poland now that the borders were closed with tall barbed wire fences and ferocious German shepherd dogs on patrol? How could she possibly get her family to Wentorf, Germany, when it was illegal to do so?

> *How was it possible for her and the children to escape from communist Poland now that the borders were closed?*

She wrote back: "Do you have a job? And what kind of a home do you have for us?"

He responded: "I live in a room in a displaced person's camp. I don't have a job."

She wrote back: "Why should we come to Germany? We have a lovely home here in Slawno, and I have started a good business. I'm making lots of money buying and selling clothing, home furnishings, and other needed items. You come here!"

He responded: "I will not live in a communist controlled country. You come here so we can all go to America."

She wrote back: "That's impossible. You don't have any money. I'm making lots of money. You come here."

He responded: "I will not give up my dream for freedom. Displaced persons are being shipped out weekly to places like the USA, Australia, and South America."

She wrote back: "Get a job!"

Obviously, all this writing back and forth was not accomplishing anything. Elza was becoming more and more determined to stay in Slawno where she was safe, had plenty of money, enjoyed a good church family, and had a comfortable home. In addition, the children had started school. And she didn't have to deal with an opinionated husband!

By now, she had lived for almost two years without Wladek. She was beginning to doubt whether or not it was a good idea to pursue the idea of reuniting the family. If their apparent conflicts were escalating through correspondence, what would it be like if they were actually together? Plus, it was illegal to cross the border. And if she and the children got caught trying to do so, it was punishable by imprisonment, a lifetime in Siberia, or death! The risk was just too high!

Wladek was also realizing their letter writing wasn't working. In counseling with his friends in camp, he learned that he was not the only husband who was having difficulty getting his wife and family into Germany. That's when the idea came to hire someone who had successfully escaped through the closed border between Poland and Germany. Perhaps someone with experience could go back to Poland and bring their families out.

"I know just the person who could do this," one of Wladek's friends suggested. "Her name is Mrs. Gatzki."

"Of course," Wladek exclaimed. "My family actually knows her. I remember now. She has been looking for her husband. At first, she heard he was in Poland, so she went back there to search. When she couldn't find him, she escaped back over the border in a wagon with a false bottom. They jabbed pitchforks down into the hay covered wagon. The spikes hit the false bottom, and thinking the wagon was empty, the people underneath were able to get across the "closed" border into Germany. I think she has been talking about taking another trip back into Poland to once again search for her missing husband."

And so the plan was developed. Wladek and Mr. Guzi, who was a very successful judge and businessman in his former life, each promised to pay Mrs. Gatzki 500 marks if she could successfully get their families across the border. Wladek even offered to look after Mrs. Gatzki's three children while she was away.

Word spread, and a man from Krakow also asked Mrs. Gatzki to bring back his family. Mrs. Gatzki decided to leave as soon as possible since every day they waited it became more difficult to escape from communist Poland.

The Knock on the Window

Early one Sunday morning in May 1946, Janek heard someone knocking on the window pane. "Who could it be at this time of the morning?" He and his sister pulled back the curtain, and Danusia recognized Mrs. Gatzki, an old family friend from Plock. When Elza opened the door, and Mrs. Gatzki saw the children, she announced, "Your father has sent me to bring your family to where he is in Germany so you can all go together to the United States of America."

Was it true? they wondered, *Or could the police be trying to trick us to get some private information to use against us?*

Mrs. Gatzki then pulled her knapsack off her back and opened it. "Here are some yummy things I have brought for you from America to show you what a wonderful place it is." First, she opened a can of Planter's Peanuts. The children had never in their lives eaten a peanut. They each hesitantly took one from the tin, put it in their mouths, and began to chew. "Wow! It tastes good." Then, they took several more.

The next treasure Mrs. Gatzki pulled out was a package of soda crackers. Once again, the kids had never eaten soda crackers, and they thought they tasted like manna from heaven!

"These are just some of the wonderful things you can have when you go to the United States," she teased. Well, by then, the kids were ready to leave behind their comfortable Slawno house (including Hexa) and head off on the adventure of their lives, escaping from Poland, finding their father, and going to America.

Elza, however, was more practical. It would take more than peanuts and soda crackers to convince her that escaping from communist Poland with four little children was a good idea. She and Mrs. Gatzki talked for quite some time. Elza honestly asked, "Why should I risk my life and the children's lives to go back to live with someone who is hard to get along with when the kids and I are doing just fine here? He doesn't even have a job! Wladek can easily cross the border and return to Poland. And I'm not even sure I still love him. All we seem to do is argue!"

Mrs. Gatzki was a woman on a mission. "I'm sure he loves you very much," she countered, "or he wouldn't have paid me to bring you back." Then she explained how she had been asked by Wladek and Mr. Guzi to bring both of their families out of Poland. Her plan was to visit Mrs. Guzi and her two sons, who were similar in age to Janek. She also had a family from the Krakow area that she wanted to join their group. After all of the families were ready, she would set a date; hopefully, in a few weeks, they would all meet together in the border town of Szezecin, and from there, they would finalize the plan of how they would get across the border.

Elza was not easily persuaded. "It just doesn't make sense when crossing the border is illegal—and dangerous!" To get her point across, Elza raised her voice to emphasize her negative feelings about the whole idea. The children couldn't help listening.

That's when Mrs. Gatzki started talking about freedom, what it meant to be free to make choices without government intervention, and what opportunities were possible when people were free to make decisions without being controlled by a godless state. She brought up how controlling the Nazi German government had been, and now Soviet Communism was even worse. If Elza chose to stay in Poland, what hope did she have that her children would have educational opportunities and be free to choose any occupation they wanted or that they would be granted religious freedom? All of that could be denied them. And then Mrs. Gatzki asked, "Elza, is that what you really want for your children? Do this for them and the opportunities that America will give to them. Don't do it for yourself—or even for your husband. God has gifted your children. Anything is possible in the USA, but not under communism! We don't know if this escape plan will be successful. But you owe it to your children to risk everything for freedom. Your husband has a dream to go to America where his family will be free. Don't rob him of that!"

After Mrs. Gatzki left, Elza sat down with a sigh. She couldn't believe what had just happened. In the end, she had agreed to attempt an escape across the border with her four children! If she were alone, she would have put up with communist control as long as she could make a decent living and she wasn't being harassed. But the possibility of freedom and having young children who needed a father in their lives changed everything. They would never forgive her if she selfishly stayed in a comfortable and safe place and missed this opportunity to reunite the family. She prayed, had morning worship with the children, and then started to make a list of all the things she needed to do in the next few weeks.

First on the list was to try and sell as much as possible. It would mean taking a cut in the prices she had been asking, but she reasoned some money was better than none. She hated to leave her things again—as she had done when forced to leave Plock and then again when forced to leave Belgard. Now, once again, she was planning to leave her comfort zone and all her earthly possessions that she couldn't carry across the border. *How much more would God ask of her?*

Danusia's Baptism

Danusia was excited when she learned about the plan for escaping, until she heard the proposed time schedule: *as soon as possible!* She was fourteen and taking Bible studies from Elder Zielinski, the district pastor, and she was looking forward to being baptized in July or August along with six of her girlfriends. "I won't go until I'm baptized," Danusia emphatically stated to her mother. "What if I die and haven't been baptized? I will never go to heaven!"

Her mother tried to reason with her that although baptism was an important step in one's growing relationship with Jesus, that accepting Jesus into your life was the prerequisite for salvation—not baptism. Baptism was just a public symbol of your commitment.

Nothing, however, would convince Danusia to leave Slawno without first being baptized. "We have to get ahold of Elder Zielinski and see what he can do for me," she asserted. It was still May, so the rivers and lakes were freezing cold, and swimming pools were far too public because it was now illegal to participate in religious activities such as baptisms in communist Poland. Even so Elza contacted Elder Zielinski, and they quickly made plans for the secret event.

Danusia recalls that her baptismal day was one of the most memorable experiences in her life. Here's how she described it. "Early one Sabbath morning, I left my house at 5:30 in the morning with a towel and my mother. I wish Krysia and Janek could have come, but we had to keep it a secret, so the fewer people there were, the better. We walked a long way—probably two or three miles. We crossed a big meadow and then saw trees further on where there was a stream. It was so special. The sun was rising, the birds were singing, and the water was icy! All seven of us were dressed in white robes. It was so beautiful! So quiet! So touching! Some older women sang as my friends and I dunked in that freezing cold stream. It was an amazing experience, which I have recounted many times. After my baptism, we went home and had breakfast. All day, we celebrated at our secret church meeting in the Lehmans' living room." Elder Zielinski gave a beautiful sermon, but what made the day even more special was that we also celebrated communion—foot washing and the Lord's Supper."

God Chooses the Right Leader

God knew what He was doing when He guided Wladek to escape from the Nazi German Army and make his way *alone* across the Polish/German border in the middle of one of the worst winters of the century. Wladek's burning desire for freedom would keep him alive and moving toward the goal. His call to freedom was stronger than the hunger and freezing cold he endured that would have made a lesser man surrender to the physical exertion, the deprivation, and the blizzard conditions and freeze to death. Wladek may not have been a physically strong giant, but he was a spiritually strong giant, and God rewarded his faith and guided him over the frozen tundra until he reached the safety of the displaced person's camp in Wentorf, Germany. It was a treacherous journey that might have discouraged or killed men with less stamina. *What kept him going?* His determination, courage, and passionate desire for freedom drove him to risk everything!

God also knew that Wladek's Polish nationality would be a handicap when it came to his wife and children escaping from communist Poland. Not only did he not have a German heritage, but he also lacked the cunning, creativity, and political know how necessary for the task.

God, however, knew the "right" person for the job. He knew exactly what it would take to bring four young children out from the clutches of communism and navigate them through the maze of communist Russian control and German politics to get those children safely to their father. Just the thought of what was required to mastermind this trip was something that the Kuzma kids doubted their father would have been able to accomplish. Of course, any one of them would admit that "anything is possible with God" (see Mark 10:27), but in their hearts, they knew God did the right thing by putting their mother in charge of this part of their journey.

The children loved their father. They knew he was an amazing provider. They knew he had a super-sized faith, but he was not street smart. He was never interested in politics and never seemed to know how to get what he wanted in a secular world controlled by devious dictators.

Here's how Danusia explained this difference in her parents: "If we as a family were going to navigate through hell—which basically we were going to have to do if we were to make a successful escape from communist Poland, then God gave us the very best leader.

"When we were living under Nazi domination, and my mother wasn't available, I'll admit, I was sometimes afraid because I didn't know if Tata would know how to outsmart the enemy. But all of us kids knew we could trust Mama to always do what was best.

"When the folks were together, I never worried. I trusted that Mama would take control when necessary and tell our father what he should do to get the response we needed. Mama may not have had much formal schooling—only three years, but she was a quick learner and a savvy person. She had what we called 'Spritna!' I never doubted that Mama could do anything. First of all, I knew God led her (just as He led my father) but she was also clever, quick-witted, and knew how things worked in a world controlled by dictators. With her expertise and cunning, along with God's guidance, I knew I was on a winning team."

Preparing for Escape

A few days later, Elza received word from Mrs. Gatzki that she had arranged with the other families to meet in three weeks at the Szczecin[30] train station on the Polish/German border. She told Elza that she was to get her family's papers in order, dispose of their money because it was illegal to take zlotys across the border, and get approval from the government to move from her current location and settle in Szczecin.

The next few days were pretty intense emotionally. Elza warned her children, "Just go on acting as if we were going to stay here forever because we can't take a chance that one of our neighbors might catch on to what we're planning and turn us in." So, the older kids continued going to school. Elza dropped the prices on the items she was selling and told her clients to spread the word that she was having a big sale because she had too much inventory and needed to get rid of as much as possible. Once again, Elza depended on her older daughter to help her take care of baby Jurek while she was busy. At one point, Danusia rebelled and refused to pick him up or even change his diaper. When she was again asked to help, she turned to her younger sister and demanded, "Krysia, you take care of him. After all, you're the one who wanted him." The pressure of too much to do in too little time was getting to the whole family!

One day, when the older children were in school, Elza took baby Jurek and caught the train to Lodz (her birthplace), where she needed to get official Polish passports and other papers for the family. All this she explained under the guise of trying to get her life reorganized after the war. But actually, she would need those papers to get into a displaced person's camp once they escaped over the border.

Next, Elza had to pack. They still had baby Jurek's buggy, with slots in the mattress where important papers and money could be hidden. Elza knew it was illegal to take money out of Poland, but at the same time she had quite an impressive amount and didn't want to travel without some cash, just in case they might need it for emergencies. So into the mattress it went along with the Polish papers.

One of the final things Elza had to do was go to the city hall in Slawno and get permission from the police to move to Szczecin. They easily

---

[30] pronounced "shteh-cheen"

approved her application. They were actually happy to see her go so they wouldn't have to be responsible for monitoring her business.

Finally, Danusia, Krysia and Janek each packed two suitcases with their clothing and other belongings. Then, before she could catch her breath, Elza was once again standing on the railroad platform with baby Jurek in his buggy. He was now just six weeks shy of being two years old. And her three older children were each holding on to their suitcases, waiting for the train to take them to the border town of Szczecin—and hopefully freedom!

Elza finally settled herself and her children in the coach section of the train and presented her tickets to the conductor. Then she sighed an exhausted sigh and thought, *"What am I doing? I must be crazy. I hear every day of people trying to escape and getting caught and sent to Siberia, or almost getting over the fence and being killed by the communist guards or mauled by the specially trained guard dogs. What makes me think there is even a slight possibility that three kids and a woman with a toddler in a baby buggy can somehow get across the border?"*

Mrs. Gatzki had explained her plan to Elza. "We'll hire a hay wagon with a false bottom and hide underneath."

No way, thought Elza, *that might work for adults who don't have hay fever, but children? How am I going to explain to little Jurek that he can't cry? Or what if Janek does something to tease his sisters, and they retaliate without thinking? We'll all get caught. There has to be a better way!*

At last, Elza closed her eyes in prayer, "Help us, God!" she said as her thoughts faded away in sleep.

Chapter 23

Szczecin: Escape from Poland
(1946)

It was early June, 1946. Jurek was almost two, Janek was ten, Krysia was a few weeks shy of twelve, and Danusia was fourteen. Now, they were planning the biggest gamble of their lives. To escape from the tyranny of communist Poland and make their way to their father in a displaced person's camp in Germany, and then hopefully go on to America, the "land of the free!"

The instructions given to Elza by Mrs. Gatzki were that a group of three families would all meet on the same day at the train station in Szczecin on the Polish/German border. Mrs. Gatzki got there first and began exploring options. Elza had heard about a camp near the Szczecin train station for German citizens who wanted to go back to Germany, but when she and her children arrived, she was afraid to ask anyone about it for fear they would guess what she wanted to do. So, instead, she went with Mrs. Gatzki to scout out the town, discuss options, and listen for any information that might be helpful in making their plans for escape while they waited for the other families to arrive.

When Elza and Mrs. Gatzki returned to the train station, the Guzi family and the family from Krakow had arrived. Without warning, a railroad official came up to Elza and said secretively, "I know what you are planning, and I can help you."

"What are you talking about?" Elza countered. "I'm meeting my friends before going into town to find a place to stay."

"Don't tell me that! I know you are trying to escape across the border and I can help you. It will be dark soon, and you have a lot of children with you. I have a safe place for you to stay tonight. Come with me!"

Immediately, Elza feared she was being trapped and she tried desperately to avoid the man. "No!" she said, "I am waiting for someone!"

"Don't lie to me!" the man reprimanded Elza. "Come with me!" He wouldn't take no for an answer. Finally he grabbed Jurek's buggy and started to walk away with it. Janek was holding on to one side and Krysia the other. Danusia was in the middle, desperately trying to hold on to the handle, but eventually lost the tug of war. The man started pushing the buggy with Jurek in it away from the railway station. Elza screamed. "Wait!" She called the others, "Grab your suitcases and follow us!"

That's exactly what the man wanted. In just seconds, he had turned the entire situation around and was now in command of four women, six children, and two young men from Krakow.

The railroad official looked like a mother duck leading "his" ducklings as they walked to a long barrack-like apartment building a few blocks away. He opened the door, and they saw that the room was filled with beds. As Janek crawled into bed that night, he noticed an ax under his bed. Curious, he looked under the next bed and the next, and there was an ax under every bed!

Should they trust this man? The problem was—they didn't have a choice!

Becoming German

They stayed in the apartment for a week, planning what they should do next. Mrs. Gatzki was still pushing them to accept her plan of escaping in a false bottom wagon. Elza knew there had to be a better way. During the Nazi occupation, she had five years of experience working with the Germans—and pretending to be a German citizen. As cruel as they were to the Poles and the Jews, they had always taken care of their own people. They had provided transportation out of Plock when the Russian invasion was imminent—even though it was by cattle car. And she had seen how the German government had provided transportation back to Germany for the German families who were being forced out of Polish towns like Belgard and Slawno. She knew if she could somehow persuade the authorities that she was German—she might be able to get her family across the border "legally." Her ethnic background was German, but she had been born in Poland and married a Polish man. However she still spoke perfect German! And because the kids had attended German schools for almost five years, their German was fairly good—unless they got angry and found it was easier to argue in Polish! *This scheme just might work!*

But what about the other families? Mrs. Guzi couldn't speak a word of German. Her boys knew a little, having lived under German occupation, but they didn't know enough to really communicate. The other family was about the same.

"What if we could get German papers for everyone in our group?" Elza asked. "If we can prove we are German, they are offering free transportation for citizens to return home."

"No way!" Mrs. Gatzki exclaimed. "Mrs. Guzi can't speak German. She'd have to pretend to be deaf and dumb!"

"I can do that!" offered Mrs. Guzi. "I'll do anything to get back to my husband."

"I suppose it could work," Mrs. Gatzki hesitantly admitted. "But as for myself, I have seen what the Gestapo does to people who try to beat the system. I personally don't want to have anything to do with this scheme! I'd probably get caught and sent to Siberia!"

"Well," Elza argued. "What other option is there?"

And at this point, everyone merely shrugged their shoulders.

"Okay then," Elza replied, "I think we have our answer. I'll have to find out what Germans have to do to get citizenship papers when their documents have been lost in the war."

Once again, the railroad official turned out to be helpful and told Elza exactly what to do. Then he added, "There are hundreds of people waiting in line for papers. You might want to consider offering a *lapowka* (bribe) in order to speed up the process."

Elza knew what he was saying was true. She had seen it happen numerous times at the Plock train station when the authorities dragged their feet.

She also knew she only had one opportunity to make an appeal for German papers. Now she understood why she had felt so impressed to stuff Jurek's buggy mattress with all that paper money. She took out a handful, rolled each bill like a cigarette, and filled a silver cigarette case with a thousand zlotys.

Next, she gathered all the necessary information from each person who needed German papers. Then, she went to the office of the German Citizens Processing Camp. The man at the front window asked in German, "May I help you?"

"Yes," Elza replied in perfect German. "My four children and I have lost our German papers in the war. My husband was in the German army and is now in Germany. We would like to be reunited with him, but we need new German papers. I have prepared all the information you need to know about our family. And by the way, we have two other families who also need papers."

She then handed the man an organized stack of papers with all the information the authorities would need to make new German papers for everyone. Finally she placed the silver cigarette case on the very top.

Elza guessed by the look on his face that he was just about to say, "I'm sorry your request is impossible," when he picked up the cigarette case and opened it, hesitated, and for a moment didn't say anything. Finally, he continued, "Well, this is a major request, but it just might be possible for me to get those papers for you. Come back in three days."

Elza smiled a confident smile as she thanked the man. Then turned and left.

Three days later, she went back and there was a perfect set of German papers for each person in the group, with instructions to present the papers in the next day or so to the officials at the entrance to the German processing camp. If you pass the inspection, you will be admitted to the camp. You will stay there until a train is ready to depart for Germany. One usually leaves every two or three weeks."

Elza was praising God for her good fortune. It was a miracle. Now, the only problem was getting Mrs. Guzi and her sons, with their limited knowledge of German, into the camp and making sure her own children remembered that their last name was now the German name Kutzman and not the Polish name Kuzma!

> ***Her children must remember their last name was now the German name Kutzman and not the Polish name Kuzma!***

She then started repacking in hopes that their family would pass the inspection and be granted permission to enter the processing camp—and Mrs. Guzi began pretending she couldn't hear or speak.

Next, Elza took out all the Polish papers that she had brought with her: her passport, her marriage certificate, each person's birth certificate, and the children's school papers. She couldn't destroy these papers because they would be needed to prove that she and the children were actually Polish so once they were in Germany, they could get into the displaced person's camp in Wentorf.

Where could she hide her Polish papers? Finally, she decided—in Janek's school books. In order to protect the covers of the books, she had previously taped heavy paper covers over each book's hardcover. Now she took a sharp knife and carefully removed the tape, slipped an important Polish paper behind each cover, and then re-taped the covers so no one would suspect anything was underneath. Then she put the school books back into Janek's black leather satchel (backpack), which he carried to school each day.

Next, *where should she hide the money?* Although she knew it was illegal to take any Polish money into the German processing camp, she reasoned that she might need it—if for nothing else as another "incentive" sometime in the future. Finally, she decided the camp officials might not search the children as carefully as they would an adult. Janek had a uniform-type outfit with lots of pockets. She decided to have him wear this uniform, fill his pockets with money, and then put another outfit over the top. No one would ever guess he was wearing two sets of clothing. Then she filled his pockets with coins and told him, "When they ask, 'Do you have any money?' simply empty the coins from your pockets."

It worked! Janek walked through the gates into the German processing center loaded with money![31]

The others in their group were also able to enter the camp without a problem. Getting in, however, was easy, compared to staying in! Each family was shown a room where they could stay and stack their suitcases and other belongings until they were ready to leave on the train for Germany. The first thing Elza noticed was that German soldiers and the NKVD (the Russian secret police) were everywhere. They were listening to every person who entered the camp, watching carefully what they did, and basically looking for people, like the Kuzma family, who were there illegally. A couple of times, the Kuzma kids got angry and started to argue in their native tongue. Suddenly, they remembered the soldiers and the NKVD and immediately switched to German.

Although food was served in the camp—it wasn't much and the kids at times complained of being hungry. God solved this problem in a unique way. One of the kitchen workers, when leaving camp one day asked Danusia and Krysia, "Are you hungry?" When they admitted that they were, he replied, "I work all night. When I get off each morning, I will bring bread and cheese and push it under the chainlink fence over there," pointing to the place. "Be sure you come early and pick it up so no one discovers what I am doing because I could easily lose my job." For the next two weeks, this kind "Samaritan" made sure the kids had enough to eat.

The Black Satchel

Then it happened! The NKVD discovered that the two older boys from Krakow had smuggled some gold coins into the camp, and their family was immediately thrown out. Now the soldiers and NKVD were watching the "Kutzmans" closely, especially the girls, because they had noticed the boys

---

[31] A few months later, the Polish zloty money was devalued, and what they had carried illegally across the border was basically worthless.

talking to the girls and suspected they may have shared some coins with them, so without warning, an NKVD policeman walked into the "Kutzman" family's private room and demanded to search their belongings.

Elza and her children immediately realized the danger they faced. One family in their group was already gone. *Would they be next?* What if this policeman picked up the black satchel, searched through it, and discovered their Polish papers? It would be a one way ticket to Siberia, bitter imprisonment, or a life of hard labor in the salt mines. Plus, they would never see their father again. Each one of the family immediately started praying, *"Lord, help us! Don't let the man look in the black satchel!"*

Elza and her children were standing next to their belongings as the NKVD official demanded in a threatening voice, "Don't move," then started opening suitcases and boxes and carefully searching through their belongings. Closer and closer, the man came to the black satchel. Mama, Danusia and Janek were standing on one side of the pile, but Krysia happened to be on the other side and rather close to the black satchel. If only Krysia could pick up the black satchel when the Russian wasn't looking and drop it on the pile of already searched items, maybe he wouldn't notice and wouldn't find their Polish papers. Elza made eye contact with Krysia, then looked at the black satchel and indicated with a head movement to throw it onto the pile of suitcases already searched.

Krysia knew exactly what Mama wanted her to do. She watched for an opportunity. At last, the secret policeman looked away to check what was in a box, and Krysia made her move. But as the satchel landed, the metal clasp hit the cement floor and made a clinking sound. In a flash, the NKVD official straightened up and shouted, "I told you not to move!" The whole family stood stiff and looked straight ahead. The man knew something had happened, but he couldn't figure out what it was. After a minute, he gave up and continued searching through the rest of the suitcases. As he came to the last item, he stood up, breathed deeply, and paused.

Elza and the kids thought he was finished and were beginning to silently praise God that the man hadn't searched the black satchel, when suddenly he turned toward the pile again and announced. "I have a feeling I missed something! I think I should look through this pile again."

Now, the family could hardly breathe. They had thought they were safe, but instead, there was no way this man would miss the black satchel the second time. And now, to make matters worse, he made the family move away from the pile. Then he knelt down and began searching through everything again.

From where the family was now standing, it was impossible for them to move the satchel as Krysia had done before. They absolutely had no way of helping themselves. All they could do was fervently pray!

Closer and closer, the secret policeman came to the black satchel. It was obvious to the whole family that all the boxes and suitcases were now opened with their contents in full view. Only the black satchel remained closed. At last, his hands touched the black satchel. *This was it! They were doomed!*

He picked it up. The room was so quiet you could hear a pin drop. The family continued petitioning God for their lives. Then the man did a very strange thing. He lifted the satchel, looked at it strangely, shook it slightly, and said, "I looked through this, didn't I?" and tossed it onto the other pile. Then he stood and left their room.

The family was stunned. They had prayed for a miracle. They had hoped for a miracle. They had even thought God might work a miracle for them—until the man picked up that satchel and shook it. Then, they knew it was hopeless. No sane person would say what this man had just said. It was obvious; the leather satchel had NEVER been opened.

God had worked many miracles for the Kuzma family, but nothing like this had ever happened before. Janek often said when he later told the story, "If God never again worked another miracle for me, the 'black satchel' experience was enough to know that God was a God of miracles—and with Him nothing was impossible. Sometimes, God's miracle is to give us the courage to help ourselves. But when we are utterly helpless—and God breaks into our world in such a forceful way to make a competent, highly trained secret policeman do something so irrational, *that's really powerful!* Because of the black satchel, I have never in my life doubted God. And I can say with Isaiah,

The Lord was ready to save me;
Therefore we will sing my songs with stringed instruments
All the days of our life, in the house of the Lord." (Isaiah 38:20, NKJV)

Catching the Train to Germany

The last two weeks in the German processing camp were two of the toughest weeks Elza and her children had ever endured because of the unrelenting presence of the NKVD and the threat that at any time, because of a wrong move or a suspicious word, they could be removed from the camp and denied any hope of enjoying the freedom of living outside of communist Poland. *They were so close to their goal—and yet so far away.*

At last, the announcement was made; the train departing for Germany had arrived. It was on a sidetrack about a mile from the camp. The people were told that they should get ready and prepare to carry their own luggage to the train early the next morning.

Around eight o'clock in the morning, the announcement was made that the train was ready for boarding. The Kuzma family—now the Kutzmans—got in line and began to slowly make their way to the train. By 9:30, it was so hot and humid that most of the people were grumbling. Everyone was thirsty. In the rush to pick up their suitcases and boxes, few had thought to bring along something to drink. Half an hour later, as the family loaded their baggage onto the train, they learned there was no drinking water available on the train at this time.

"No water!" sighed Krysia. "I'm really, really thirsty."

"Me too," Danusia complained. "I'd give anything for a drink."

Elza shook her head, "I'm sorry, kids. We just need to be thankful we're all here. It won't be long now, and we will be on our way. Earlier this morning, they announced that the train was leaving around noon, but now I hear there may be some delay because of not having adequate fuel."

"Well, if we're not leaving until noon, why don't I go to town and get some water? Better yet, why don't I buy some lemonade," volunteered Janek as he patted one of his pockets where the zlotys were hidden.

"I don't know," Mama said. "I don't want you to miss this train."

"You don't have to worry," volunteered Janek. "If this train isn't leaving until noon, I have plenty of time."

So, with a nod of approval from Elza, Jan grabbed an empty aluminum container and headed toward town about a mile away. But with all that Polish money in his pockets, Janek wasn't thinking of just getting lemonade. Since this would be his last time in Poland he was thinking about using some of that money to buy himself something special. So when he got to town, he started window shopping.

It wasn't long until he spotted a small pair of opera glasses, black with beautiful gold sleeves that twisted out to change the focus. Janek reached under his outer shirt, found a pocket that had some zlotys in it, pulled out a wad of money, went into the store, and purchased the opera glasses.

"Now," he thought, "Where can I find some lemonade?" It took a while, but his persistence paid off, and he asked the storekeeper to fill his aluminum container. The lid didn't fit tight, so he had to walk rather slowly so the lemonade wouldn't slosh out. He glanced at the sky. The sun was straight overhead. "Umm," he sighed. "It looks like it may be about noon. Maybe I better walk a little faster."

As Janek came over the last little hill, his heart nearly stopped. The train was pulling away. He could see his mother near the engine. She was screaming at the train dispatcher. "You can't leave. My son isn't here!"

Janek yelled as loud as he could, "STOP!" "STOP!" and began running faster than he had ever run in his life. "STOP!" "WAIT FOR ME!" Lemonade sloshed out, but that was the least of his worries.

When his mother saw him, she screamed at the dispatcher and pointed toward her son. The dispatcher took one look, whistled to the engineer, and the moving train ground to a halt. Elza grabbed Janek and raced to the nearest passenger door, pushed Janek up onto the train steps, and jumped on after him as the train once more began moving away from the platform.

Janek knew he was in trouble. He found the closest empty seat, glued his face to the window, and watched as the electric poles began racing past. Elza sat down beside him and had a few "not so pleasant" words for her son. He never said a thing throughout her entire speech!

Later, he learned that his mother had delayed the train for twenty minutes. She couldn't believe he had been gone so long—and with tears, she had pled with the dispatcher. "Please don't leave my son."

The ironic thing was that the train dispatcher was the very same railroad official who had met the family three weeks before when they first arrived in Szczecin and had said to them, "I know you want to escape." Now, here he was again, having a major encounter with Elza beside the train that was allowing her and her family to escape from communist Poland. He could have easily turned her in—and that would have been the end of their westward journey. After all, he was a Polish communist railroad official. But he didn't!

If the situation of having to wait for Jan had not occurred, Elza would have been sitting in one of the coach cars with her children and would have never seen the man who was dispatching the train—nor would he have seen Elza. Interesting, isn't it, how God, at times, opens our eyes to see more clearly the miracles He is working in our lives?

When Janek learned that if he had missed the train, his mama was going to let the other children go on to Germany, and she would stay with him—giving up her chance for freedom—that incident made him realize just how much he was loved.

Survival Strategies

As the train click-clacked toward the German border, Elza considered her next move. On her German application, she had given a name and address of a relative her family could stay with in Germany. Elza had written: *Husband: Wilhelm Kutzman in Hamburg*. She also knew the German papers she had been issued at Szczecin were not official German citizenship papers. Those would be issued to her in Hamburg at the end of their journey, but if she got those papers, she and the children wouldn't be allowed into the Wentorf displaced person's camp with Wladek. *She had to somehow avoid Hamburg!*

She knew there was a train stop at a small station in Bergedorf, which just happened to be the closest stop to Wentorf—*and* the last stop before Hamburg. Hopefully, her family could disembark in Bergedorf without anyone realizing what she was doing.

Elza's plan was complicated by the fact that the train she was on was not heading directly to Hamburg. Rather, they were first traveling south to the small town of Oberau, Germany, close to Germany's border with Austria. It was in Oberau where they would officially enter Germany. There, they would receive the papers and food stamps necessary to purchase food for the trip and would also be given the tickets to their final destination.

Somehow, in Oberau, as soon as she got processed for German welfare benefits and received her tickets to Hamburg, she had to escape the German system and once again become Polish!

Mrs. Guzik (who couldn't speak or understand German) was still playing deaf and dumb. For safety's sake, however, the two families acted like strangers so if either family was arrested because of their Polish backgrounds, it would not endanger the other. Elza was well aware of the risk. She had accidentally overheard a conversation between two people on the train discussing their suspicions that the Kutzmans were not true Germans, so she and her family kept a low profile.

It was late in the day when their train arrived in Oberau on Germany's southern border. Elza and her children disembarked with their luggage and cued up to receive processing papers and a pass to travel to their final destination. Then her prayers were answered; Elza found that she and her children were basically on their own until the train left for Hamburg. She quickly found the International Red Cross office, which contacted UNRRA (the United Nations Refugee Relief Association) and gave them their arrival time at Bergedorf. The UNRRA officials said they would contact Wladek Kuzma in Wentorf's displaced persons camp and give him that information. Thankfully, no one asked for her German papers.

CHAPTER 24

Germany: Existing as Displaced Persons
(1946-1951)

The "Kutzman" family was at last traveling north on the train to Hamburg, the last leg of their journey. It was time to once again become Polish. Sitting in a sheltered compartment, Janek's school books were retrieved from the black satchel, and the covers slit once again. This time, their Polish Kuzma passports and papers were retrieved. Taking their place behind the taped covers of Janek's books were the German Kutzman papers.

Now Elza began praying that when the train stopped at Bergedorf (eight kilometers before Hamburg) that no one would notice their early departure. They had to avoid Hamburg where the German citizenship processing was to occur. Elza shook her head in amazement. *Was this really happening? In a few hours, she would be in the arms of her husband, whom she hadn't seen for two years.*

Meanwhile, back at Wentorf, Wladek was excited when he got the news that his family would be arriving and he hired a horse drawn wagon to pick them up. He also invited a handful of friends from the camp (who had known his family in Warsaw and Plock) to join him in welcoming Elza and the children.

Danusia, Krysia, and Janek excitedly looked out the train window as it neared the Bergedorf station. They had no idea whether or not their tata had gotten word about their arrival. As soon as the train screeched to a halt, they grabbed their suitcases and jumped onto the platform. When they spotted their father, they dropped their bags and ran to him. What a reunion! They hugged, kissed, and vied for his attention.

"Oh, my little pearl," he said to Danusia, "you are such a beautiful teenager."

"And my special Krysia. Oh, how much I have missed you. You look so grown up, I can hardly recognize you."

"And Janek, what a fine young man you have become."

While all this was happening, a few passengers helped Elza negotiate the train steps and lift Jurek's carriage onto the platform along with her suitcases. Elza's friends (the Hincs and the Klutzs) embraced her and admired two-year-old Jurek.

Elza looked around. *Where was Wladek?* At last, she saw him gazing at her with a surprised expression—and not paying any attention to baby Jurek in her arms. *What was wrong?* He should have been the first one of the crowd to embrace her, and to notice the baby he hadn't seen in almost two years—but he wasn't. He just stood there as if in a trance. Elza was embarrassed and deeply hurt by Wladek's odd reception. *What rejection!*

Finally, Elza walked up to her husband and held up the baby, "Wladek," she said, "this is your son, Jurek." Wladek finally reached out and took Jurek in his arms to get a better look at his chubby little face, and then he said with a smile, "Jurek, you're such a big boy—I didn't recognize you. You were so tiny when I saw you last."

Finally, after handing the baby back to Elza, he kissed her on the cheek and said, "I can't believe you and the children are actually here!"

It could have been assumed by his friends that Wladek was acting like a proper Polish gentleman who didn't believe in showing public affection, but it had been almost two years since he had seen his wife. He could have at least shown a little more enthusiasm!

But what stabbed Elza's heart and left her emotionally assaulted and empty was what Wladek *didn't* say to her. He didn't say, "I have missed you so much. I have looked forward to this day with all my heart. You mean everything to me. Now that you're here, my life is complete." He didn't even say, "I love you!"

Because it was getting late, their friends grabbed the luggage and motioned toward the horse drawn cart. "Come, we know you're tired. Let's get you home."

As the horse plodded down the unpaved road toward the old German army camp that was now a large displaced person's camp, everyone was chattering. They were so happy that Wladek's dream about the five white geese alighting on the evergreen tree had come true. The Kuzma family had not only survived the war but had successfully escaped from communist Poland, and they were once more together.

It had been almost two years since Wladek was taken away from the family and forced to work for the Nazi German military. Although distance can make the heart grow fonder, it can also negatively impact a family and weaken the bonds that are necessary to survive tough times. In this case, both Wladek and Elza had anticipated an emotionally high reunion—and it just didn't happen!

Elza was deeply disappointed. Not only did her husband seem like a stranger, but the Germany she was returning to was not the Germany she had known before. She remembered how organized and efficient it was when she had traveled to Berlin in 1942 accompanying Wladek to the hospital. Now, everywhere she looked, there were bombed-out buildings and piles of rubble. She knew Hamburg had been heavily bombed by the Allies in the last few months of the war—but even in her wildest imagination, she could not have known how much had been destroyed. And the train stations they had passed on the trip across the country had been full of what appeared to be lost, discouraged, and confused people. Germany *after* the war was a cacophony of confusion and despair, not a well oiled and carefully maintained society that she had once known.

> *Everything Elza had observed since she stepped off the train confirmed to her that her nightmares were real.*

The war had shattered lives and left homeless over eleven million people of many different nationalities in Eastern Europe (Armenians, Poles, Latvians, Lithuanians, Estonians, Yugoslavs, Jews, Greeks, Russians, Ukrainians, and Czechoslovaks). Eighteen thousand of these people were or had been temporarily housed at Wentorf, which was a transit facility to process displaced persons (mostly from Eastern Europe) and assist them in finding homes.[32]

Elza had so hoped that when she arrived in Bergedorf, her concerns about whether or not she and Wladek's marriage could survive would disappear like nightmares at dawn. However, everything she had observed since she stepped off the train confirmed to her that her nightmares were real. It was as if she and Wladek were separated by a ten-foot brick wall topped with broken bottles and barbed wire.

As they drove through the front gate of the camp, she read the sign "Wentorf Camp: Regional Resettlement Processing Centre." When they were greeted by a British military guard, Elza felt as if she were entering

---

[32] Two years after the end of the war, there were still 850,000 people in Germany classified as displaced persons. The Kuzma family was part of that number.

a "prison." But the cement wall around the camp was only two feet tall, so obviously, it was meant to keep vehicles out rather than people in! She could also see quite a number of large three-story red brick buildings (approximately twenty), called *kaserna,* that the German army had first used to house enlisted men. There was also a mess hall and a number of smaller buildings that had been used for offices and living quarters for army officers. These buildings were now offices for the many doctors and politicians who would cross-examine the populace of the camp for immigration purposes and request all kinds of documents and papers in what would become, to Elza, an almost endless interrogation process.

When Wladek described their living space in his letters, Elza had pictured a hotel-like building with private rooms, but as she walked up the three flights of creaking wooden stairs and then down a long corridor running from one end of the building to the other, passing an area for women's toilets and one for men and then a little further down, a number of public wash basins in the hallway, she quickly realized that her imagination had been overly optimistic.

What a disappointment to find there was no such thing as privacy. In fact, it was shocking to realize that two families had to occupy the same living/sleeping room, separated only by a clothesline strung across the room holding up army blankets to give "privacy" to the families. And since this was an old army camp, the beds were narrow bunkbeds—meant for soldiers, not couples. To take a shower, you had to walk to the communal shower area at the time allotted for your building to have hot water. The only other hot water came from a faucet outside a designated building for the purpose of washing your own dishes after meals—so the water was only hot for a short time.

There was no central heating. Every room had a potbelly stove—but people had to find their own kindling—which was almost nonexistent. There were no kitchens or cooking facilities in the rooms (although later Elza learned that some families cooked their own meals on hot plates they had purchased). Everyone was served from a common kitchen where they had to queue up three times a day with their food cards to be stamped and wait their turn for a meager meal prepared by camp residents. A typical dinner consisted of dill pickles, potatoes, and an entrée, like canned corned beef hash. Or maybe they would get a hard bun and soup. Two favorites were borscht (beet soup) and *zupa mleczna* (milk soup) which was thickened with flour and seasoned with salt. Fresh fruit and vegetables were rare.

What had she done? Elza had given up the beautiful little home with a red gate, with all its privacy, lovely home furnishings, a thriving business, fresh fruit and vegetables, and hot water for this!

It was depressing to realize how, almost overnight, she had gone from having enough money to live modestly almost anywhere in Poland to now having *nothing*! And it wasn't as if she could just leave. If they ever wanted to experience life in the United States of America, they would need to stay in the displaced person's system until arrangements for immigration could be made. There was no other way! Her situation seemed hopeless.

When she complained to Wladek about the terrible accommodations, he reminded her that this wouldn't be forever. As soon as they could get someone to sponsor them in America, they would be on their way. Elza imagined that it might take a month or maybe two. But she was soon to find out the process was much more complicated and time consuming.

Someone of less stamina, determination, and faith may have given up had they been told the process would take over five years! First, three months in Wentorf, then two years in Eckernforde, then back to Wentorf for a couple of years, then to Lubeck, and finally, back to Wentorf in 1951 for the final processing necessary for immigration.

The Fight

With each new week the tension built between Elza and Wladek. Passing the health standards was the first immigration requirement for all incoming displaced persons. Somehow, Elza and the children endured the three weeks of intensive health examinations, blood tests, and injections. The process started with having to submit to being deloused. That meant they had to be scrubbed with a delousing solution and have delousing powder put through their hair. And then they had to endure endless health exams and lab tests.

Elza tolerated the humiliating delousing procedure and her disappointment concerning the living conditions for the first few weeks. She endured the public bathrooms, the sleeping arrangements, the horrible tasting meals that always left her feeling hungry, the cold water, the children complaining of nothing to do, and Wladek—who not only was distant but didn't have a job.

And she somehow made it through the first two weeks of health examinations and the never-ending lab tests, which caused her to exclaim, "I now know why some people pay for complete blood transfusions, or they present another family member's urine sample when their own is repeatedly rejected!"

At last, the third week of medical tests was over and they were given the results. That's when Elza lost it! "What do you mean that three of us failed?" Elza cried in shock!

The physicians tried to soften the blow by saying, "You were fortunate that the contagious disease that three of you have has been found while it was still dormant. At any time, it could have become active and not only caused you physical discomfort but finally killed you by destroying your nerves and brain. Do you know how fortunate you are that it has been found and that we have medication that can cure it?"

Basically, the tests showed that Elza, Krysia and baby Jurek had been exposed to a highly contagious disease, and even though it was currently dormant, they would need to have extensive doses of penicillin to "kill" it and stop its possible spread. This finding meant that the family would not be allowed to proceed with plans for immigration until they could pass the health exams—and no one knew how long the process would take. In addition, until the infection could be killed, the infected ones had to be careful not to contaminate the rest of the family.

How did this happen? The results of the health examinations shocked everyone, *and broke Elza's spirit.*

When Wladek heard the lab results, he immediately assumed Elza had gotten the disease by being raped or by having an affair and had given it to the children. She tried to explain to him about the sick baby in Belgard with the terrible infection and how she and Krysia had tried so hard to care for the baby's puss-filled sores. There was no doubt in Elza's mind that they had caught the disease at that time. But she couldn't seem to get Wladek to understand or accept the truth. All this grated on her psyche. She couldn't sleep! Her emotions were raw!

After weeks of humiliating treatment and then to be hit with severe disappointment, something had to give…and in Elza's case, she poured out all of her frustration about their living conditions and irrationally blamed her husband with explosive, pent up anger! "I can't stand how we're living! No privacy, No double beds. Terrible meals! I can't stand this for one more minute!" she exploded. "Why did you lie to me about this place?" she yelled.

Her pent up anger caught him off guard. "I didn't know it would be this bad!" he tried to explain.

"What do you mean, you didn't know? You had been here for almost a year before you found us. You knew exactly what the living conditions were like. I put my life and the lives of our children on the line to escape from Poland for you, and now we have nothing! *You don't even have a job!* Plus, you ignore me. You treat me like I'm a stranger instead of your wife. You never even told me you loved me when I got off the train. Now, you don't believe me when I explain the infection. How do you think we can put our marriage back together when you don't trust me and you treat me like I mean nothing to you?" She started to cry.

"Well," he finally admitted, "I was shocked at the way you looked when you got off the train. I thought you were pregnant. I thought maybe you got raped by the Russians or were messing around, and I didn't know what to say. And then it flashed into my head that maybe Jurek wasn't mine! All this hit me the moment I saw you!"

"Why are you always so quick to accuse me of being unfaithful? How can I prove to you that I'm not that kind of woman? You have no idea what I have gone through. I knew I was in a dangerous situation with the Russians advancing toward Plock. I could have left earlier, but I was hoping you would return to Plock so we could escape together. But you never came. So, with the Russians invading Poland and the front coming closer to Plock, I didn't even try to lose weight! It was my way of looking so unattractive that the Russians would leave me alone! I've always been faithful to you, but you can't seem to get this fact through your head!"

"Well, I can't even sleep with you now because you sleep with Jurek," he shot back.

"That's because you've been gone for two years, and I'm all that Jurek knows. I can't just make him sleep alone when he is in a strange place—and there's no way I'm going to let him cry and disturb another family who is sleeping in the same room with us! It will take time for him to adjust to change—and besides, he's still nursing. And two grownups in a single bunk bed is NOT what I call comfortable!"

"You are impossible!" Wladek shot back. "And now, after all these medical exams, I discover that you have contracted a contagious disease. What am I to think?" And at this point Wladek got so angry that he threw the book he was reading out the window and yelled, "IT'S NOT MY FAULT! You're not the only one who is hurt, disappointed, and frustrated!"

By this time, the children were cowering in the corner. They had never before seen or heard their parents act this way. The kids knew their parents had their share of arguments, but they never threw things nor made so many insulting accusations, and they never had so little love for each other, which was the glue needed to hold them together. The kids actually feared that this might be the end of their family.

But somehow, throwing the book out the window shocked both parents into silence. The kids never heard exactly how their folks made up. But they did. And no one ever brought up that terrible argument again. It was as if it went out the window with the book! And from then on, things went better between them.

The Organization of Displaced Persons Camps

To process the millions of post-war displaced persons and either send them back to their home countries, or get them established in Germany, or monitor their immigration papers to a new country, camps were established in each one of four allied governmental zones in Germany: the British, American, Soviet, and French. In an attempt to give people an environment where they could enjoy a common language, entertainment, and customs while they were being processed, the refugees were sent to different camps depending on their nationalities.

Each of the one hundred-plus displaced persons camps was organized and governed pretty much the same way. Wentorf's displaced persons camp was in the British zone (as were the other two camps where the Kuzma family was eventually sent). This camp was self-governed with a British camp director and representatives to help govern the camp selected by the different nationalities of the residents. All camp inhabitants were free to move in or out of the camp, to get jobs outside the camp (if they could), and to purchase goods in town (if they had the money).

Since there were few, if any, employment opportunities, each family had to figure out how they were going to exist. Some had little garden plots where they grew vegetables. Others grew tobacco and learned how to process it. Some went into the scrap metal business and sold pieces of tin, copper, and zinc to recycling centers to manufacture vehicles and machinery. Some collected bottles and glass and received money from recycling centers. Some people even took trains to locations where they could buy inexpensive supplies or food, such as apples, salted herring, or tobacco, and sold these items for a profit back at the camp. Some raised chickens or pigs. All of these activities were encouraged to not only keep the people busy while they waited endless weeks and months for the necessary papers for immigration but they also provided an incentive for the refugees to learn new skills that would make them more employable—wherever they finally settled.

Since camp residents had time on their hands and little if any money for entertainment, the camp administration started theater groups, organized concerts by vocal and instrumental musicians, and sporting events where camp residents could use their talents—or just be entertained. Plus, there were long periods of time when the people just sat around and talked. Unless they were on kitchen or bathroom cleaning duty, there wasn't much to do. Many ended up drunk. Wladek kept busy repairing shoes with the equipment he had purchased when he first arrived in Germany. Sometimes, he worked late into the night with a towel over his head so the rest of the family wasn't bothered by his light. But Wladek didn't earn much because most of the displaced persons in Wentorf didn't have money for shoe repair.

Eckernforde Assembly Camp

By the time Elza and the children arrived at Wentorf, schools had been established, both for children and various trade schools, to teach skills that would allow the residents to get jobs. But before the Kuzma children could start school in Wentorf, the initial processing of the Kuzma family was completed, and they were transferred in August, 1946, to Eckernforde on the Baltic Sea, about 30 kilometers northeast of Kiel and 130 kilometers north of Wentorf.

Eckernforde was a much smaller camp than Wentorf. It was actually called an "assembly camp." At peak capacity in 1947, the camp only housed approximately 2000 displaced people in three different sections (mostly from Poland, Lithuania, and Estonia). There were about 500 in the Polish camp.

Instead of large three-story buildings like Wentorf, Eckernforde had small one-story barracks with smaller living/sleeping rooms, but regardless, most residents had to share their space with another family. Each room had a potbelly stove. It may at first have seemed like a better situation, but within a few weeks, the family realized that living conditions in Eckernforde were worse than in Wentorf.

There was running water in their barracks but no indoor flush toilets. Instead, the toilets for each barrack were in a separate wooden shed-like building consisting of six round holes with a trench—and no stalls or doors. The Kuzma children remember trying to wait as long as possible before making their way to these smelly "facilities."

Eckernforde was the selected destination for the Kuzma family because it not only had a "Polish" camp and school, but it also had a small hospital (known mostly as a maternity hospital) that was located in a mansion on the hill next to the camp. The hospital had the medical personnel who could monitor the health status of Elza, Krysia, and Jurek on a weekly basis with blood tests and injections. Their family wasn't the only one in camp trying to overcome health problems. For example, in the Lithuanian Camp at Eckernforde, 30 percent of the children were infected with tuberculosis.

Eckernforde was also one of the holding camps for the people who had indicated that their first choice for immigration was the United States. There were three immigration locations available from this "assembly center." The USA was first. Australia was the second most popular and South America (either Paraguay or Uruguay) the third.

The USA was the most difficult country to enter. In fact, there was a saying among the displaced persons that it was easier for a camel to go through the eye of a needle than for a family to get qualified to go to the United States. Not only were there strict health requirements, but each applicant had to have a sponsor who would be responsible for the family for one entire year, promising them an inexpensive place to live and giving them a guaranteed job so they could earn enough for their living expenses.

In addition, the USA had established certain immigration quotas. At first, they only took singles and couples without children, then families with one child, then two, then three children, so families like the Kuzmas with four children were way down on the list.

They may have been able to qualify for other destinations sooner, but Wladek had a burning desire to go to America. His passion and stubborn insistence were so strong that Elza and the children soon learned that it was useless to argue. They would just have to make the best of their situation and wait until God took away all the hurdles and they met the qualifications.

> *The USA was the most difficult country to enter. In fact, there was a saying among the displaced persons that it was easier for a camel to go through the eye of a needle.*

Dealing with Deteriorating Camp Conditions

When the German displaced persons camps first opened, conditions were fairly decent, but as the years went by, it became more difficult to meet people's needs. For example, the Kuzmas arrived at Eckernforde in the winter of 1946–1947, which was a record breaking frigid winter—and living conditions suffered. Everything was so snowed in and frozen that supply trucks could not get to the camp, which meant people were hungry, and many suffered from malnutrition. Food was so scarce they were forced to mix sawdust in the bread to increase the volume, making it dry and crumbly[33].

---

[33] It was not until a number of years later that the Kuzmas realized that the Soviets offered little cooperation with the American and British humanitarian efforts for the displaced persons in Europe. This made it very difficult for the other two countries to provide all the supplies needed for these people, especially during the winter of 1946–1947.

It was heartbreaking for Elza to see her family going hungry. This forced her to make a difficult decision. When first crossing the border in Oberau, Germany, the "Kutzman" family had been processed into the German welfare system which allowed her to obtain monthly ration stamps for food. All she had to do was show her German papers, and monthly food stamps would be issued to her. But since her family was being fed three meals a day at Wentorf, she never followed through and registered for food stamps. Now, she had to make a choice. *Should she, or should she not, finish the paperwork at the welfare center of Regensburg, Germany, which would allow her to supplement her family's diet?*

The food shortage at Eckernforde became so acute that she finally pulled out her German papers from the covers of Janek's old books, got dressed in her warmest winter wear, and boarded the train to Regensburg, where she picked up the "life-saving" ration stamps to feed her family. What a blessing the extra food was for the rest of the long, cold winter. Elza considered the ration stamps "manna" from heaven. The family also wrote to the General Conference of Seventh-day Adventists in the United States, explaining the dire living conditions and asked for care packages because they knew their worldwide church was very involved in humanitarian causes.

Once the weather improved enough to allow Wladek to leave the camp on his bicycle, he ordered two leather pouches to be made for his bicycle handlebars so when he delivered repaired shoes, his customers could pay him with food products which he carried back to camp in the leather pouches.

Prolonged living in the camps impacted not only people's material needs but also their emotional health. Clothing that had been adequate when the refugees first came into the camp was now wearing out, but there were no new clothes to offer the people. Some refugees had been able to bring their savings into camp, but now their money was either gone—or quickly disappearing. The value of the Deutsche Mark was declining. This severely impacted the refugees who had gotten jobs but now found the money they earned was almost worthless. Plus, the crowded conditions, lack of privacy, and the growing sense of hopelessness were tearing down people's morale. The Kuzma family wasn't the only family that was experiencing heightened tension, resulting in arguments and alienation.

Life in Eckernforde

During the family's first year in Eckernforde, Danusia, who had finished the last two years of grade school with top scholastic honors, was qualified to go to gymnasium (high school) instead of trade school. The closest high school with a Polish faculty was a boarding school in Penniberg (Polskie Liceum), 120 kilometers from Eckernforde.

Krysia and Janek attended "Polish" school in the camp. Krysia was in fifth grade when they arrived. Because of not being able to attend school regularly in Belgard and Slawno after the war, she needed to catch up. Help came in an unexpected way. Her teacher got sick in the middle of the first year in Eckernforde and had to be hospitalized. Krysia was able to visit him. He was very understanding and, without the distraction of other children, he took time to explain the concepts in a way that she could understand. It was just what she needed!

Janek was ten and was not at all interested in school. But he had a great time playing in the large field behind their barracks, where the kids flew kites, picked wildflowers, and enjoyed games of cops and robbers. It was in Eckernforde that Janek learned how to play the Polish game of palant (which many think was the forerunner of American baseball). It is played with a bat (a wooden stick) hitting a rubber ball and then the batter running around four bases. Jan was also introduced to soccer, which soon became his passion.

When Jurek was three-and-a-half years of age and the harsh winter months were over, it was time to wean him—and Elza needed her freedom! Jurek, however, rebelled. He was now strong enough to reach into Elza's blouse and pull out his "feeding machine," which at times was quite embarrassing. Finally, Elza's doctor suggested she put mustard on her breasts. And within a month, Jurek was eating and drinking on his own!

The doldrums of the displaced person's camp life were accented with a touch of warmth when Elza's family, who now lived in Germany, came to visit. First, Elza's brother Emil, her sister, Truda, and Truda's boyfriend, Martin, came. Then, later, Emil brought their mother, Pauline, for a visit. Oh, how much they had to share! Emil then took Pauline to Penniberg to see her favorite granddaughter, Danusia. The future was uncertain and they realized this might be the last time they were together.

By the summer of 1948, when the family was still struggling to meet the health requirements for immigration, and the Eckernforde camp was in the process of closing down, the Kuzma family was again transferred back to Wentorf, where their friends were still living. The Hinc family had to spend another year at Wentorf and the Klutzes another year and a half before their families immigrated to the United States. *Who would have thought that it would take almost four more years for the Kuzmas?*

Growing Up in Camp

Spending your teenage years in a displaced person's camp wasn't exactly ideal. Danusia had completed her first year of high school before the family was sent back to Wentorf the second time. Now she had her own friends, and she preferred to be with them rather than taking care of her younger siblings. She had spread her wings and loved the freedom of attending the Polish boarding school in Penniberg. She was happy not to have the responsibility of helping her sister with schoolwork or being tied down with the care of her little brother, Jurek. She was bright, talented, and determined to make her own way in life. What a wonderful world she had discovered beyond the awful camps where her family was forced to live.

Krysia and Janek, at thirteen and eleven years of age, were pretty much homebound at Wentorf. The Polish school and library for Krysia and Janek were two barracks. Because of the lack of qualified teachers, Krysia's class was in the same room as Janek's. This soon became a problem.

Krysia loved and admired Janek, but she needed him to achieve in order for her to feel good about herself. If he did well, she was proud. But if he didn't study because soccer and palant were more important, she was embarrassed. It didn't help that the Gatzki boys, who also happened to be in the same classroom, were jealous of Janek and delighted in teasing Krysia by reporting to her all of Janek's faults. They bullied Janek, demeaned him in public, and cruelly laughed at him in class, especially when he didn't know an answer. None of this seemed to faze Janek but it was *devastating* to Krysia until she'd yell, "You guys have nothing going for you that would beat my brother." Her defensiveness only egged on the Gatzki boys, which resulted in more cruelty.

> *The teacher made Janek sit on the dunce stool in the corner or kneel on pebbles.*

The teacher didn't help. When Janek didn't know his lessons, he made Janek sit on the dunce stool in the corner or kneel on pebbles when he wore short pants or lederhosen and keep his hands in a circle drawn on the chalkboard above his head. If Janek's arms got tired and his hands started to drop out of the circle, the Gatzki boys would point this out to the teacher. Then, before the teacher could whip him, Janek's arms would shoot up to the circle again.

And if that weren't enough, Krysia made the dysfunctional pattern even more severe and physically painful. She was beside herself because Janek wouldn't study, so she would tattle to her father, who then whipped him. She did this hoping that it would motivate Janek to show the Gatzki boys how smart he was. But this strategy didn't work. Janek never retaliated when Krysia tattled on him. He just continued doing what he loved—and that was excelling in sports.

One of the teachers, Mr. Przygodski, was particularly harsh on Janek when he didn't know his lessons. He not only had him kneel on pebbles but whipped him with a willow switch or hit his knuckles with a ruler. Mr. Przygodski got the teaching job because he had advanced degrees, but he had a mean, sadistic nature—and should have never been allowed to be around children.

In winter, when it was too cold to play outdoors, Janek did well in school, but when spring came, Janek played soccer every night instead of doing his homework. Then, once again, the cycle of tattling and punishment would begin. Playing ball was so important to Janek that he just endured the pain. And he never seemed to resent Krysia or his father—he figured he deserved the punishment he got! One of the consequences, however, was that Janek began to stutter. To relieve Janek's stress, Elza immediately took him away from camp for a time and the stuttering stopped.

Elza Takes a Break

Going back to Wentorf was especially painful for Elza, as it brought back memories of that terrible fight where Wladek threw the book out the window. By 1948, the stress of living without any privacy and still suffering from all the penicillin therapy—and then the disappointment of seeing others finish the immigration process and leave camp for America while the Kuzma family had no idea how much longer they would be living in limbo, was too much for her. She, too, needed a break.

Elza had started taking short breaks from the terrible living conditions in Eckernforde after the horrible winter of 1946–1947. On one of Elza's monthly trips to Regensburg to get her food ration stamps, she had met a friendly German couple who invited her to visit them at their vacation home near Chiemsee. (Elza called the lake Konigssee. Others called it the Bavarian Sea because it was the largest lake in Bavaria.) Elza accepted this couple's invitation for three summers in a row and called it *"eine kur for mental restitution"* (a cure for good mental health).

Wladek could not understand why Elza needed a "vacation" when she didn't have any work to do in camp. He complained, "Why do you need to go all the way to Bavaria when we're living a few kilometers from the Baltic Sea, and you can enjoy the beach at Eckernforde for the day?" When she tried to convince Wladek of her need for the life-restoring beauty of Bavaria, he accused her of having a boyfriend. She tried to reason with him but finally just gave up, packed a suitcase, gave instructions to Danusia and Krysia who were on summer vacation, and caught the train.

There was something about spending the summer in the Alps that nurtured Elza's soul as nothing else. She hiked in the mountains, prayed as she watched the beautiful sunsets, and daydreamed as she sunbathed by the lake. She also took walks, read, and went on outings with her host family. She knew herself well enough to know that taking a three or four-week vacation *alone* was the only way she would be able to come back and cope with another year of camp life.

Fulfilling Immigration Requirements

As soon as Wladek and Elza realized that finding someone to sponsor them in the United States was a requirement for immigration, they made contact with the General Conference of the Seventh-day Adventist Church in Washington, D.C., about the possibility of finding a sponsor.

In 1949, they learned that a Seventh-day Adventist farmer (Ralph Jensen) from Elgin, Texas, was willing to sponsor their family. The Jensens had a large farm that produced watermelons and cotton. There was a house on the property where they could live and they could work for Mr. Jensen for a year. And the good news was that the USA was starting to take families with four children!

Now, all they had to do was pass the health qualifications. So, in 1949, the family was sent to a camp in the city of Lubeck where better medical services were available. The procedure the doctors had previously followed was to treat the infected family members and then wait a year to see if the disease was still active. Two years of treatment had not worked! It was now time to get serious. Plus, the penicillin that was currently available was significantly better than what was used previously. Hopefully, they would now see some progress.

After the family arrived in Lubeck, all three infected family members were hospitalized for a week and given penicillin shots every two hours for seven days. It was difficult enough for Elza and Krysia but torturous for little Jurek. Finally, it appeared that Elza and Jurek were cleared, but to make sure they had to take blood samples each month and then every two months. Finally, in 1950, both of them were cleared for immigration.

Krysia, however, was another story. When they moved to Lubeck, she enrolled in school at the camp for a couple of months, took the Latin test, and finished eighth grade—but then had to skip school for a whole year because of her health. She was admitted to a hospital in Hamburg for three days of extensive testing. Next, she had to go back to Wentorf because that was where the administration of the camp's health system was located. While she was there, she shared a room with another lady who had a daughter her age.

From Wentorf, she was again sent to Hamburg. She had to take a bus to Bergedorf, then a train to Hamburg, then the trolley to the medical center. Her condition was improving, but when would this nightmare be over?

Living in Lubeck

Lubeck was a welcome change for the family. The camp was large, consisting of three-story buildings like Wentorf. But there were not as many people, which meant that the Kuzmas were at last able to have their own living quarters.

Wladek was not around as much. He loved big cities, and this was his chance to explore, meet people, and sell his wares. Thankfully, when Wladek was first in Wentorf, he had purchased equipment for mending and making shoes. Now that he was in a large city where people had an income, making money from his shoe business was much easier. He also started selling books again, as well as the German *Signs of the Times*. But the years of uncertainty had an effect on his health, and in 1949, at 54 years of age, he was once more having stomach problems, which made him even more irritable when he was with the family.

Elza, as soon as she had been cleared for immigration, felt better. She liked the city and the opportunities it held. She especially enjoyed taking the kids to the beautiful resort town of Travemunde, which was located just northeast of Lübeck on the Baltic Sea and next to a beautiful pine forest. How relaxing to enjoy swimming in the crisp, clear water and sunbathing on the beautiful, long sandy beach. In fact, it was so refreshing to Elza's spirit that she no longer needed to travel to Cheimsee in Bavaria. When she had a down day, all she had to do was take the short bus trip to Travemunde, and she felt her spirits lift.

But unfortunately, Wladek and Elza were still fighting—about almost everything. For example, now that Wladek had saved some money, he wanted to buy all sorts of gadgets, while Elza, the more practical one, knew they would just have to leave the gadgets behind when they went to America. She wanted to save their money. And Wladek just couldn't get over his suspicions about what Elza was doing when she wasn't at camp. She had almost given up trying to rebuild his trust. Nothing she said or did seemed to convince him of her love. And to be truthful, at times, she was so frustrated with him that she wondered whether there was any love left. But she never gave up her faith that God could heal their marriage. And she was still determined to honor their marriage vows they had made to each other twenty years earlier: *"for better or worse!"*

Even though they were living in a camp, the children seemed to be doing better in Lubeck.

Danusia loved boarding school, finally taking two years in one year so she would be able to graduate in 1949, two years before the family left for the United States.

Krysia, receiving aggressive treatment for her infection, had given Elza hope that she would soon be medically cleared for immigration. She had also been baptized on March 15, 1949, by Elder Kaufmann. Both of the girls were now enjoying the attention of the opposite sex and spent their free time playing ping pong, watching movies, and flirting with the boys!

Janek was doing well in school now that he didn't have his sister pushing him around. Plus, he now had teachers who recognized his potential and encouraged him. One teacher, in particular, knew Janek was smart and encouraged him to compete with German kids his age. How proud Elza and Wladek were when Janek was honored by the German school system for his achievement in math based on his high scores on the standardized tests that he took with German students. In fact, he scored so high that his teachers talked to Elza and Wladek saying that they should definitely send him on to gymnasium when he graduated from eighth grade.

Wladek had always wanted his son to play a musical instrument, as he had done himself as a child, but during the war and then the chaos of the post-war years, it never seemed possible. Now, Wladek had enough savings to buy Janek an accordion, and Janek took lessons during the two years the family spent in Lubeck.

In 1950, Jurek, now five years old, started school, leaving Elza with more time for herself, reading her Bible and praying. In anticipation of going to America, Elza also began selling some of the dishes and other things their family had accumulated while living in the displaced person's camps.

The family had a good church they attended and had made friends—especially in the Bergedorf Seventh-day Adventist Church that they had attended when they were at Wentorf. Now, after years of despair, heartache, and disappointment, it seemed that their dreams were about to come true. God was good!

Back to Wentorf—and Beyond

In February 1951, the family at last received the news for which they had been eagerly waiting. Krysia had been medically cleared. The disease was dormant. It would always be there and might flair up in the future, but at this time, she met the health requirements for immigration to America.

The Seventh-day Adventist General Conference representative was contacted. That person, in turn, checked with the potential sponsor. The Jensens were still willing to sponsor the Kuzma family. Everything was set to go, so the family went back to Wentorf for the final processing. The date of departure for the USA was set for April 18, 1951.

In March, Danusia and Krysia were offered classes in English to get them ready for their departure. They were shown films of Micky and Minnie Mouse going through all the forty-eight states, acquainting them with their new county. The girls laughed at a mouse dressed in clothes and going traveling. They then showed an American speaking English with giant English words on the screen to get them familiar with reading English.

It was now time for Danusia to be **Donna**. Krysia to become **Christine**, Janek to become **Jan** (as in January), Jurek to become **George**, and Wladek to no longer be called Wilhelm as he was called in Germany, but **William** in English.

At last, the day came when the family took the train from Bergedorf to Hamburg and then on to the port at Bremerhaven, where they were to depart for America. What a memorable farewell for the family to have three of Elza's brothers (Emil, Alfred, and Gerhard) travel by car to see them off. Their last words were directed to Donna, "You are the oldest child. Your parents are getting older, so you will need to be responsible and make sure everyone is taken care of in the USA."

William and Elza were leaving their beloved country of Poland (and the displaced person camps of Germany) for the last time. After all the years of waiting, they could hardly believe they would soon be boarding the naval ship, USS *General Harry Taylor*, ready to sail for the land they had dreamed of for so long, *"America the Beautiful."*

Donna summed up the years they had spent in displaced persons camps with these words: "Having survived a horrible war and looking forward to freedom was the most important thing in our lives. We didn't need money and things. I was just thankful for my siblings. They meant more to me than toys and books. And the miracle was that regardless of the dangers and hardships we experienced, no one was hurt or disfigured with war injuries. God obviously blessed and protected our family. We never gave up hope. We knew there would be something good beyond our time as displaced persons."

The USS *General Harry Taylor* was the first thing from America that the Kuzma children experienced since peanuts and soda crackers back in

Slawno. It was April 17 when the Kuzma family boarded the ship. It left Bremerhaven the next day.

Now, the Kuzmas stood united on the deck of the old navy ship, watching the first sunset on their voyage to America, breathing the salty mist of ocean spray, and thanking God for all the hardships and disappointments that had culminated in this amazing adventure. They were together, and their dream of freedom was coming true. In America, *the land of the free*, they could begin again.

Visions of a land flowing with "milk and honey" filled the heads of each one as they watched the shores of Europe disappear into the distance. They knew the streets of America wouldn't be literally paved with gold, but at least they knew America would offer better living conditions than they had experienced in displaced persons camps for the last six years. Thankfully, no one shattered their dreams and, except for the seasickness, they had a pleasant trip. However, on the other side of the ocean, reality hit!

CHAPTER 25

America: The Land of the Free

(1951 to 1978)

The first stop of the USS *General Harry Taylor* was Caracas, Venezuela, where 400 immigrants disembarked. The Kuzmas arrived in the port of New Orleans, USA, on Saturday, May 5, 1951, seventeen days after leaving Europe. Donna was eighteen, Christine was sixteen, Jan had his fifteenth birthday on board the ship on April 24, and baby George was six.

When the ship slowly glided into the mouth of the muddy Mississippi, the family had their first look at their new homeland—which didn't exactly look like "America the Beautiful." But it was the weather that really bothered them. They had never in their lives been so hot and sweaty. "Hopefully, Texas won't be this hot and humid. I can hardly breathe!" Donna lamented. "At least in Germany, when it's cold, we can put on a coat and be comfortable!" (What they didn't realize was that Louisiana's springtime was mild compared to the muggy heat they would experience hoeing cotton in the blazing summer sun in Texas!)

The New Orleans port may not have been the most beautiful entrance to the U.S., but it was one of the largest and busiest ports in the world, with as many as fifteen big ships in port and giant cranes unloading huge containers.

After docking, their papers were checked, and their baggage was unloaded. Their first question was voiced by Donna, "How will we ever find our sponsor, Ralph Jensen? There are thousands of people on the dock working or waiting for passengers!"

"And we don't know what Mr. Jensen looks like, and he has no idea what we look like! Plus, we don't speak English, and Mr. Jensen doesn't speak Polish or German," Christine added.

"Don't worry," Jan said, "I'll find him," as he ran down the gangplank praying the whole time, "Lord, help me find Mr. Jensen."

As soon as Jan stepped on land, he noticed a middle-aged gentleman standing next to some crates. He went up to the man, pointed, and asked, "Mr. Jensen?" Jan was shocked when the stranger pointed back and asked "Kuzma?" It obviously was a God thing! What were the chances that among the thousands of passengers, people waiting for passengers, and the dock workers, the very first person they met in the U.S. was their sponsor?

After greeting the entire family, Mr. Jensen led them to his big 1949 Chevy flatbed truck with wooden side panels, helped them load their luggage, which included two big crates approximately 2 ½ x 4 feet, into the back, and motioned for them to get in. *Were they really going to ride in the open back of that truck the entire 500 miles[34] to their new home in Elgin, Texas, a little town near Austin?* This was quite a change from the fast moving, comfortable European trains on which they were used to traveling!

> *Kuzmas had imagined a lovely brick house with an indoor bathroom and stylish furniture—like what they had in Poland.*

Mr. Jensen drove all night and stopped in the morning at a gas station. For the first time, the family tasted Baby Ruth candy bars and a bright orange carbonated drink called Orange Crush. That was an incredible experience—almost better than peanuts and soda crackers!

They arrived in Elgin late the second night.

Home in Texas

It was Mr. Jensen's promise of providing work for a year and a house where they could live inexpensively that made it possible for the Kuzma family to come to America. Their sponsor gave what he had, and it was enough to make the dreams of this immigrant family come true. The local church rallied to the challenge of hosting a refugee family and helped furnish the vacant house. The dishes didn't match, and the furniture was well used—but it was all the church members had—and it was all the family needed.

Expectations, however, don't always match reality. And that's what happened when the family first saw the old farmhouse that Mr. Jensen's parents had built years before. They tried to hide their reactions, but they were disappointed! It was not anyone's fault that the Kuzmas had imagined

---

[34] approximately 800 kilometers

a lovely brick house with an indoor bathroom and stylish furniture—like what they had in Poland.

Instead, their house in Texas had a corrugated tin roof and was made of flattened cardboard boxes nailed to studs and covered by tar paper that looked like red bricks. It had no running water and no indoor plumbing. To get a drink, they had to pump water from a well in the backyard. Their "bathroom" was an outdoor privy, and for baths, they had to use the creek's "running water"—after first scaring off the water moccasins. There wasn't even an indoor refrigerator! Instead, Elza had to use a small fridge that was located in the chicken coop across the backyard area that was fenced for the chickens. The closest store was over two miles away— and they had no way of getting there since they didn't have a bicycle or motorcycle. And even if the Jensens had provided a car, no one in the Kuzma family knew how to drive.

Elza, however, made the best of the situation. She never complained. At heart, she was a farm girl. That's what her grandparents did for a living—and that's what her mother had done when she and Emil moved to Ostrowo.

Elza loved fine things, but she could get along without them. What was important to her was the freedom to choose and worship without persecution. All she wanted for her children was that they would be able to take advantage of the educational and occupational opportunities that America offered. To her, the dilapidated old house with its tin roof and sagging veranda was a symbol of that freedom. It was a stepping stone to the abundance that she knew was available to those who worked hard in America.

Elza quickly assessed her family's needs and asked Mr. Jensen for a short term loan which she promised to repay by working in his fields. She then mail ordered 100 leghorn chicks for eggs and meat and planted a garden. Mr. Jensen loaned them a cow with a newborn calf. The cow produced more milk than they could drink, and Elza churned butter and skimmed off the top for buttermilk. Fruit trees produced an abundance of produce, and the kids found wild grapes growing nearby, which she made into juice and even canned some for the winter. Elza had all she and her family required. Plus, she had the freedom to cook her own meals (even though it was on an old wood stove). How blessed she felt to be able to provide for her family's nutritional needs.

The little home nestled among the green pine trees with a well and a little creek running next to it was all Elza needed to be content. In the fresh air and freedom of country life, she could lift up her eyes to the Lord and feed her soul. Her little family could survive. Elza, at last, was free to become the person God designed her to be—*and she flourished*. But not all of her family adapted so easily.

Donna and Christine were shocked at the poverty they saw in rural Texas. Plus, there were spiders everywhere—inside their home, and in the neighbors' homes. Outside, they had to shoo away the poisonous snakes and swat the mosquitos and flies. It was hard for the girls to adjust. Years later, Donna commented on her first impression of America—and of Texas in particular. "If there were a bridge across the ocean, Christine and I would have walked back. First of all, Texas was too hot! And second, the Texans didn't speak the English we had learned from Mickey and Minnie Mouse movies. The English spoken in Texas was gibberish to us and almost impossible to understand. We were so discouraged that we expressed the foolish wish, 'If only we could return to Europe where civilized people live!'"

When the girls tried to make friends with teenagers their age, they were shocked to discover that some of the families had sixteen-year-old sons who were married to fifteen-year-old girls—girls younger than they were! It was as if the people in Texas were living on a different planet!

The longer Donna and Christine lived in Texas and the more they worked and went to church with the people, the more the good hearts of the Texans stole their hearts. What finally broke their will to remain in Texas, however, were two things: the heat, and the outdoor bathroom facilities!

At first, the whole family worked picking cotton, hoeing weeds, and hauling watermelons for 30 cents an hour. After just a few days working in the sweltering heat and coping with no running water—except for the creek—the girls began to look for other employment. They were willing to work anywhere that offered indoor plumbing! They soon found jobs cleaning and babysitting for families in Elgin and nearby Austin.

Right after arriving in Texas, William shared the gospel with three Polish boys who had immigrated to Texas in 1949 to work in a brick factory. (Elgin was known as the Brick Capital of the Southwest.) Bruno was the only one who argued with William about religion. In fact, he argued so much that he convinced himself of Bible truth and was baptized. Bruno, like William when he was younger, had a great yearning to live a better life and to know the truth about God.

But William wanted to do more. And, like his daughters, he was discouraged by Texas. The dirt and grime, the hot sun, and the bugs didn't meet William's life goals. He admitted there was a certain pleasure he got in picking his own produce, but nothing on the farm built his self esteem like selling Christian literature and sharing Bible truth. He was NOT a farmer; He was a literature evangelist!

Now, after years of religious persecution in Europe, where his dream job was difficult or illegal, he was free to share his religious beliefs. Of course, doing what he loved meant he needed to speak English. That never worried William. Languages came easy to him. He could not only speak German and Polish fluently, but he also spoke a little Russian, Ukrainian, French, and Esperanto. *He would learn English.* And meanwhile he could witness to the Polish and German people living in the United States—but he couldn't do that in the middle of rural Texas. He would have to go to where the people were, perhaps the big cities of Chicago or Detroit.

After a couple of months in Texas, William couldn't take the heat and the farm work any longer. His stomach was giving him trouble, making him irritable and short tempered. But more importantly, he had a burning desire to return to selling Christian literature. He finally told Elza, "I'm sorry, but I was not born to work on this farm for 30 cents an hour. At this rate, we will never earn enough money to buy a home of our own or have the money necessary to pay for our children's education."

Elza didn't argue with him. He was right. The year's contract could easily be fulfilled by her and Jan working on the farm. It was time that William was set free to do what he was called to do. Perhaps this was best for the whole family—for their marriage—and for his health.

> *Elza waved goodbye to her husband as William boarded a big Greyhound bus to seek his fortune in the great unknown.*

So, in the middle of the blasting heat of July, Elza waved goodbye to her husband as William boarded a big Greyhound bus with his small satchel of belongings to seek his fortune in the great unknown of the United States of America. As the bus pulled out and turned north, Elza shook her head, took a deep breath, turned south, and made her way back to her children and the old patched together farmhouse she now called home. It wasn't exactly the way she had envisioned life to be in the Promised Land, but they were living free. This was merely the first step in taking advantage of that opportunity. She had faith in her husband's dream, and she was determined to joyfully do her part as she waited patiently as God worked things out.

William was headed for Chicago. That's where his Polish friend and colleague, Pastor Klutz, was now living and working. But when he arrived, Pastor Klutz discouraged him from staying. Instead, he said, "William, the Polish church in Detroit needs a strong leader. They could really use you and your pastoral skills. Pastor Klutz made some contacts for him, and within three days, William was back on the bus, heading east.

The Polish church in Detroit was made up of not only Polish but also Germans, Russians, Ukrainians, and other Eastern European people who could all speak Polish. Before long, William was teaching Sabbath School and contributing to the church in a meaningful way.

William's first priority was making enough money so that he could buy a house in Detroit for his family. He wanted the family to have a place to live as soon as the one-year contract with Mr. Jensen was fulfilled. He found a job working for a shoe repair business and made good money as he practiced his English. He was even able to live in a small room off the shoe shop workroom, so he didn't have to waste money on rent. Five days a week, after repairing shoes, he took a bus down to the center of Detroit and did janitorial work at night in the famous skyscraper called the Penobscot Building with forty-five floors above ground and two basement floors.

William knew his daughters were unhappy in Elgin, and even though they were both working for good families, their wages were extremely low. If they were working in the Detroit area, he knew they would be able to make a lot more money, and the more money they made, the quicker his dream of buying a house could be realized. He began to write to Donna and Christine, urging them to come to Detroit—the sooner, the better.

Finally, when the girls couldn't stand the inconvenience of the "outdoor bathroom" (the outhouse and the creek) any longer, they quit their jobs and talked their friend, Bruno, into taking them to Detroit. They left on October 27, 1951, and stopped to rest in Chicago at Pastor Klutz's house, where Bruno met one of the pastor's daughters—and later married. After a short stay, Bruno fulfilled his promise and took Donna and Christine on to Detroit, where their father was working. The girls immediately got jobs and started saving their money.

In Texas, life for Elza and the boys settled down into a comfortable routine. George began first grade at seven years of age in the little Seventh-day Adventist Church School in Elgin. There were eight students in the ten-grade school! George loved it. In this small school, he learned English quickly, made friends, and did so well that by the time his family moved to Detroit, he was able to skip second grade.

There were two things in Elgin, however, that George liked more than school. First, he loved his mongrel dog, Rex, who chased rabbits with a passion, even in his sleep with running leg movements and an occasional yip! The second thing George treasured was the Friday evening sundown worship times with his mother and brother on the veranda of their old, rickety house, watching the sun set behind the stately pine tree forest and singing hymns together to begin the Sabbath. Elza's favorite English song was, *"It is morning; it is morning in my heart. Jesus made the gloomy shadows all depart...."* It was her personal testimony.

Later, George would comment, "That year in Elgin with my mom and brother (and my dog) was the best year of my life. That was the year that Mom had time to share with us boys just how much God meant to her and how rewarding her life had become once she had discovered Bible truth. She was always sharing a new gem from God's Word, like Philippians 4:8, about how only talking about good things could change our lives if we really lived by that admonition! I believe that time together in Elgin was a pivotal year for the character development of my brother and me. We asked God for everything, and He provided it. What a revelation that God does answer our prayers—not just the prayers of our parents. Mom had a special relationship with Jesus, and it made us want to have the same."

Every school day, Jan took the bus to the Elgin High School. One day, his high school English teacher called him aside and said, "Jan, even though your first language is Polish and you speak fluent German, you are getting better grades in English than the kids who have spoken English all their lives." His French teacher also encouraged him. "Jan, even though you're still learning English, you are doing so well in your classes that if you grasp all the opportunities of a good education, you will go far in this world and do something meaningful in your life."

Jan was sometimes teased for his accent and called a "Polack" by the "tough" Mexican kids who sported knives and had little interest in learning. But having teachers who saw his potential and encouraged him to apply himself made a significant difference in his attitude toward school. He worked hard, completed his homework, mastered the English language, and got top grades, even though, in addition to going to school, he worked daily for Mr. Jensen on the farm. He felt honor-bound to complete his family's work contract. And he was motivated to earn money—even if it was only 30 cents an hour.

During cotton-picking time, the workers were rewarded for how much cotton they picked rather than receiving an hourly wage. Jan realized that if he could figure out how to pick cotton faster, he could earn a lot more than

30 cents an hour. He soon became the fastest cotton picker on the farm! The hard work was good for him. It honed his muscles and taught him valuable lessons such as working with livestock, fixing farm equipment, managing his time wisely, and learning to drive tractors, motorcycles, and the farm truck—which was not really "work" for a fifteen-year-old boy!

Ralph Jensen grew so many watermelons that he was known in the area as the "watermelon king." Watermelon season was Jan's favorite time. He liked nothing more than cracking a big juicy melon in two and eating out its heart with the juice running down his neck and arms! This was truly an American experience—since he had never tasted watermelon in Europe! Plus, having access to a cow that he milked meant he had all the milk he could drink—perhaps as much as a gallon a day! The good food and healthy exercise did wonders for him. He had grown almost a foot by the time he left Elgin in August of 1952. Plus, Jan had become a disciplined, hardworking, dedicated teenager who studied his Bible daily and was baptized on May 10 in Austin. Jan was determined to take advantage of every opportunity that America offered.

Elza was happy in Elgin. She enjoyed watching her two sons grow with the good homegrown food she was able to prepare, and she loved the wonderful Texas sunshine, which made Elgin's autumn, winter, and springtime so pleasant—and so different from the freezing cold winters in Europe. But even more important to her was the invigorating fresh air of religious and political freedom that confirmed in Elza's mind that God had kept His promise to protect her family from the ravages of the horrific war and had brought them to a country as close to heaven, this side of heaven that you could find.

Detroit and a Home of their Own

With a burst of excitement and pride, William wrote to Elza. "I have good news. I just bought us a house in Detroit. It is brick and has a solid cement basement. It has a big upstairs attic plus a nice kitchen, a living area, and plenty of bedrooms. And it has a vacant lot across the street that we can use as a garden." William had pooled the money he had made repairing shoes and doing janitorial work with what Donna and Christine had saved, and he was able to put $2000 down on a $13,000 home. They could make payments on the balance.

Elza was overjoyed when she got the news. "Just imagine," she thought to herself, "a house of our own!" The Kuzma family had never been homeowners! Elza informed Mr. Jensen and her Elgin church family of the good news about the house in Detroit and gave notice that they would be leaving in August. It was a sad farewell. The church members had grown to love Elza and the boys—and they had grown to love their church family.

Elza packed up their few belongings and put them into an old crate that they had used when crossing the ocean. It was sad to leave her Texas home with the little creek. The comfortable old farmhouse with no indoor plumbing would always hold fond memories. Jan was leaving behind his life as a farm boy—and an endless supply of milk and watermelons. And George cried when he had to say goodbye to Rex.

They left on a Greyhound bus bound for Detroit in the middle of a hot, muggy day in August. With great expectations, the boys watched the miles go by until the big bus finally pulled into the Howard Street bus station in Detroit, where their dad, Donna, and Christine were waiting.

What a great reunion! The U.S. had been good to them. It had only been a year and a couple of months and look what they had accomplished. Having fulfilled their obligation to their sponsor, they now had a lifetime to enjoy the riches and freedom of America.

Elza loved the home William had purchased. She immediately organized the kitchen, found furniture, and set up housekeeping. Soon, she was busy cooking three meals a day. While she was working alone in the kitchen, she listened to the local Polish/German radio station. She enjoyed the news reports, the latest political intrigue, the human interest stories, and the programs that featured classical music, like the Danube Waltz, or popular big band music like Guy Lumbardo or Benny Goodman. How wonderful it was to be able not to have to hide the radio for fear the authorities would find it! When the family got a TV, her favorite shows were the Loretta Young Show and Liberace on Saturday nights. Liberace's first name was Wladziu (no one ever used his Polish first name). He was the son of working class immigrants and his mother was Polish. It was inspiring to see how successful a person could become in America with such humble beginnings.

English programming helped Elza understand the language, but unfortunately, she never immersed herself with enough English-speaking friends so she could speak the language fluently. Since their family continued to speak Polish at home, she never forced herself to practice conversational English.

When Elza moved to Detroit, automatic washing machines were fairly common. But Elza didn't want one. In fact, the kids actually bought her one, but she refused to use it, and they eventually returned it. And she never had an automatic dryer. She hung her clothes outside or on clotheslines strung in the basement.

William set up his "office" in a corner of the basement with bookshelves and a single bed for napping. Especially during the summer, the cool basement was a welcome place to rest and read.

As soon as the Michigan snow melted, William tilled the vacant lot across the street from their house the old fashioned way—with a shovel! He never lost his European attitude that vacant land was meant to be used by someone, even if you didn't own it. Soon he had a good garden growing and had planted some trees. He continued to use the land until the owner decided that a small house could be built on the land and excavation began. William then moved his garden to a vacant lot behind their house.

Attending Church and Other Special Events

When William first arrived in Detroit, he became active in the Polish church, but after a few months, he said, "I will never learn English here." So, by the time the girls arrived in Detroit, he was already attending the local English-speaking Van Dyke Seventh-day Adventist Church. Listening to the English services and talking to people who only spoke English forced him to practice the language. He was determined to learn English as quickly as possible so he would be able to restart his bookselling career. And before long he was once again peddling his bicycle loaded with books and *The Signs of the Times* magazine. One of the most receptive communities he found was a Jewish community approximately three miles from their home. It felt good to be doing the Lord's work once again.

When Elza arrived in Detroit, she was not ready to join the Van Dyke church with William because getting spiritual food from the sermons and the Bible study in Polish was more important to her than learning English. So on Sabbaths, as soon as Jan was able to buy a car for the family, he would drop his mom off at the Polish church, and then the rest of the family would head to Van Dyke. The kids enjoyed the Friday night JMV (Junior Missionary Volunteer) meetings, as well as the Saturday night socials and recreational activities, like ice skating or roller skating with their friends. They loved attending summer camp at Camp Au Sable in Grayling, Michigan. Not only did they make lifelong friends and great memories from camp, but they were spiritually recharged.

Elza's social needs seemed to be met at church. On weekdays, she seldom entertained company unless it was her children and their friends. Her home was her mansion—and her sanctuary. She loved the solitude and her Bible study time during the week. Her exercise was a walk around the block. On Sabbath afternoons, snow, rain, or shine, she would encourage whoever was home to go for a walk with her. For many years, George was the only child at home and remembers her saying, "Breathe deeply. Fresh air is good for you." And then she would share a lesson she had learned from the Bible. George said, "I never had the same closeness with my dad. I think it was all the years during the war and immediately after when I was a baby or toddler that she protected me, fed me, and slept with me to help me feel secure in a very chaotic world that bonded us in a special way. Father's absence during that critical time in my life had a lasting effect on our relationship."

Elza and William never learned how to drive. If Elza's destination couldn't be reached by walking, riding a bicycle, or taking a bus, she was totally dependent on others. William sometimes bicycled to the market for supplies. When George got older, he did the shopping for the family by first checking the sales coupons and then riding his bicycle and putting the produce into leather bags on the handlebars, just as his dad used to do in Europe. At fifteen, because the older kids were away from home, George started driving the car to take his folks to church or special events.

After church, Elza and William (or the children) would often invite someone, like a visiting pastor or a Polish or German-speaking guest, over for a Sabbath meal. Everyone loved Elza's cooking. If someone refused a second helping or if they didn't finish something on their plate, Elza would ask with concern, "Is something wrong with the food?" Then, they would enjoy a pleasant afternoon together, sharing stories and life experiences.

Elza loved Belle Isle Park, a 985 acre island park located in the Detroit River near downtown, especially in the summer when the family could listen to the free Saturday night concerts. What a delight to sit on the grass, look up at the stars, and listen to beautiful music. Christine once commented, "For mom, music filled her soul needs in ways that father was never able to do."

The cultural events held at the local Masonic Temple were also a family highlight. Elza's favorite performance was a folk dancing tour group from Warsaw. It brought back fond memories of better times in Poland, but Elza never had a desire to return to her homeland.

On Sundays during the summer, Bishop Lake (about an hour from their home) was a big attraction. The kids would swim while the folks enjoyed the sand, sun, and the family comradery. Then, everyone delighted in Elza's picnic lunch. When they went to Bishop Lake during blackberry season they came home with buckets full of the luscious berries—then it was jam making time.

School Days in Detroit

After the first year in Detroit, Donna attended one year of college at Emmanuel Missionary College (EMC, soon to be renamed Andrews University) in Berrien Springs, Michigan, and was planning to return. That summer, she got a great job as a secretary at Electrical Specialties in Detroit. Because her family needed her income, she chose not to go back to college. After working for a couple of years, Christine, instead of finishing high school, attended two years of college at Emanuel Missionary College. She then decided to go to Loma Linda, California, where she got a great job working for the registrar at the College of Medical Evangelists (soon to be renamed Loma Linda University). She finished her education at La Sierra College in Riverside, about twenty miles away.

Jan chose to attend Wilbur Wright for his last two years of high school because it offered a work/study program where he could earn money to help his family while going to school. He was industrious and got a summer job at General Motors, where he worked on the assembly line until he got beat up and his life threatened by Union members because he refused to join the Union. He then bought an apartment building in a rough neighborhood and made money on rent until some of the tenants looked at the young kid collecting the monthly rent and refused to pay him. He finally gave up his big idea of being a landlord and concentrated on his education.

When Jan decided to attend college at Emmanuel Missionary College (EMC), he learned about the literature evangelism program where he could earn a scholarship by selling religious books—just like his father. He prayed and got the training, but weeks went by without a sale. Even Elza, who thought her son could do anything, said, "Jan, maybe you're not as talented as your father when it comes to selling books."

Jan just prayed all the more. He made his first sale of a set of children's storybooks to a pastor who knew what this young lad needed to be a success, and he gave Jan his church membership list with an introductory letter saying how valuable the books were for building children's characters. That was all Jan needed to open doors, and for the next four years, he paid his entire college tuition with the scholarships he earned selling books.

George went through grade school, first in public school, and then, when his sister Donna offered to pay his tuition, he attended the Van Dyke church school for four years. His high school years were spent at Cass Technical High School. Then he went on to Emanuel Missionary College, which by then had been renamed Andrews University.

By encouraging and financially supporting each other, the Kuzma kids were able to apply themselves and pay for their educations, which obviously made their parents extremely proud.

Becoming Citizens

William's passionate dream was that his family would become American citizens as soon as possible. His greatest fear (because of his experiences in Europe) was that someone could accuse them of doing something illegal, and they would be deported. It was not enough that his family was enjoying American privileges, William wanted them to *belong*. He wanted to make sure that America was their home legally. He wanted them to be able to say, *"We are Americans!"*

He carefully checked off the citizenship requirements:

- ✓ The ability to read, write, and speak English.
- ✓ The basic understanding of the fundamentals of U.S. history and government.
- ✓ Good moral character and an affinity for the principles of the U.S. Constitution, such as paying taxes and having no criminal record.

After five years—on May 5, 1956—*on the very first day of eligibility*, the Kuzma family went down to the Detroit Courthouse and were sworn in as citizens. (George had to wait until he was eighteen.)

It was time to celebrate! But not for long, for on October 4, 1957, Elza had her first stroke, which left her almost completely paralyzed. After a few weeks of physical therapy, most of Elza's functions returned, all except her left arm, which remained almost useless for the rest of her life. Her bicycling days were over. Now, she was even more dependent on William and her children.

At the time of Elza's stroke, George was the only kid at home. Donna was married and was working part time for the Reisens (a local family); Christine and Jan were away at college in Berrien Springs, Michigan; but all three lived close enough to enjoy many weekends together. Christine fondly remembers Jan entertaining the family with stories about school. Or he talked about politics with his mom so she could understand what was happening in the U.S. government. Christine said she was amazed at the way Jan could delight his parents and hold his siblings' attention. "My brother is incredible," she thought. "He will do well in life."

Relational and Health Challenges

Elza had so hoped that having their own home in America where they could make their own choices would give her marriage a new start, but bad habits are sometimes difficult to change. She had also hoped that William's stomach problems would go away when he didn't have to worry about the physical safety of his family. But that didn't happen, either. Instead, the pain got worse—and the only temporary relief he found was "overdosing" on baking soda. Every time he felt stomach pain, he took another spoonful. The problem was that although the baking soda neutralized the acid in his stomach, it didn't cure the problem.

As William's pain intensified, he took it out on Elza. In turn, Elza became a master at needling him until he spat out hateful words. He was even known to throw things—as he once threw a book out the window in the displaced persons camp in Wentorf. Then, when the pain subsided, they were both repentant.

Elza and William knew all the Bible texts about turning the other cheek and the Golden Rule to treat others as you would like to be treated. But somehow, those admonitions were difficult to put into practice. And instead of their marriage improving, it at times got so bad that William slept downstairs, leaving Elza weeping into her pillow from the pain of rejection.

Elza soon learned that things went best when William had a successful day selling books or when he had a meaningful conversation with someone about the Bible. Elza tried to compliment him more, to listen to his stories, and encourage him in his work, but whatever she did, it was never enough.

Finally, in 1960, when the pain became unbearable, William went to the Detroit Receiving Hospital, which was a city owned hospital dedicated to caring for everyone, regardless of their ability to pay. An excellent surgeon, who just happened to be Russian, said, "Mr. Kuzma, you have a very bad ulcer problem. I can help you." William had surgery to remove two-thirds of his stomach. At last, no more pain. And with the pain gone, so was the irritability. Elza now understood the source of her husband's cantankerous behavior, and the bickering, the blaming, and the fighting subsided.

It was during this time that the Kuzma kids smiled to see their father putting his arms around Elza and calling her pet names. It didn't happen as often as they may have wished, but when the folks were getting along, the kids could feel the geniality of their affection. It was heartwarming to see their parents having fun and enjoying the camaraderie. But unfortunately, it didn't last long.

William was easily influenced by externals. When bad things happened, he would come home with comments like, "Why did he do that?" or "The man didn't have to be so rude." On "off" days Elza would respond to his comments with her own negative statements, like, "Why didn't you just come home," or "You shouldn't have stayed out so late."

Neither one intuitively knew how to turn the negative into the positive. Neither one knew how to break the tension with a joke or compliment.

And without that intervention, one could expect "Polish" fireworks that sent William to the basement to quietly read a religious journal or Elza to the kitchen to chop vegetables.

Moving to California

In 1963, only the folks, and Donna and her growing family were still living in the Detroit area. George was in college at Berrien Springs, Michigan, and Christine and Jan had married. Jan was teaching at the University of California in Los Angeles (UCLA) and planning a career teaching for the School of Health at Loma Linda University in Loma Linda, California. Christine had her degree in social work and was living in Riverside, California. Maybe it was time that the folks sold their home on Fleming Street and moved to California.

William began to dream about owning more land. He found a notice about an Adventist family selling a seven-acre farm in Middletown, California, a small town with a tiny church where students from a nearby Adventist College (Pacific Union College) provided special music and a sermon each Sabbath.

The miracle happened—they began to work as a team rather than sparring partners.

The Detroit home was sold, and they purchased the farm—sight unseen. The children rallied around and helped the folks pack and move. At last Elza had her farm, her own chickens, cats to keep away the rodents, and five baby calves to nurture.

And it was in Middletown where Elza and William experienced a sweetening of their relationship. They were now alone. They had no family members or friends who lived nearby. Each had a specific role they needed to fulfill to take care of the farm. They were totally dependent on each other, and the miracle happened—they began to work as a team rather than sparring partners. Elza had her daily work to take care of the house and to cook. William fed the calves and rode his bicycle into town to collect the produce the markets were throwing away so their chickens could be fed fresh food. They tried to plant a garden, but William finally gave up and declared, "This rocky, sandy ground is cursed!"

They were getting older now. Elza worked hard, even though her left arm didn't work well. But it was the strange behavior in William that now concerned the family. It was as if he was on a roller coaster. Professionals would call this behavior manic-depressive, but for years, it was not dysfunctional enough to cause him to go to a doctor. At one point, on a high, William bought twenty-one dress shirts all alike but never took them out of the plastic wrappers. Then, a few days later, he locked himself in a room and wouldn't come out.

Finally, in 1969, Jan drove to Middletown to bring his dad back to Loma Linda Medical Center to be examined and hopefully get him the medical help he needed. By this time, George was in medical school at Loma Linda University, so between doctor's appointments, William stayed in George's apartment.

After extensive testing, the internist explained to Jan and George, "Your father, because he had so much of his stomach removed, is suffering from what we call a 'dumping syndrome.' He eats a big meal, insulin kicks in, his blood sugar "dumps" and at times it is so low that it is a miracle he can still walk. Others who experience a blood sugar that low would be in a coma." The answer was actually a fairly simple one: eat small meals more frequently so small amounts of insulin are released, and there is not a significant drop in blood sugar. If only they had that information years before, life for both William and Elza would have been much easier.

In 1971, everyone in the family agreed that it was time for the folks to give up the Middletown farm and "retire." They moved to a small house on Barton Road in Loma Linda, California, where they had just enough room for a garden and a few fruit trees. Now, they were near their children and grandchildren.

It was in Loma Linda where old age crept up on them. As for their marriage, it was what it was. They loved each other, but neither knew how to consistently meet each other's emotional needs. William continued to be the visionary; Elza the practical one. William found fulfillment in the stimulating university environment; Elza found solace in her home and garden.

Commitment kept them together. Elza would always be thankful for William introducing her to Bible truth. God was her source of joy. Both continued to be spiritually strong—but, except on rare occasions, both were emotionally needy. America was good for them—but they found the greatest delight in their children's lives.

Mining "Gold" in America

Donna expressed her thankfulness for the freedom the family found in America in these words: "We heard that the streets of America were paved with gold, and the land was flowing with milk and honey. *It was obviously not Texas in the summer!* But here in America, we could help ourselves. Good things didn't happen by us picking cotton, necessarily, but by giving us opportunities to get the things we could never dream of getting in the old country. The gold that we found in the U.S. was in our education."

It was America that offered the Kuzma children the freedom to mine the gold of opportunity. Donna would never have been able to express herself so beautifully verbally, and in the written word, without her college education. Christine would have never become a social worker meeting the needs of so many people. Jan would have never been able to get his Ph.D. in biostatistics and become a beloved professor and respected researcher in medical science. George would never have been able to get his M.D. and have a long career as a physician helping so many to be restored to health.

In the 1940s and 50s in Europe, others made your career decisions while you were still in grade school. Most children were groomed for a specific job, such as a baker or machinist—or for some other industry. Many were trained through apprenticeships to follow in their parent's footsteps. Few were given the educational opportunity to prove themselves and choose their own destinies. For the Kuzma children, America gave them the freedom to choose to be who God inspired them to be.

Elza loved hearing about her children's and grandchildren's achievements. She never regretted leaving Europe and coming to America. In Elza and William's later years, she often said that it was worth the fear, the separation, the misunderstandings, the wait, the pain, and the sacrifice of their own lives to be able to give the gold of an education to their children.

In 1977, Elza suffered a massive stroke causing expressive aphasia, which is a coma-like condition where she couldn't move or in any way express herself—and there was no way of knowing whether she could understand what was happening around her or what was said to her.

The family members remember William clinging to his wife, kissing her forehead and cheeks, and whispering through his tears, "Oh, Elusia; my Elusia. I love you so much. Please come back to me, my precious Elusia!" She died without being able to respond on July 22, 1978.

Epilogue

Time, location, events, friends, family, and even antagonists are God's way of shaping our characters. As you close this book and perhaps wipe away a tear for what life could have been for Elza if she and Wladek had been born in a different time or place, remember this chaotic world is not the end.

The stories inside Elza's favorite book, the Bible, are fascinating and filled with hope. That's where Elza found her joy in the Lord and her courage to face the future. Whatever you're going through now, you don't need to worry! If you feel trapped and persecuted, help is on its way. And you know how all this misery ends. God says, "Behold, I am coming quickly" (Rev. 22:7). Yes! God is coming to your rescue. He will right the wrongs. God wins.

Our loving heavenly Father closes His book with a blessing to you, His child—regardless of your age. "The grace of our Lord Jesus Christ be with you all. Amen" (Rev. 22:21). I'd like to close this book with that same blessing to you and your family.

The Kuzma Family Album

Elza and Wladek's wedding day, 1931.

Elza's mother, Pauline Gartz, on the family farm in 1938.

Elza (seated at right beside her three-year-old, Danusia) poses with her mother and siblings, 1933.

Mrs. Betzel and her daughters, Jasia and Marisha, 1939.

Marta, the Kuzma's nanny from 1937-1939.

Slawno church members in 1946, with Elza and Jurek seated at left, Janek behind her, Krysia with head bent toward Danusia at left rear.

Elza and children in 1945 after Wladek was taken to a forced labor camp.

Children's Sabbath School at the Wentorf Displaced Person's Camp. Front row: Jurek Kuzma, center; Lydia Klutz Boyanic's granddaughter, Ela, right. Middle row: Romek Hinc, center; Krysia Kuzma, far right. Back row: Janek Kuzma, far left, with Jurek Hinc next to him.

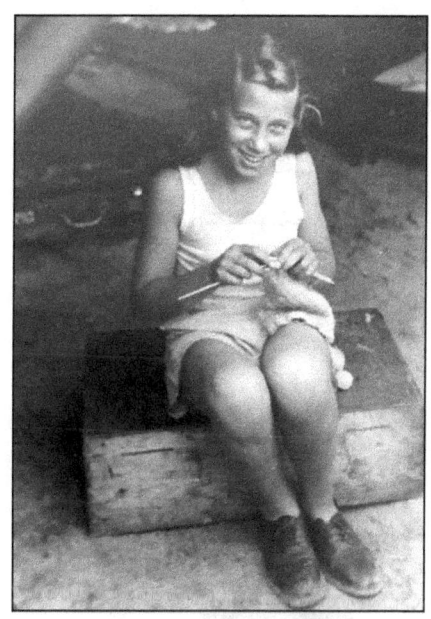

Krysia as a fifteen-year-old in 1947, during the stay at Eckernforde.

Danusia with friends, 1947 (L to R: Danusia, unnamed boy, Hania Hinc).

Elza as a railroad employee, 1941.

Janek, age fourteen, plays his accordion at Lubek, 1950.

Jan aboard the U.S. bound ship on his fifteenth birthday, 1951.

Kuzma children in displaced person's camp, 1947 (L to R: Danusia, Jurek, Janek, Krysia).

Jan and Christine at Emmanuel Missionary College, Michigan, 1959.

Kuzma family in 1953 (front: Elza and William; their children L to R: Christine, George, Jan, Donna).

The family in front of their Detroit home, 1953.

Elza in 1954.

Elza with her first two grandchildren, Corinne and Mark Ranzinger, 1961.

Jan Kuzma and his family meet with Gen. Jarilzelski, then president of Poland, in 1986.

Kuzma siblings in Florida as young adults.

The Kuzma siblings in 2014 (L to R: George, Donna, Christine, and Jan).

TEACH Services, Inc.
P U B L I S H I N G

We invite you to view the complete
selection of titles we publish at:
www.TEACHServices.com

We encourage you to write us
with your thoughts about this,
or any other book we publish at:
info@TEACHServices.com

TEACH Services' titles may be purchased in
bulk quantities for educational, fund-raising,
business, or promotional use.
bulksales@TEACHServices.com

Finally, if you are interested in seeing
your own book in print, please contact us at:
publishing@TEACHServices.com
We are happy to review your manuscript at no charge.

www.ingramcontent.com/pod-product-compliance
Lightning Source LLC
Chambersburg PA
CBHW071148160426
43196CB00011B/2039